ART IN CRIME WRITING

Essays on Detective Fiction

ART IN CRIME WRITING
Essays on Detective Fiction

edited by
Bernard Benstock

St. Martin's Press   New York

ART IN CRIME WRITING. Copyright © 1983 by Bernard Benstock. All
rights reserved. Printed in the United States of America. No part of this
book may be used or reproduced in any manner whatsoever without
written permission except in the case of brief quotations embodied in
critical articles or reviews. For information, address St. Martin's Press,
175 Fifth Avenue, New York, N.Y. 10010.

Library of Congress Cataloging in Publication Data
Main entry under title:

Art in crime writing.

  Includes index.
  1. Detective and mystery stories—History and criticism—
Addresses, essays, lectures. I. Benstock, Bernard.
PN3448.D4A77   1985   809.3'872   85-1760
ISBN 0-312-05397-5 (pbk).

Contents

Notes on the Contributors

Leon Arden was born in New York City and attended Columbia University before becoming a freelance photographer. His novels include *The Savage Place*, *Seesaw Sunday*, *The Twilight's Last Gleaming* and *One Fine Day*. An early play of his has seen three summer-stock productions, and his new comedy, *Hi-Fidelity*, has been optioned for production in the West End. Mr Arden is married and has a four-year-old daughter. He and his family divide their time between London and Connecticut.

Bernard Benstock is Professor of Comparative Literature at the University of Tulsa. He has published several books on James Joyce and Sean O'Casey, and spent 1982 at the Camargo Foundation in Cassis on a grant from the Center for Advanced Study of the University of Illinois to work on a book, *Private Faces in Public Places: The Writer and Political Commitment in the 1930s*.

Allan J. Dooley is Associate Professor of English at Kent State University. Educated at Wabash College and Northwestern University, he is a specialist in Victorian literature. He is a member of the editorial board of the authoritative *Complete Works of Robert Browning*, for which he is editing *Men and Women* and other works, and is the author of articles on Browning, Arnold and other nineteenth-century writers.

Linda J. Dooley is Associate Professor of English and Assistant Dean of the College of Arts and Sciences at Kent State University. She was educated at Ohio Wesleyan University, the University of Aberdeen, and Northwestern University and is a specialist in medieval English literature and linguistics. She is currently completing a book in the latter field.

David I. Grossvogel is the Goldwin Smith Professor of Comparative Literature and Romance Studies at Cornell University. Among his books are *The Self-conscious Stage, Four Playwrights and a Postscript, Limits of the Novel, Divided We Stand* and *Mystery and its Fictions*. He has written articles on literary criticism, dramatic theory, motion picture semiotics, and detective fiction. He is the founder of the review of contemporary criticism, *Diacritics*.

Bruce Harkness has taught English at the Universities of Illinois and Southern Illinois. He was Dean of Arts and Sciences at Kent State University until he resigned to work as general editor of the Cambridge edition of Joseph Conrad.

James Hurt is Professor of English at the University of Illinois and has written on a variety of subjects, including Old English literature, modern drama, and the literature of the American Midwest. He has also had several plays produced.

Bruce Merry is the author of books on the Italian poet Montale, and of *Anatomy of the Spy Thriller*.

Eric Mottram is Reader in American Literature at King's College, London. He is the author of *Towards Design in Poetry* as well as books on William Burroughs, Allen Ginsberg, Paul Bowles, William Faulkner and Kenneth Rexroth and (with Malcolm Bradbury) of a *Companion to American Literature*. He has published twelve books of poetry including most recently *Precipice of Fishes, 1980 Mediate, Elegies* and *A Book of Herne*.

James Naremore is Professor of English and former Director of Film Studies at Indiana University. His writings include *The World Without a Self: Virginia Woolf and the Novel* and *The Magic World of Orson Welles*, as well as monographs on Alfred Hitchcock's *Psycho* and John Huston's *The Treasure of the Sierra Madre*. He is currently writing a book about performance in the cinema and is a visiting professor of literature and film at the University of Hamburg in Germany.

Carol Shloss teaches English and American Studies at Wesleyan University and is an editor of *Canto: Review of the Arts*. Her writings include essays on Nabokov, Crane, Joyce and Beckett and a book on Flannery O'Connor. She is currently at work on a second book, *The Privilege of Perception: Photography and the American Writer: 1840–1970*.

Pierre Weisz is Associate Professor of French at the University of Illinois at Champaign-Urbana. He was educated at the Sorbonne where he wrote his dissertations on Hemingway and James Thurber. He is the author of *Incarnations du Roman* and has published articles on Jacques Prévert, Benjamin Constant, and Jean-Paul Sartre.

Introduction

The auteur theory, which has had an important impact on film criticism, would hardly be applicable to works of literature, where it would seem both obvious and redundant. Yet detective fiction is a subgenre that allows for a rather special approach: the importance and pervasiveness of the detective as the instrumental personality has always held a dominant position in reader response. That almost every fictional detective has a serial role to perform and becomes so well known book after book – in some instances in dozens of novels over scores of years – has resulted in the cultic significance of a Sherlock Holmes or a Lord Peter Wimsey. Not that Sir Arthur Conan Doyle or Dorothy L. Sayers have been relegated to obscurity, but they often have to share the limelight with their fictional creations, and on occasion find themselves somewhat eclipsed by these phantoms. *Essays in Detective Fiction* focuses on the authors who have written some of the most enduring and important works in that genre – as authors who have created not only compelling fictional sleuths but works of fiction.

For a corner of literature that has usually been dismissed as repetitively given to formulaic constructions, detective fiction has indeed proven itself an unusually diversified form, as much so as any other branch of the literary family. Sayers is as different from Conan Doyle as Jean Renoir from D. W. Griffith – and not just in the gap between generations. Contemporaries are sometimes remarkably unalike: few would mistake the work of John D. MacDonald for that of Ross Macdonald, or Ruth Rendell for P. D. James. The Amsterdam of Nicolas Freeling has been replaced by the Amsterdam of Janwillem van der Wetering, with distinctive changes in the population and fictional landscape. The really dedicated writer of crime fiction strives for individuality of style and tone, and more often than not achieves uniqueness. Most of them publish a regular succession of books with a central detective (or, as in the case of Dame Agatha Christie, two or three), while rare authors like Josephine Tey and Dashiell Hammett defy the conventions by working outside the serial-detective form and produce only a handful of novels.

Productivity has also been an uneasy factor in evaluating crime fiction as a serious component of our literature. That Erle Stanley Gardner could grind out books by the dozens has relegated him to the status of a competent hack, yet Raymond Chandler, who expressed the wish that Gardner had taken more care with his work, none the less used one of his narratives as a model from which to learn the craft. Georges Simenon has provided a certain respectability for the prolific writer of crime fiction, and although we are as much aware of his structured approach to his material as we are of the genuinely specific Simenon touches, few have ever faulted Simenon as careless or uncaring. For every Chandler who needed two or three years in order to polish a finished piece of work, there is the novelist who can offer highly literate and exquisitely styled books at a yearly pace. The twenty Nicholas Blake volumes (most of them Nigel Strangeways crime novels) seem to be a reasonable output for a practising poet and essayist, and only when a John Creasy manufactures a multitude of works under a multitude of pen names does an application of the auteur theory begin to founder.

The essays in this volume are by various hands on a handful of detective writers, a dipping of the skimmer into the reservoir. The operative process of selectivity has been the choices made by those who agreed to participate, and by the good fortune that comes from having expert critics involved, the selections offer an excellent cross-section, from the English classical puzzle specialists to the American hard-boiled school of private operatives, from the writers of the Golden Age to the New Wave of realists, and from the Anglo-American hegemony of the international genre to the continental Europeans who have successfully exported their national products. And the critical yardsticks applied by the essayists here are as diverse as the authors under consideration. *Essays in Detective Fiction* takes a close look at some of the finest writers, a good sampling of those who have made the fictional form as internationally respected as it is universally read.

BERNARD BENSTOCK

1 Death Deferred: The Long Life, Splendid Afterlife and Mysterious Workings of Agatha Christie

DAVID I. GROSSVOGEL

It is not uncommon for the demise of an author's popularity to coincide with his actual death, the chance of resurrection awaiting the archaeological whims of future scholars and critics. Not so Agatha Christie: even though she has been gone since 1976, even though the worlds she described are, for the most part, no longer with us, even though the very genre she helped fashion is largely obsolete – in great part because of the disappearance of those worlds – Dame Agatha, her worlds and her particular notion of a genre still seem to be defining for an exceptionally large readership.

Part of this anachronistic phenomenon seems to be due to the truly huge size of that readership developed by Agatha Christie during the course of a career that spanned well over half a century, a hundred titles (titles that number, in addition to her detective stories, plays, romantic novels written under the pseudonym Mary Westmacott, an autobiography, and so on), translations into more than a hundred languages: the size of that readership is impossible to evaluate accurately, but close to half a billion is the figure generally guessed at.

We are still tied to a past we never knew through a few strands that fray even as we hang on to them and, sooner or later, disappear: Agatha Christie is one of those strands. We believe that the detective story as we know it began with Edgar Allan Poe and, some forty years after his death, was popularised by Sir Arthur Conan Doyle. What we may be less aware of is that we are linked to these historical inceptions through the presence of Agatha Christie. The author of Sherlock Holmes was writing, and would still be writing for a number of years, when young Agatha

1

Mary Clarissa Miller decided to try her hand at the genre. This was towards the end of the first world war: Agatha, born in 1890, was in her late twenties. For many years, she and her sister had been avid readers of Conan Doyle and they 'had always argued a lot about whether it was easy to write detective stories':[1] challenged by her sister, Agatha began writing what was to be *The Mysterious Affair at Styles*, first published in 1920. From then on, and until 1973 when she wrote her last detective novel (*Postern of Fate*), Dame Agatha supplied an increasingly large and expectant audience with a steady flow of stories that owed to Conan Doyle two fundamental attributes which are unmistakably his even though they are not generally mentioned: a fondness for bucolic settings and a strong admixture of improbable occurrences (when one considers the supreme urbanity of Sherlock Holmes, it is striking to note how many of his adventures take place on distant moors and within halls of rural estates, drafty with an unurban otherness; and if one considers further that Sherlock Holmes is the child of that *esprit de finesse* Auguste Dupin, a reader of exceptional good will is required to grant their authors a criminal who turns out to be, against every rational expectation, an orang-utan, as in *The Murders in the Rue Morgue*, or a trained snake, as in *The Adventure of the Speckled Band*). It was only after Conan Doyle that rules of fair play evolved, owing perhaps to an increasing desire of the genre to be the accurate reflector of a sociological scene (as with, for example, the 'hard-boiled' Americans).

When Agatha Christie began, she opted for a sunnier countryside than Doyle's, and one which she could people with the homey or homespun types that may have been the romanticising of her own Devonshire youth. Its crystallisation was the village of St Mary Mead (in the 1930 *Murder at the Vicarage*), with its representative spinster, Miss Jane Marple, who was to become, after Hercule Poirot, Agatha Christie's most ubiquitous detective. Miss Marple enjoyed from the very start an acuity and acquaintance with evil that belied her grand-auntish frailty. Over the long half-century of her author's writing, she became more and more that disabused acuity while the bucolic dream faded in England, as elsewhere, and the discontents of an industrial civilisation reached from urban centre to urban centre across a dwindling rural space that had been able once to better conceal a less expected evil. (It was that undisguisable awareness that things were no longer what they had formerly been, however much they might still appear to be, that allowed Miss Marple to perform successfully in one of the more interesting of Agatha Christie's later stories, *At Bertram's Hotel*, in 1965. Even before that, in the 1950 *A Murder Is Announced*, Miss Marple had begun noticing what upward and other mobilities had done to traditional structures and how amenities and a security formerly taken for granted had systematically eroded.²)

It is therefore in the nature of a cavil to note that, in a more enduring world, Miss Marple remained a sleuth in the tradition that assumed the unconditional omniscience of the detective and preserved that omniscience by imparting information to the heroine that had not necessarily been vouchsafed the reader, or by contriving circumstances so improbable as to be acceptable only to that heroine and her entourage of fictional listeners at the final disclosure.

Agatha Christie came to fame in 1926 with *The Murder of Roger Ackroyd*, and aroused the susceptibilities of such defenders of fair play as were already about by turning the narrator into the murderer; she ended Poirot by making *him* one of the killers – but by this time the defenders of fair play had all yielded to Dame Agatha, who had meanwhile turned the supposed victim into the assassin in *Peril at End House* (1932), and done the same to a corpse in *Ten Little Niggers* (1939). In the words of Robert Barnard, 'When the time for a solution came round, the most unaccountable rabbits were produced from her hat: the murderer was the investigating policeman, he was a child, he was one we had thought already dead, he was all the suspects together.'³ And all along, that inveterate gardener, Jane Marple, led uncomplaining generations of readers down primrose paths known only to her (usually by offering those readers a great diversity of paths, all but one of which they were supposed to pay any attention to).

And so did Poirot. But Poirot was also walking – even as was Jane Marple – a more interesting path, one leading, at least in the fiction, from Styles Court to Styles Court, through some fifty years and as many adventures, across the changing landscape of our times. On that long journey, moral notions evolved, social circumstances changed, what had once been clear markers became either difficult to read or were obliterated altogether, leaving the journeyer with the residual sense of our times, an anxiety that filtered at last beyond the covers meant to contain the adventure, and which transcended the spurious suspense of the detective genre.

I have analysed elsewhere (*Mystery and Its Fictions*, 1979) the (relatively) innocent world of which, and within which, Agatha Christie first wrote. In that innocent world, the detective-story writer did not propose so much a solvable problem as a disposable one. Agatha Christie's first readers read her in order to purchase at the cost of a minor and passing disturbance the comfort of knowing that the disturbance was *contained*, and that at the end of the story the world they imagined would be continued in its innocence and familiarity.

The nature and consequences of that disturbance are crucial, for ultimately they are the key to Agatha Christie's huge popularity and her yet-enduring readership. A sense of Dame Agatha's climate in her early works will be obtained instantly through contrast with the hard-boiled variety mentioned in later chapters. In the latter, a relatively sordid private eye does battle with openly sordid forces loosed by the urban chaos. That private eye – Sam Spade, Philip Marlowe or Mike Hammer – encounter what is intended to be 'real' corruption, whether in a politician, a sexuality (most frequently a woman's, against which is success-fully matched the demonstrative virility of the detective), a corpse. This 'reality' entails a specificity; the detective performs acts that particularise him even though they have nothing to do with the functional gestures required of him by the case he is on: he drinks, he makes love, he lets all and sundry know that he is 'tough'. He walks the back alleys of a city whose surfaces are fully analysed. As Zola discovered a century before, such 'slice-of-life' realism not only entails specificity, it also assumes a burden of 'truth' which, more often than not, it feels able to demonstrate only by exposing its seamier parts.

Agatha Christie was far more stylised. For her, the game was merely a puzzle (or a series of interlocking puzzles) told in the form of a story. The story required people, of course, but their creation was left largely to the imagination of the reader.

Writing in the years immediately after the end of the first world war, Agatha Christie was instinctively striving for a delicate balance, but one that was still possible at that time. It consisted in an intrusion upon the reader's ideal world, but an intrusion not so intense as to cast doubt on its eventual dissipation. She achieved this balance by identifying accurately her middle-class audience

and its hankering for an Edwardian gentility.⁴ Dame Agatha
offered these readers recognisable posters of a world which they
had experienced only through posters: they were offered a
journey to a land that they knew well, but only in the world of
their social fantasising and bygone dreams of empire. Poster and
book served the selfsame purpose: they preserved the awareness of
a world that must have existed for someone; it was a far better
world than the known world and doubly comforting because of a
suspicion that if it had indeed existed once, its days were now
numbered.

In 1920, Styles Court was the province of the upper-middle
class.⁵ Like most parts of the worlds which it supposed, it endured
mainly in the reader's private storehouse of prides and prejudices.
Styles Court was a functional set of lexical stimuli, never anything
more precise than a 'fine, old house', with 'a broad staircase'
which you descended in your mind's eye after having 'dressed' for
'supper . . . at half past seven' (due to wartime conditions, 'We
have given up late dinners'). It had an 'open French window' in
order to disclose 'the shade of a huge sycamore tree' beneath
which 'tea' was ritualised in summer, and beyond which was
located the leisured class's tennis court.

Part of the world adumbrated by Styles Court was a poster
village, Styles St Mary, which was exactly like Jane Marple's St
Mary Mead (ideal images being perforce identical), nestling in a
small verdant world of scrubbed and loyal people – working or
farming – with its quaint vicarage for an effortless accommoda-
tion of spiritual needs and a half-timbered inn for the mundane
counterpart.

Through these postcards of rural England walked a few other
stock types – a suitable clergyman for the vicarage, a jovial
landlord or two for the pub, a third-generation solicitor for the
competent handling of material vexations, servants whose
starched surface hid a heart of gold, matrons on their way to the
local flower show, elderly majors retired from colonial wars. The
reader knew these people without having encountered them and
they were therefore exactly suited to his expectations.

Murder within this English pastoral was not so much an evil act
as one whose consequences would be unfortunate for a prescribed
moment. Whereas a Mike Hammer or a Sam Spade might right
their little piece of the corrupt, urban jigsaw puzzle while the
complex itself remained corrupt and awaited the private eye's

attention to the next area of his concern, murder upon the mead was more in the nature of a washable and cathartic stain. For a while, these good people would become each and every one suspect (Agatha Christie, who built her reputation early on a disregard for established rules, showed as little unwarranted sentimentality here: however much tradition might have endeared a particular type to the reader, none was above suspicion). Within this dream of rural England, murder was trivial enough; the corpse upon which Philip Marlowe stumbled might not have had quite the stench of Laius', but in St Mary Mead or Styles St Mary the murder itself was antiseptic – already a part of the cleansing process (there were always half a dozen compelling reasons to kill the victim – and as many evident suspects). It was the wake of the murder that made things momentarily disagreeable: the country inn would lose its ruddy bonhomie; the vicarage might be pressed uncomfortably close to moral quandaries; and, worst of all, aliens would walk the pristine land. For just as the reader was able to people fully a world to which he aspired, the reader would temporarily jeopardise through his own malaise the harmony of the world he had conjured from his fiction. And here again, Dame Agatha remained supremely aloof, giving the reader only such few and accurate stimuli as were needed.

In the shadow of evil, clean-shaven Styles St Mary would begin to see beards with all the unEnglish and other unfortunate implications of that facial indecorum. Alfred Inglethorp, who is only very nearly the villain of the piece, strikes 'a rather alien note', according to bland Hastings, the narrator (*The Mysterious Affair at Styles*). Hastings understands instantly why Inglethorp's son-in-law objected to the beard: 'It was one of the longest and blackest I have ever seen .... It struck me that he might look natural on the stage, but was strangely out of place in real life.' 'Real life' is of course Styles St Mary, and since Styles had never been under anything like the present cloud, the unnatural beard is contrary to what is normal and becomes a litmus of evil.

But that litmus comes from elsewhere as well, as demonstrated by another of the characters – Dr Bauerstein. Dr Bauerstein is merely here as a red herring – he turns out to be a spy who has nothing to do with the nasty business at Styles. But the early Christie readers thought they knew Bauerstein just as they thought they knew the Cavendishes and Styles St Mary itself. The way this red herring affected those readers was articulated by Hastings – even though Christie had done no more than name Bauerstein and mention that he was a 'tall bearded man': 'The sinister face of Dr Bauerstein recurred to me unpleasantly. A vague suspicion of everyone and everything filled my mind. Just for a moment I had a premonition of approaching evil.' Bauerstein is after all a Polish Jew – twice an alien. He comes by his beard naturally. The Polish Jew has no 'natural' place in the average reader's imaginings of Styles: Bauerstein brings to those fictional imaginings a parafictional unpleasantness from a world that is more intimate and habitual to that reader. Or so it was at least in 1920.

There was always a suspicion that Agatha Christie and Jane Marple had quite a bit in common.[6] There were of course their moral and social beliefs; but there was also an acuity, a depth of *insight*. Just as Miss Marple was able to see the hidden snake lurking in Devonshire Edens, Agatha Christie was able to discern precisely what would give her reader the surest of twinges, though neither she nor that reader ever identified the causes to which they both referred.[7] This being so, it might be unmannerly to repeat here that Dame Agatha was one to take unfair advantage of even such fundamental intuitions: in *Styles*, not only did the culprit turn out to be the most upright and prototypical of British stereotypes, but the author added insult to injury by hiding the culprit behind a (false) beard.

It was within a world distracted only momentarily by this kind of curable malaise that was born the detective destined to become one of the most famous of the genre: Poirot was able to dissipate the uneasiness, but he was also created and shaped by it to a great extent.

Like his prototypes, Dupin and Holmes, this sort of detective demonstrates a perfect intelligence within a multitude of flaws. The structural reason for this contrast results from a fundamental identity between the fictional detective and his circumstances: that detective is the reader's assurance that his expectation of an end to a number of small annoyances will be met – the detective's acuity is therefore absolute; but the reader's concession in that contract requires that a semblance of doubt be maintained for as long as it takes to tell the tale – all else in the detective is therefore flawed.

However, the strangeness of Dupin and Holmes confirmed

their intelligence even as it removed them from the common world of mortals; Dupin and Holmes dwelt in remote worlds, isolated by books, drugs, laboratory or musical instruments – all awesome objects that extended the awesomeness of their brains. Poirot's flaws, on the other hand, represented a compendium of what marred the idyllic landscape once it became the temporary site of the sombre event that brought Poirot into it. When Agatha Christie first described Poirot, he was in fact a part of the negative consequences that followed the transgression of the bucolic dream.

To start with, Poirot was a foreigner, another alien note within the pastoral harmony. The evidence of his foreignness was multiple, but because of the specific area of Poirot's first trespass, it was peculiarly unEnglish. Starting with his ridiculously short stature, most of his obvious traits were intended to amuse, but also to annoy, his English reader:

> Poirot was an extraordinary-looking little man. He was hardly more than five feet, four inches, but carried himself with great dignity. His head was exactly the shape of an egg, and he always perched it a little on one side. His moustache was very stiff and military. The neatness of his attire was almost incredible. I believe a speck of dust would have caused him more pain than a bullet wound. Yet this quaint dandyfied little man who, I was sorry to see, now limped badly, had been in his time one of the most celebrated members of the Belgian police.

Hastings' initial awareness and dismissal of the physical Poirot spoke for his reader, and Hastings' voice was subsequently echoed by countless others – villains, chambermaids, gardeners, romantic leads: just about everyone was to be taller than Poirot, treating him until the final moment of revelation and awe with either amused contempt or patronising tolerance.

Lack of stature made Poirot's aping of British virtues something halfway between a joke and an affront: dignity sounded like an unseemly overstatement in one so short, while the military moustache became a ridiculous attribute. As for Poirot's sartorial fastidiousness, something that would have been praiseworthy in an Englishman of more normal size, could at best be quaintly dandifying in an undersized foreigner.

But Poirot added to even these shortcomings. Having been

denied the grace of British birth, he compounded his misfortune by refusing to hide it, indulging an unBritish propensity for exuberance and exaggeration. He was from the first a boaster, one given to stressing the subject pronoun through the apposition of his own name, and using his hands with abandon for even greater emphasis. And to bring the picture to its full dejection, this master of the little grey cells never learned to speak English correctly. To the end, Poirot's sentences were marred by Gallicisms, even though they became more probable over a lifetime than the porcine 'Ah! Triple pig!' or 'you remain there like – how do you say it? – ah, yes, the stuck pig' that flavoured his original speech.

Poirot's very intelligence, before even his unseemly boasting about it, was yet another exaggeration, and one which he displayed with equal lack of tact in his all too apparent egg-head. Aloof as ever, but knowing full well from which vantage point *she* observed her creation, Dame Agatha named him after the least favoured of vegetables (*poireau*: the leek, which also means 'wart' in French) and then stressed the dismissiveness by pairing it with a singularly grandiloquent Christian name, Hercule – itself turned into still another overassertion by the diminutive size of its bearer.

Seemingly self-removed, Agatha Christie kept a gimlet eye on her reader at all times, knowing the disposition of his afferent nerves as accurately as might an acupuncturist. Where Mike Hammer's or Sam Spade's readers were drawn through a world which they either knew or knew to be there, Christie's readers were returned to their own imagination in order to flesh out the otherwise abstract puzzle. And though they only assumed that the enviable world of the fiction must exist, they tainted it for a while with fears that were as imaginary but which they knew to be real beyond the fiction. Pre-eminently, Christie knew how much her reader did not know: if that Edwardian world still existed for some in 1920, it is unlikely that it could ever have appeared as desirable or as easily jeopardised as it did to those for whom it was only a dream. For the latter, the bulk of Christie's readers, dream and jeopardy derived from aspirations and fears that the author intuited with unfailing accuracy. But as Agatha Christie wrote for a long time, and as her sense of her reader remained acute, the nature of those parafictional fears changed over the years.

Robert Barnard has called the quarter of a century of Agatha Christie's *maitrise* (1925–50) her 'classic period': it is certainly true that by the time the euphoria of second-world-war victories evaporated, the delicate balance she had hitherto maintained could be maintained no longer. By the time of his end, it was possible to read in Poirot the deep alterations of the world upon which he had intruded only briefly at the start: Agatha Christie continued to write, but she and her readers were now affected by other fears and other longings.

At the end of the forties, Poirot and Hastings met in *Curtain* for the last time at the place of their first meeting, Styles. By now, Agatha Christie was writing with a sense of many deaths;[8] not only was the writer aware of her own future death – from now on, an awareness of the passing of familiar worlds imparts an unmistakable shade to her writing. The war collapsed many social structures that wishful thinking had supported beyond their term: already in *Five Little Pigs* (1943), Poirot had gone back through memory lanes of better known and better liked times. So doing, he was starting to express Christie's growing sense of dismay at the assertion and vulgarity of new money, the deterioration of values formerly held, knowledge previously shared, the anxiety of exile from old assumptions into a world of rapid and radical change, where social contact could be only tentative and tenuous.

By the end of the forties, Sytles stands for much more than simply its own demise. There is much to be read into the fact that it is now a 'guest house' whose once 'old-fashioned large bedrooms had been partitioned off so as to make several smaller ones'. Along with comfort, a style has gone: it is now 'furnished in cheap modern style'. The water is lukewarm, the towels thin, and Hastings muses.

> I remembered the clouds of steam which had gushed from the hot tap of the one bathroom Styles had originally possessed, one of those bathrooms in which an immense bath with mahogany sides had reposed proudly in the middle of the bathroom floor. Remembered too the immense bath towels, and the frequent shining brass cans of boiling hot water that stood in one's old-fashioned basin.

Styles can survive its eviction from Edwardian times only by becoming a part of the new mercantile world. The class structure that once supported it (and its hot-water basins) no longer exists.

Nowhere is this loss more apparent than in the efforts of the
author to sustain her stock characters. They are still there, but
their presence is shadowy and unsure to the extent that their
supporting world has largely vanished. Gone is the ideal working
class that gave the village its solid and immaculate under-
pinnings. Gone, as a matter of fact, is the village itself: 'I
realised the passage of years. Styles St Mary was altered out of all
recognition. Petrol stations, a cinema, two more inns and rows of
council houses.' The gardens are overgrown and the tennis court
has presumably moved out of the private park and into the public
playground. Class stereotypes have been replaced by others for
which there is as yet no mythology; it is difficult to maintain the
old mainstays within such a world:

> He looked as though he had led an out-of-doors life, and he
> looked, too, the type of man that is becoming more and more
> rare, an Englishman of the old school, straightforward, fond of
> out-of-doors life, and the kind of man who can command.
>
> I was hardly surprised when Colonel Luttrell introduced him
> as Sir William Boyd Carrington. He had been, I knew,
> Governor of a province in India, where he had been a signal
> success. He was also renowned as a first-class shot and big-
> game hunter. The sort of man, I reflected sadly, that we no
> longer seemed to breed in these degenerate days.

These 'degenerate' days extend into other ethical and social
areas: a new rudeness is now currently permissible ('His manners
were not what one would call polished to anyone'), the mere
surface of a deeper and more pervasive corruption: 'Norton, the
gentle-hearted, loving man, was a secret sadist. He was an addict
of pain, of mental torture. There has been an epidemic of that in
the world of late years – *L'appétit vient en mangeant.*'

The very family is disintegrating. Parental authority is flouted
– Hastings' daughter tells him, when he tries to warn her about
an obvious cad, 'I think you have a perfectly filthy mind.' And the
generations look at each other with pitying contempt across the
gap that separates them: 'So vulnerable they are, these children!
So ready, though they do not recognise it that way, to take a
dare!'

This is the atmosphere of the times after the rural dream has
ceased to be possible (or better, once it is no longer possible to

write about it). It informs the present with a sense of failure: 'That's the depressing part of places like this. Guest houses run by broken-down gentle-people. They're full of failures − of people who have never got anywhere and never will get anywhere − who have been defeated and broken by life.'

The end of possibility is heightened by a pervasive sense of what used to be: 'To me there was a charm in his slightly old-fashioned way of putting things. It conjured a picture of old-world charm and ease.' 'I saw the scene in my mind's eye. I could imagine Daisy Luttrell with a young saucy face and that smart tongue − so charming then, so apt to turn shrewish with the years.'

The stock character hardest to sustain in this altered world is undoubtedly Poirot himself. Of necessity, he is still the little man who speaks gallicised English, who brags (a little), whose grey cells work as hard as ever. But constrained by the mood of the times, a new Poirot displaces much of the old caricature − a more 'living' character (as are many of the other characters similarly affected), one burdened by the darkened world, a longing for the past, an unstated apprehension of tomorrow.

The Poirot who brought disturbance in his wake (like Chaucer's Pandarus − through his *book*), and then disappeared Pied-Piperlike, taking the disturbance and its causes with him, that Poirot could no longer be effectual within the circumstances of which Agatha Christie was now so keenly aware. Though he could still solve the crime, Poirot could no longer return a world bereft of former bounds or norms to a definitive closure or normalcy: today's disturbances were simply not what they used to be. And as Agatha Christie's reader intuited that worlds formerly conjured from a putative reality could no longer be sustained by that reality, that same post-war reader also knew that former small and disposable irritations caused by the bearded alien, the foreign and quirky detective, the transitory interloper, the outlandish fashion, were no longer there to be disposed of in a world that now lacked the normative criteria against which these minor annoyances were once stated: they were now supplanted by the more insidious malaise of being in a world that lacked those normative criteria.

The last Poirot is therefore an awkwardness, a necessary aggregate of former traits that are without resonance once the codes of class structures, of social mores, of ethical modes, are no longer what they appeared to have been at the time of his creation. The functional caricature now throbs with a consciousness of the times, a nostalgia and a gloom. And the loss of that functional caricature causes the purity of the detective story to be lost as well. The deranged heiress, the pilfering solicitor, the two-timing butler may be removed at the end, but in a world of far more insidious threats, their removal does not return the world to a pristine innocence, and the non-functional reality of the former caricature endures in the reader's enduring anxiety.

After Poirot's premature passing, Agatha Christie would resurrect him, off and on, for still another quarter of a century, even as she would Miss Marple through the depletion of rural possibilities. Dame Agatha tried valiantly to have her people swing with the new, as in *They Do It with Mirrors* (Marple, 1952), *Hickory, Dickory, Dock* (Poirot, 1955), *The Mirror Crack'd from Side to Side* (Marple, 1962), *Third Girl* (Poirot, 1966), but she did not feel any easier in those new spheres than did her protagonists. The best of her later work shows people who feel themselves as she does to be spiritual outcasts and who may find in their marginality a new acuity of detection, reading a more accurate palimpsest through the modern surface. But, in general, the difficulties evidenced in *Curtain* were simply repeated.

Why then her continuing popularity? A part of the answer was intuited by the directors (Sidney Lumet, Don Guillermin, Guy Hamilton) who have recently turned into films *Murder on the Orient Express*, *Death on the Nile*, *The Mirror Crack'd*, peopling them with old-time actors now seldom seen on the screen – Lauren Bacall, Richard Widmark, Bette Davis, David Niven, Angela Lansbury, or, in a new, Queen-Motherish avatar, the enduring Elizabeth Taylor. These actors represent the cinema of a shinier moment, over a third of a century ago, before they were swept aside by the new forms of the present cinema. Seeing them once again on the screen, we re-enter that world briefly. This is especially felicitous casting for Agatha Christie, since we now regress through her books to something more real than the times she described: the period pieces that those descriptions themselves have become now attract us. There may have been a time when Agatha Christie mediated for her reader unattainable worlds: now her archaic books have become those worlds. We acknowledge our present discontent in retrospections that make us smile at what once constituted the measure of our passing cares, the sense of how comfortable we felt in a world of referable absolutes (after all, Dame Agatha herself tells us in her autobiography that she came to the detective story out of a comforting sense that Evil could be hunted down and that Good would triumph – an avowal that explains not a little her sombre mood within, and tenuous grasp on, the world that followed the second world war).

In that world, our present one, a residual pull of pyschological gravity draws us to the evidence that we once had faith in the possibility of control, of knowledge and of the power of reason against the irrational. We are still drawn to the old writings of Agatha Christie.

NOTES AND REFERENCES

1. See Nancy Blue Wynne, *An Agatha Christie Chronology*, p. 264.
2. This is the book into which, belatedly and cautiously, Lesbianism backs.
3. *A Talent to Deceive*, p. 40.
4. See the anonymous 'Commentary' in *The Times Literary Supplement*, 18 Sept. 1970.
5. See J. Ritchie, 'Agatha Christie's England, 1918–1939', in *The Australian National University's Historical Journal*, 9 (Dec. 1972).
6. It is interesting that Margaret Rutherford was Jane Marple in so many of the films made from these stories, even though she did not look at all like Miss Marple; she did, however, bear a certain resemblance to the older Agatha Christie.
7. In 1939, she had no qualms about calling one of her most famous stories *Ten Little Niggers*: she had, after all, a nursery rhyme to justify her. Her American publishers were more sensitive – they changed the title to *And Then There Were None*.
8. The book was supposed to appear posthumously. In fact, it was published in 1975, the year before Agatha Christie died. (I have used for quotations from *Curtain* the 1977 English edition by Fontana Books.)

BIBLIOGRAPHY

Barnard, R., *A Talent to Deceive*: *An Appreciation of Agatha Christie* (Dodd, Mead, 1980).

Cawelti, J. G., *Adventure, Mystery, Romance* (University of Chicago Press, 1976).

Christie, A., *An Autobiography* (Dodd, Mead, 1977).

Feinman, J., *The Mysterious World of Agatha Christie* (Book Award Books, 1975).

Grossvogel, D. I., *Mystery and Its Fictions: From Oedipus to Agatha Christie* (Johns Hopkins University Press, 1979).

Keating, H. R. F. (ed.), *Agatha Christie: First Lady of Crime* (Holt, Rinehart & Winston, 1977).

Ramsey, G. C., *Agatha Christie, Mistress of Mystery* (Dodd, Mead, 1967).

Wynne, N. B., *An Agatha Christie Chronology* (Ace Books, 1976).

CHRONOLOGY

Dates of first publication; US titles (in parentheses, English titles if different) unless otherwise stated the publisher is Dodd, Mead (New York) and Collins (London).

1920 – *The Mysterious Affair at Styles*
1922 – *The Secret Adversary* ([Dodd, Mead] London: Allen Lane)
1923 – *Murder on the Links*
1924 – *The Man in the Brown Suit*
1924 – *Poirot Investigates*, short-story collection
1925 – *The Secret of Chimneys*
1926 – *The Murder of Roger Ackroyd*
1927 – *The Big Four*
1928 – *The Mystery of the Blue Train*
1929 – *The Seven Dials Mystery*
1929 – *Partners in Crime*, short-story collection
1930 – *The Murder at the Vicarage*
1930 – *The Mysterious Mr. Quin*
1931 – *Murder at Hazelmoor* (*The Sittaford Mystery*)
1932 – *Peril at Endhouse*
1932 – *The Tuesday Club Murders* (*The Thirteen Problems*), short-story collection
1933 – *Thirteen at Dinner* (*Lord Edgeware Dies*)
1933 – *The Hound of Death and Other Stories*, short-story-collection
1934 – *The Boomerang Clue* (*Why Didn't They Ask Evans?*)
1934 – *Murder in the Calais Coach* (*Murder on the Orient Express*)
1934 – *The Listerdale Mystery*, short-story collection
1934 – *Mr. Parker Pyne, Detective* (*Parker Pyne Investigates*), short-story collection
1935 – *Death in the Air* (*Death in the Clouds*)
1935 – *Murder in Three Acts* (*Three-act Tragedy*)
1936 – *The A.B.C. Murders*
1936 – *Cards on the Table*
1936 – *Murder in Mesopotamia*
1937 – *Death on the Nile*
1937 – *Poirot Loses a Client* (*Dumb Witness*)
1937 – *Murder in the Mews*, English short-story and novelette collection
1937 – *Dead Man's Mirror*, American short-story and novelette collection
1938 – *Appointment with Death*

1938 – *Murder for Christmas* (*A Holiday for Murder*; *Hercule Poirot's Christmas*)
1939 – *Easy to Kill* (*Murder is Easy*)
1939 – *And Then There Were None* (*Ten Little Niggers/Ten Little Indians*)
1939 – *The Regatta Mystery*, short-story collection
1940 – *Sad Cypress*
1940 – *The Patriotic Murders* (*One, Two, Buckle My Shoe; Overdose of Death*)
1941 – *N or M?*
1941 – *Evil Under the Sun*
1942 – *The Body in the Library*
1943 – *Murder in Retrospect* (*Five Little Pigs*)
1943 – *The Moving Finger*
1944 – *Towards Zero*
1945 – *Remembered Death* (*Sparkling Cyanide*)
1945 – *Death Comes as the End*
1946 – *The Hollow* (*Murder after Hours*)
1947 – *The Labours of Hercules*, short-story collection
1948 – *There Is a Tide* (*Taken at the Flood*)
1948 – *Witness for the Prosecution*
1949 – *Crooked House*
1950 – *A Murder Is Announced*
1950 – *Three Blind Mice and Other Stories*, short-story collection
1951 – *They Came to Baghdad*
1951 – *The Underdog and Other Stories*, short-story collection
1952 – *Murder with Mirrors* (*They Do It with Mirrors*)
1952 – *Mrs. McGinty's Dead* (*Blood Will Tell*)
1953 – *Funerals Are Fatal* (*After the Funeral*)
1953 – *Pocket Full of Rye* (London & Sydney: Collins)
1954 – *So Many Steps to Death* (*Destination Unknown*) (London, Toronto & Sydney: Collins)
1954 – *The Spider's Web*, play
1955 – *Hickory, Dickory, Death* (*Hickory, Dickory, Dock*) (London & Sydney: Collins)
1956 – *Dead Man's Folly*
1957 – *Spider's Web*, play
1957 – *What Mrs. McGillicuddy Saw* (*4:50 from Paddington*)
1958 – *Ordeal by Innocence*
1958 – *The Unexpected Guest*, play
1958 – *Verdict*, play
1959 – *Cat Among the Pigeons*, play
1959 – *The Unexpected Guest*, play
1960 – *The Adventure of the Christmas Pudding*, short-story collection
1961 – *Double Sin and Other Stories*, short-story collection
1961 – *The Pale Horse*
1962 – *The Mirror Crack'd* (*The Mirror Crack'd from Side to Side*)
1962 – *Rule of Three*, 3 one-act plays
1963 – *The Clocks*
1963 – *Rule of Three*, one-act plays
1964 – *A Caribbean Mystery*

1965 – *At Bertram's Hotel*
1966 – *Third Girl*
1967 – *Endless Night*
1968 – *By the Pricking of My Thumbs*
1969 – *Hallowe'en Party*
1970 – *Passenger to Frankfurt*
1971 – *Nemesis*
1971 – *The Golden Ball and Other Stories*, short-story collection
1972 – *Elephants Can Remember*
1972 – *Fiddlers Three*, play
1973 – *Akhnaton*, play
1973 – *Postern of Fate*
1974 – *Hercule Poirot's Early Cases*, short-story collection
1975 – *Curtain* (written during the second world war)
1976 – *Sleeping Murder*
1979 – *Miss Marple's Final Cases*, short-story collection

2 Dorothy L. Sayers: Mystery and Demystification

BRUCE MERRY

Dorothy L. Sayers' novels are long and do not age well. Yet intellectually they are resourceful and highly refined. In the delightful extravagance of the plot of *Five Red Herrings*, for example, we have six painters living in Kirkcudbright. All six of them have a motive of some kind for killing a seventh painter in the area, Campbell. We know that it must be one of the painters who kills Campbell, because beside his body near a high mountain stream is a recently finished landscape skilfully faked in his manner but not done by him.

Timing of *rigor mortis* proves this, as it does in many of Sayers' plots. It turns out that all six painters have alibis, some rough, some good, some perfect. We remember that E. A. Poe in *The Purloined Letter* argues that the more perfect and watertight an alibi is, the more suspicious it should look to a good detective. Sherlock Holmes is quoted in the last chapter of *Have His Carcase*: 'Only a man with a criminal enterprise desires to establish an alibi.' The breaking of the key alibi by Wimsey is ingenious, absurd, breathtaking, all at once. He is quite removed from real police work, however hard Sayers fights to include the police hierarchy in the unravelling of motive and manner, from chief constable Sir Maxwell down through inspector Macpherson, to sergeant Dalziel and the humble constables Duncan and Ross, all of whom have different theories about which of the six suspected painters must be the killer.

Patricia Craig writes that 'if you take away the detective-content of Sayers' books (as she tried to do herself, to an extent, in her least impressive novel, *Busman's Honeymoon*), you are left with popular, insipid, middlebrow writing.'[1] She quotes Q. D. Leavis's opinion of two late Wimsey novels as 'popular and romantic while pretending to realism'. Such views push the point about realism too hard. Sayers is not writing detailed studies of fly-fishing and landscape painting in Scots dialect (*Herrings*), nor of bell-ringing and lowland drainage (*The Nine Tailors*), nor of the law of intestate inheritance (*Unnatural Death*). Rather she is assembling an intense intellectual structure, tapering at its apex and based on a single revealing idea, which explains the whole plot: the purchase of a printing set to fake a punched and countersigned railway ticket (*Herrings*), the dissection of the actual murder corpse by the surgeon who did the killing (*Whose Body?*), or the exact date when a law was enacted (*Unnatural*).

The charge of superfluity of material or insipidness of treatment can certainly not be levelled against the collections of short stories (*Lord Peter Views the Body*, 1928; *Hangman's Holiday*, 1933; *In the Teeth of the Evidence*, 1939; and *Striding Folly*, 1942). The point of a Sayers short story is usually in an intense single clue which shatters or confirms an alibi. For example, the clock and time-piece is as important to Sayers as the mirror to Borges. In various stories we have the hands of a clock defining lighting-up time on a garage rather than telling the real time, or the fact that a grandfather clock should be moved forward eleven hours rather than back one hour to account for the striking pieces, or again a clock striking in a London drawing-room heard over the telephone 40 miles away (except that the murderer has hidden in the same house and linked the London call to a parallel home telephone line). All these are elements which Lord Peter Wimsey or Montague Egg (commercial traveller in superior wines and amateur detective) can pinpoint more quickly than a police inspector.

In the story 'Dirt Cheap', Egg and other commercial travellers are sleeping overnight in a seedy hotel. The dinner gives indigestion, the steps on the landing make you trip, the bathroom noises wake you up, and the various chiming clocks punctuate the uncomfortable silence of the night. Murder is done and even overheard, but the commercial traveller with dirty photos has a firm alibi based on the hour of midnight, until Montague Egg realises that a notional travelling clock on the night-table next door may have caused the 'sweet, vibrating, mellow tone' that seemed to come from a town clock in the distance. The clue of the vibrating musical tones of a distant clock is mentioned twice in the story, but only Egg deduces that this must have been an old-fashioned repeating clock with a coiled spring, accidentally knocked against well after midnight so it chimed twelve.

Most of the short stories are based on a simple observation, the germ of an idea round which a whole text is subsequently built. In *Holiday* the three Egg stories come close to the mere mechanical expansion of a thematic discovery: thus the garage clock motif is preceded by a sketch that recurs in Dorothy L. Sayers: the commercial room at the Pig and Pewter is filled with chattering drinking men. One man is aloof, silent or hidden behind a newspaper. In other stories the scene can be a railway carriage (Sayers is extremely fond of the mystique of British railways, of duped ticket-collectors, missed connections, labelled luggage, chance meetings with would-be murderer or future victim), a hairdresser's shop, a hotel lounge, a dinner table. In 'Sleuths on the Scent' Egg unmasks a disagreeable member of the bar-room company, determining that he was a chemist by inviting him to take the stopper out of a bottle of perfume. The dominant idea is that one knows an academic from the way he handles a book (or arranges the volumes on his library bookshelves; see 'The Professor's Manuscript'), a salesman from the way he handles a wine bottle, a doctor or chemist from the way he uncorks a jar. The story 'Poisoned Dow '08' is built round the idea of an ingenious corkscrew with a fine tube inside, used for introducing nicotine poison into port without disturbing the cork. A Wimsey story, 'The Necklace of Pearls', constructs a whole Christmas gathering and party guessing-game round the idea that pearls resemble the berries on mistletoe (where they are in fact pinned during a part of the charade). Again 'The Fountain Plays' is composed to illustrate the danger of removing a body from place *a* to place *b* in order to simulate an accident. The victim was killed in the house but then transported to a garden basin. However, the wind changed after the hour when the body was placed in the fountain so that the corpse was not sprayed. The butler draws this fact to his master's attention. The blackmailer has been killed and now the butler politely requests an immediate doubling of his wages '. . . to begin with'.

'The Queen's Square' organises a fancy dress ball in which a guest is murdered, and even provides a diagram. The detection depends on realising that false lantern lights would change the colour of the dress on the murderer's accomplice. Realising this, the accomplice shifts the lantern back the following morning.

Since the victim was a blackmailer, Wimsey and the police voice the common prayer that this 'accessory after the fact' may be acquitted or let off with a light sentence. In all these stories the dialogue is light and colourful in such a way as to represent the milieu in question: party-goers, commercial travellers, stolid policemen, the apparently irrelevant patter of Wimsey (now paralleled by the absent-mindedness and head-scratching of the American TV-hero Columbo), the stiff deportment of butlers, the anxious banalities of suburban commuters. In general the most likely candidate among the suspects is sympathetic. His guilt is discarded, and then a second candidate, rude or brusque in his behaviour, is irrevocably landed with the guilt. The police inspectors are hardly characterised at all. Servants and house staff are fussy but usually innocent. Suspicion falls first on the wrong character, subsequently on the right one. In a few paradoxical pieces there is no crime at all, and the whole edifice of suspicion is seen to be misconceived. The weather may have been forbidding, the surroundings menacingly Gothic, headaches and illness induced by nerves rather than poison. This is the case in the exemplary 'Scrawns', where a body buried outside the gloomy country house turns out to be a marble statue which the owner could not bear on his property, but which has to be disinterred when the donor aunt comes down to stay.

The twelve stories in *Lord Peter* are more ingenious puzzles, all featuring Wimsey in an eccentric environment (often aristocratic, Gothic and charged with sinister violence) and decked in bizarre titles which provide an initial clue to the reader: 'The Abominable History of the Man with Copper Fingers', 'The Piscatorial Farce of the Stolen Stomach', 'The Bibulous Business of a Matter of Taste', 'The Fantastic Horror of the Cat in the Bag', and so on. In one story, Wimsey tells his valet Bunter that 'the unpremeditated course is usually the safest'; indeed practically every murder in a Dorothy Sayers mystery is preplanned. There is fell intent and nefarious design. This liberates the plot from the need for a court-room ending, which would show motive, degree of guilt, possible innocent involvement. Only *Clouds of Witness* ends in a trial scene, and this is because Wimsey's bumbling brother, the Duke of Denver, refuses to give an alibi which might dishonour a farmer's wife. We never learn the eventual length of a murderer's prison sentence. If the murderer is to be hanged, he is headed for hanging in a single·

sentence (or less) after his identity is revealed. Thus the police feature in Sayers as enforcers of the law rather than protectors of the public. The judiciary does not have a part to play, though lawyers are often consulted on points of information (as in *Unnatural*).

Inquests and coroners' courts provide in fact a more favoured stamping ground for the hunters and the hangers-on than the police station and the criminal court. Journalists and men-about-town seem every bit as knowledgeable as detectives and professional men. These reflections lead Sayers' everyman reader very easily to the story 'The Man Who Knew How', a brilliant composition based on irony and misunderstanding. Also, in the modern vogue, this story has strong leanings towards being a meta-novella. Aspects of Sayers' own art are analysed in the course of it. There is a perfect explanation for the coincidence of several chance meetings between the suspicious private citizen Pender and the mysterious man who claims it is simple to get away with any murder. The two men meet in the canonical ambience: a railway carriage. They are rattling along from Birmingham to Rugby but Pender can't keep his attention on *Murder at the Manse*. He offers *The Paper-Clip Clue* to his irritating companion in the carriage. Both titles, with their banal alliteration and stylised reference to Gothic scenario and minuscule circumstantial evidence, seem to demysticise Sayers' own vocation as she writes this very story which is in the same genre. The plot Pender is reading errs by being too studied, forcefully elaborate in a way that one would casually associate with Sayers herself:

> But the story was of the academic kind that crowds all its exciting incidents into the first chapter, and proceeds thereafter by a long series of deductions to a scientific solution in the last. . . .
> Twice he had to turn back to verify points that he had missed in reading. Then he became aware that his eyes had followed three closely argued pages without conveying anything whatever to his intelligence.

Such a story precariously spins too thin a 'thread of interest'. Sayers astutely shows the deficiency in reader performance which will inevitably flow from a grade-B plot ('Twice he had to turn . . .').

She then puts together a cunning study in curiosity and recurrence. The anonymous railway passenger hints that 'sulphate of thanatol' plus a hot bath will kill anyone without trace. Pender starts noticing bath deaths in his daily newspaper. He starts attending inquests on them. The stranger is usually there too. The stranger comes to his home for a drink, calling himself (of course) 'Smith'. Pender falls ill, suspecting 'Smith' of doctoring his whisky. Eventually he confronts Smith with attempted murder, after a meeting at an inquest; he is restrained by the police. After a further inquest Pender pursues Smith through the fog and kills him with a blow from a sandbag. In an artificially staged finale Pender goes to a journalists' pub and hears Smith's death discussed. He was a crime journalist and the life and soul of every railway carriage, terrifying poor citizens with stories of perfect killings and sulphate of thanatol. At which he faints clean away.

The short story 'The Man Who Knew How' is exemplary in its morality. Convinced that he is doing right, the duped Pender commits a moral killing and therefore Sayers does not make him get caught. He is like the plucky wife, the accomplice in the ballroom story 'The Queen's Square'. The trickster Smith carries out the deception with the fantastic aid of coincidence: Pender gets a chill after they drink together. The police do not tell Pender that Smith is a crime reporter, and so forth. But the preposterousness of these coincidences is mitigated by the sparse grey railway carriage and the universal travelling companion who insists on starting a conversation.

The pathetic fallacy derived from the mist and fog, in dark London streets, in 'The Man Who Knew How', makes the coshing of Smith easier to understand and tolerate morally. In Dorothy Sayers' art it shows that private citizens in England are truly interested in murder. It confirms a sharp insight expressed in Sarah Gertrude Millin's novel *Three Men Die* (1934) that all people are interested in 'sex and destruction':

> Sex and destruction. They were the profoundest concerns of humanity, and humanity craved indulgence of these concerns at second hand, if not at first hand.[2]

Part of the thrill of Sayers' 'Whodunit How' plot is the certainty of hanging that awaits the party on whom the crime is proved. The vicarious *frisson* and atavistic reader-participation in violence and its punishment is an integral component of Dorothy Sayers' technique. It provides the reader with second-hand indulgence in crime and also allows him to co-operate in hunting down a guilty villain. The corollary of this successful pursuit is that he can rub his hands with the anticipation of a vicarious hangman. Truth comes out but the rope is tightened. Raymond Chandler seems to miss this ingredient in Sayers' work when he roundly chastises as 'her essay in critical futility' the introduction which she wrote to the first *Omnibus of Crime* (1928), and goes on to criticise the glaring lack of realism in her fiction:

> It was second-grade literature because it was not about the things that could make first-grade literature. If it started out to be about real people (and she could write about them – her minor characters show that), they must very soon do unreal things in order to form the artificial pattern required by the plot. When they did unreal things, they ceased to be real themselves. They became puppets and cardboard lovers and papiermâché villains and detectives of exquisite and impossible gentility.[3]

Gaudy Night (1935), however, is more than a detective novel. It advertises itself by its very title as an 'Oxford novel'. Julian Symons castigates it as 'a woman's novel full of the most tedious pseudo-serious chat between the characters that goes on for page after page'.[4] It throws in female undergraduate slang like 'G. P.' (*grande passion*), accurately translates the Latin of the university statutes, and delicately unravels the neurosis and pain of the process of ageing. Paradoxically there is no murder and little violence. This is the only full-length Sayers study in which the police are not called in. The author is clearly repaying a deeply felt debt of nostalgia to Somerville College and to the ordered world of academic integrity. Fussy little spinsters and ex-graduates who have unsuccessfully married farmers are tossed back into the week-end world of the college reunion, the Gaudy. There is a right and a wrong way of pinning a gown, of introducing the word 'values' into a discussion over coffee, or of changing the subject when indiscreet people trample over personal feelings.

In *Gaudy* the qualities of politeness and discretion are celebrated to the point of fastidious excess. Harriet Vane, the celebrated crime novelist and notorious ex-defendant in a murder case, is called back to Shrewsbury College after the Gaudy to throw light on poison letters and a personal vendetta against lady academics. But the real subject is tact: Harriet flees from her awareness of loving the man (aged forty-five) to whom she may owe her life. This flight runs right through the novel. Wimsey proposes marriage to her on a postcard from Paris: the Latin particle '*Num . . .*' starts his single sentence. She rummages in the Latin grammar for 'polite negatives', and sends back the message '*Benigne*'.

The novel is strewn with clues and hints about Dorothy Sayers' own attitude to crime fiction and its errant human subjects. The tart, outspoken tutor says:

> 'But surely . . . you must feel that terrible crimes and the sufferings of innocent suspects ought to be taken seriously, and not just made into an intellectual game',

and in the same conversation Harriet notices that 'there is no chance assembly of people who can't make lively conversation about drains.'

Revising three of her own crime novels, Harriet reflects that

> The books were all right, as far as they went; as intellectual exercises, they were even brilliant. But there was something lacking about them; they read now to her as though they had been written with a mental reservation, a determination to keep her own opinions and personality out of view;

while a little earlier Sayers with mock autobiographical deprecation outlines a Vane plot

> in which an unhappy victim was due to fall suddenly dead in the Royal Enclosure, just at the exciting moment when all eyes were glued upon the finish of a race,

or later tries one where

> She had five suspects, neatly confined in an old water-mill with no means of entrance or egress except by a plank bridge, and all provided with motives and alibis for a pleasantly original

kind of murder. There seemed to be nothing fundamentally
wrong with the thing.

Sayers makes Vane admit to another female don that she makes
mistakes in her plots, especially over the alibis, and that every
tenth reader can spot them. But the errors don't need to be
adjusted in a subsequent edition, as the books are fun rather than
scholarship. At a deeper level than narrative badinage these
thematic pronouncements remind us of the extraordinary search
for truth in both Wimsey's detection and Dorothy Sayers' writing.
He believes in Truth as an absolute. She struggles to create right
balances and to show vanity, weakness and cleverness just as they
are, coexisting in the same person or within a tradition. Truth is
everywhere in Sayers' books, an ideal and a target, far removed
from the public prosecutor's indisputable facts before a jury.

   Much of her search for truth involves a moralising stance. Her
characters pass snappy value judgements on matters of taste,
clothing, style, grammar, speech, class, architecture, wine, food,
etiquette. There are constant glimpses of cads and bounders and
ladies in regrettable hats or Americans with brusque manners.
Yet the thrust of this opinionated research is still towards a level
of truth. Sayers is concerned to give a true account of social
intercourse in pre-war England; *Gaudy* falls in exactly the right
groove to prosecute this idealistic quest for truth and to admire it,
for example, in the unworldly behaviour to which learned and
cloistered women are prone. The crime committed in *Gaudy*
flows from a man whose career and family have been ruined by a
senior academic who spotted dishonest removal of evidence in his
thesis. His academic misdemeanour means the failure of his thesis
and the destruction of a promising local historian. But for
Dorothy Sayers the crime is caused outside Oxford, which itself
stands for Truth. Its effects carry into Oxford and therefore
create great unpleasantness. The crisis is almost a medieval one:
robust Virtue as an alternative to Chaos. By suppressing the truth
a disease is unleashed on the state. The act of denying or
repealing a cool fact warps minds and unfetters a horrifying form
of lunacy. These considerations justify the magnificent threnody
of life outside the ivory tower at the commencement of *Gaudy*.
The passage is a powerful glorification of abstract Truth amid the
base coinage of people's twentieth-century groping:

If only one could come back to this quiet place, where only intellectual achievement counted; if one could work here steadily and obscurely at some close-knit piece of reasoning, undistracted and uncorrupted by agents, contracts, publishers, blurb-writers, interviewers, fan-mail, autograph-hunters, notoriety-hunters, and competitors; abolishing personal contacts, personal spites, personal jealousies; getting one's teeth into something dull and durable; maturing into solidity like the Shrewsbury beeches – then, one might be able to forget the wreck and chaos of the past, or see it, at any rate, in a truer proportion. Because, in a sense, it was not important. The fact that one had loved and sinned and suffered and escaped death was of far less ultimate moment than a single footnote of a manuscript or restoring a lost iota subscript. It was the hand-to-hand struggle with the insistent personalities of other people, all pushing for a place in the limelight, that made the accidents of one's own personal adventure bulk so large in the scheme of things.

Once again in *Gaudy* the technical expertise, with which Sayers places the obvious lead before our eyes and subsequently surrounds it with decoy leads and less plausible suspects, is remarkable. The hoary old clichés about repressed spinsters and soured virginity are raised just often enough to lead the reader to believe that they might account for vandalism, arson and obscene inscriptions around a female-only institution. Deans, anxious students, tutors and fellows have their rooms, walks and motives scrutinised, but all along the obvious candidate is a college servant familiar with the lay-out of the place, who came there with a grievance dating back to her husband. Harriet Vane actually has an extended dialogue with one such suspect early in the book. In it the SCR scout Annie lets slip:

(a) that it is unnatural for women not to marry,
(b) that a library for women is a waste,
(c) that women should be good wives,
(d) that she has suffered hard times,
(e) that according to the Bible: 'much learning hath made thee mad', and
(f) that all the graffiti appeared since a 'certain person' joined the College.

These admissions suggest a personal grudge, a vendetta against academic women, a motive and a malevolent plan. As Dorothy Sayers says elsewhere in another context, 'It is as simple as that!' But Mrs Goodwin, the Dean's secretary, has also been poor and needed the job, and while she goes away to visit sick children, the College outrages stop. These obvious clues are fluttered very casually in the reader's face, in contiguous but unrelated sentences:

> there was no further outbreak of any kind, not so much as an inscription in a lavatory or an anonymous letter, for three days. The Dean, exceedingly busy, was relieved by the respite, and also cheered by the news that Mrs Goodwin the secretary would be back on the Monday to cope with the end-of-term rush.

Thus we have a large cast of students and lecturers (all for various reasons non-suspects). Then, by mid-book, we have a servant and a secretary (circumstantially strong candidates). But only one of them has both the motive and the opportunity to commit the outrages. Therefore, Wimsey sees that she is guilty; for him it is as simple as that; in other words he cleaves closest to Sayers' reformation of E. A. Poe's fundamental concept that 'when you have eliminated all the possibilities, then whatever remains, however improbable, must be the truth'.[5]

The novel *Clouds of Witness* develops to a keener degree than most the novelist's ear for effete humour or the intuitive aristocratic style so offensive to Raymond Chandler. Here two characters exchange a bet about the number of toes on the kitchen cat; an invitation to play billiards is couched in a throwaway formula such as 'What do you say to shoving the balls about a bit, Freddy?'; and the same characters stolidly declare that socialists and methodists are the same things as 'bounders'. Wimsey speaks, in apocope and truncated syllables, a personal dialect felt to be aristocratic and to the manner born: he says 'y'know' and 'stror'nary', and his sister refers to 'a tarradiddle' and blackmail's being 'so *beastly*'. Their mother, the Duchess of Denver, considers that left-wing people are 'given to drinking coffee and writing poems with no shape to them and generally ruining their nerves'. Yet this subjective categorisation still has its own irony, directed at the speaker herself. Furthermore, when Wimsey asks a nurse in *Unnatural Death* about the murdered Agatha Dawson and some friction that was aroused by calling in her solicitor for a will, he disguises himself as Miss Dawson's distant cousin 'Mr Simms-Gaythorpe', and refers in off-hand fashion to the lawyer as 'the solicitor-johnnie' and 'the will-making wallah, what?'.

When Wimsey says in the same book that he believes the case 'is goin' to be very excitin'', he is adopting an offhand diction to put his informant at ease, and can say later of the 1926 Property Law that he knew 'this simplifying Act would cause a shockin' lot of muddle', where both spellings of the adjective show the different levels of professional and personal involvement respectively. A novel like *Unnatural*, with its wide range of interest in British home-counties life, shows how sharply Sayers is prepared to juxtapose a scheming lesbian multi-killer, Mary Whittaker, with the placid, ongoing, prejudiced muddle of law-abiding, middle-class people. The binary division in Dorothy Sayers' *dramatis personae* is conducted with considerable vigour. Thus Miss Climpson, the independent, self-conscious spinster who conducts discreet investigations for Wimsey where men would fear to tread, is faintly but significantly an outsider in a latter-day Jane Austen world of upper-middle-class marriages, irreproachable female relatives and inherited money. Kitty Climpson, on the other hand, comes from the quirky world of boarding-house lodgers, of ladies' companions, of stifled girlish passions – and she knows it. Inspector Parker, Wimsey's departmental sidekick in Scotland Yard, is a scholarship boy, a product of Barrow-in-Furness grammar school, unglamorous, hard-working and earnest. So he is at first by definition excluded from the fabled world of professional prestige and more or less inherited money which Sayers creates for her London and county class. We can thus create a working model for the thriller's cast:

Danger	Security	Insecurity
Mary Whittaker (the murderer)	London consultancy ⟶	Miss Climpson (spinster in modest circumstances)
	London club	
Mrs Forrest ⟵ (her *alter ego*) ⟵		Bunter, the faithful valet

```
              Home-counties
              farms
                                              Charles Parker
              Fox-hunting
              Wimsey                       ←——————
              Duke's Denver
```

Inspector Parker eventually marries Wimsey's sister Mary, after some embarrassed and old-fashioned encouragement from Wimsey, the ineffectual suitor of Harriet Vane (*Strong Poison*, 1930, ch. 15). Moreover, when Wimsey is still courting Harriet unfruitfully in *Have His Carcase* (1932), Parker is emboldened to write to Wimsey a letter recommending, strictly on Lady Mary's instructions, that Wimsey should 'commit monogamy'. Thus Parker has joined the chosen fold, and sits the rest of his career on the right side of the fence both legally and socially.

In *Strong Poison*, the novel where Harriet Vane is sentenced to hang for murder by arsenic, a sleek and respectable solicitor, with a good address and a houseful of servants, Norman Urquhart, moves out of the secure fold only when suspicion is piled on suspicion that he evolved the perfect crime to dispose of his cousin and fellow-heir:

Danger	*Security*	*Insecurity*
Bohemian intellectual Philip Boyes, poisoned by N.U. ←——	London Norman Urquhart Wimsey	Westmorland Kitty Climpson fakes séance at home of N.U. and P.B.'s rich old aunt, Cremorna Garden
Harriet Vane, living unmarried with Boyes, sentenced for crime	Wimsey goes to visit H.V. in Holloway gaol	Miss Murchison becomes N.U.'s fake secretary and hunts for incriminating evidence in his office.

Dorothy Sayers feels London as a grey, cushioning mass of prestige, politics and protection. Piccadilly, Mayfair and Regent

Square, despite its ladies of dubious profession, are places that suggest solidity and repose. Outside London, in Scotland, in 'Wilvercombe' and the foggy meadows surrounding the country shooting lodge, here lie insecurity and ultimate danger. Sčéglov has traced the same structural pattern for the contrast in the Sherlock Holmes thrillers between indoors (armchair, pipe, fire, heated railway carriage) and outdoors (gas-lit streets, open moor, ambush on the high road).[6]

In some novels like *Carcase* and the minutely detailed Fen country of *The Nine Tailors*, Sayers seems deliberately to cultivate the fertile danger of lower-class, peasant, extra-London settings. The slashing and killing of the victim in both these novels (where the plot is based on a single blinding gimmick, tantalisingly unguessable till the closing chapters) is dark and broodingly violent. In *Tailors* the victim's hands are sawn off to avoid identification by finger-print; then one of the returning treasure-collectors is temporarily tied up in a belfry and leaves his mind and his life during an all-night peal of the bells. Only at the very end do we see *how* death was done; analogously in *Carcase* '*who* killed?' (Bright, Weldon) rapidly gives way to '*how* was he killed?' Once Wimsey deduces that there was a stolen horse to convey the killer to the middle of a beach where the aspirant heir of the Romanovs is waiting to be taken towards his throne in Russia, the interest shifts to '*when* was he killed?' Vane had found the Russian gigolo's corpse at 2.00 p.m. with fresh blood. All the alibis account for this period. But, hey presto, the blood of a Romanov heir might not clot because of haemophilia inherited through the female line. To make the dazzling but complacently banal solution even more sprightly, Sayers finally features Wimsey showing the police a list of eleven points, beginning like an acrostic with the several letters H, A, E. . . (-mophilia).

With these inexhaustible resources, a new trick every book, back-to-front structures, extensive intellectual or social padding, phasing out 'whodunit' in favour of 'when was it done', 'how dunit' or even 'why, with-what-motive-dunit', Dorothy L. Sayers was efficient, no respecter of persons, and the maker of boa-constrictor classics in the detective genre.

NOTES AND REFERENCES

1. P. Craig, 'Arguments for Addiction', *The Times Literary Supplement*, 9 Jan. 1981, p. 30.
2. S. G. Millin, *Three Men Die* (London: Chatto & Windus, 1934), p. 295.
3. R. Chandler, 'The Simple Art of Murder', in *Pearls Are a Nuisance* (Harmondsworth: Penguin, 1964), pp. 192-3.
4. J. Symons, *Bloody Murder* (Harmondsworth: Penguin, 1974), p. 134.
5. H. Haycraft, *Murder for Pleasure: The Life and Times of the Detective Story* (London: Peter Davies, 1942), p. 12.
6. Ju. K. Ščeglov, 'Per la costruzione di un modello strutturale delle novelle di Sherlock Holmes', trans. G. L. Bravo, in *Semiotica della letteratura in URSS* (Milan: Bompiani, 1969), pp. 101-3.

CHRONOLOGY

Dates of first publication:
1923 – *Whose Body?*
1926 – *Clouds of Witness*
1927 – *Unnatural Death*
1928 – *Lord Peter Views the Body*
1928 – *The Unpleasantness at the Bellona Club*
1930 – *The Documents in the Case*
1930 – *Strong Poison*
1931 – *Five Red Herrings*
1932 – *Have His Carcase*
1933 – *Hangman's Holiday*
1933 – *Murder Must Advertise*
1934 – *The Nine Tailors*
1935 – *Gaudy Night*
1937 – *Busman's Honeymoon*
1939 – *In the Teeth of the Evidence*
1942 – *Striding Folly*

All the above works were originally published by Victor Gollancz (London) and reprinted by New English Library (London, 1978-81).

3 Rereading Ngaio Marsh

ALLAN C. DOOLEY AND LINDA J. DOOLEY

The mystery writers whose novels not only hold up but actually improve on second reading can be counted with ease: Poe, Chandler, Sayers, Hammett – the reader is invited to fill out the short list. Such a list will probably include for the most part authors who have written a few mystery novels over a fairly long career; criticism generally holds that those who write in volume cannot write with fresh invention and intensity. Standing in defiance of that commonplace are the thirty-one novels of Ngaio Marsh, a writer whose productivity never forced her into weakness of conception or mechanism in construction. Marsh is one of the rereadable novelists because her ingenuity in plotting is always supported by sound psychology, interesting settings, intellectually stimulating problems, and outstanding characterisations. The fact that second and even third readings of Marsh's tales are as enjoyable as the first is testimony to her literary merits: knowing where her story is going in no way diminishes our interest in getting there.

One of the lasting pleasures of a Marsh mystery is the reader's entry into the world of the story. This world is a place, a time, a background, and more; it is a realm defined by an endeavour or a body of experiences that is inherently and immediately interesting. The novels do not usually take place in specific, identifiable locations. The street addresses in London are accurate enough, but Marsh's custom is to invent places that are distilled from real worlds. There is no Cloudyfold (*Overture to Death*) in the west of England, but its hills overlooking Pen Cuckoo are true to life. There is no Ottercombe (*Death at the Bar*), perhaps, but this isolated village with its dangerous and precipitous entrance is reminiscent of a dozen real villages in Dorset or Cornwall. Places in Marsh's fiction are clearly and vividly drawn, with a great deal of attention to appropriate detail. She takes care about the flora, the scenery, the architecture, and anything else about a place that can give us a concrete sense of place and time. Her most memorable descriptions are those of her native New Zealand (in *Colour Scheme, Died in the Wool,* and *Vintage Murder*); the manuka flowers, the hot springs, the mountains and unspoiled forests are rendered with loving detail. Marsh does not limit herself to evoking physical appearances; she captures the aura or atmosphere of the location she is building up in the mind. The lake island in *Photo Finish*, for example, is set down in a primeval wilderness that is in itself a harsh commentary on the artificial and corrupt lives of the people who invade it.

These settings are equally firmly located in time. Marsh always set her novels in the present (that is, the 'now' of the date of publication), and the speech of her characters (as well as their dress and manner) is true to prevailing fashions. Slang and catch-phrases change over the long course of her career, giving each novel a sense of belonging to a particular moment. Marsh's use of dialect is equally fine-tuned. Her characters speak the language of their place and station, and she had a fine ear for the varieties of English speech (including its Antipodean and American forms). With such details of time and place, Marsh's fictional settings establish what becomes for the reader an anchor in reality.

The occupants of these fictional worlds tend to be closed groups that are bound together and are also, to some extent, isolated from the rest of the world. The bonds that unite the group may be as obvious and conventional as the bonds of family, as in the case of the delightful Lampreys of *Death of a Peer* and the pathetic Claires of *Colour Scheme*, or as exotic as the absorbing and degrading bonds of pseudo-religious fervour as in *Death in Ecstasy* and *Spinsters in Jeopardy*, where strange hybrid cults made up from shreds of genuine religions are used to control and manipulate the weak and susceptible, and where the religious elements are supported and maintained by the use of drugs. On the other hand, the links among the members of the group may be as trivial as those of an ordinary house-party; but even a house-party can forge unexpectedly strong relationships. In *Death and the Dancing Footman* the party is made up of people who have good reasons to hate the other guests; in *A Man Lay Dead* the guests play at a murder-game that turns to reality. The bonds of the group may be as deep-seated as those of country families that have lived as neighbours for generations, as in *Scales of Justice*, or as compelling as those of a shared enterprise.

The shared endeavours we observe in the novels contribute significantly to the character and interest that appeal on a second reading. Several of the novels – *Singing in the Shrouds, A Clutch of Constables* and *When in Rome* – show us groups of people travelling together, strangers joined only by their common tastes or destinations. In these novels the travellers' worlds are vividly recreated; through Marsh's detailed and realistic presentations, we join in (respectively) an oceanic voyage, a leisurely trip on an English canal boat and a visit to ancient monuments in Rome. The reader's sense of entering these worlds and joining in their activities is very strong, and the settings and activities are never extraneous; they play an essential part in the working out of the murder puzzle. Some of the enterprises shared by Marsh's characters are artistic; in *Artists in Crime* the main group of characters are painters working under the direction of Agatha Troy, the famous artist who later becomes Roderick Alleyn's wife.[1] We see the artists' daily routines, the progress of their works, their shared emotions. In *Photo Finish* we enter the world of an operatic prima donna whose career and behaviour are as capricious as they are glorious. We also see the artist and her companions at rehearsals and putting on a performance, and these joint efforts are central to the plot. Here, as elsewhere in Marsh's books, the emphasis is on the ways that a shared aim creates links among characters.

Marsh's first and lasting love was the theatre. In several of the novels – *Vintage Murder, Enter a Murderer, Night at the Vulcan* and *Killer Dolphin* – we encounter theatrical troupes working on productions. Life backstage (and, in *Vintage Murder*, on the road) is carefully recreated; the routines and rituals of the actors, crews, and management become essential elements in the plots. In *Night at the Vulcan* the backstage routines of the actors during the play and the materials in their dressing rooms provide vital evidence for Alleyn. In *Killer Dolphin* a closed and neglected theatre undergoing restoration provides the setting of the novel and, through an interesting chain of events, part of the motive for the murder. Two other tales, *Final Curtain* and *False Scent*, involve professional theatre people, seen at home instead of at work. Marsh gives us three playwrights as central characters (in *Death and the Dancing Footman, Grave Mistake* and *False*

Scent), and interestingly enough she does not dwell on the practice of their art in anything like the detail we find in her treatments of painters and actors. Throughout her works dealing with the theatre, Marsh emphasises the closed nature of the theatrical community, particularly the limited community of the working company. The theatrical world she portrays is characterised by hard work, ambition, strong rivalries and strong affections. She points out repeatedly the self-conscious and rather artificial off-stage behaviour of actors, but her great respect for the artistry, dedication and loyalty of good actors is always expressed. She shows us both talented and ordinary human beings at work in a profession that looks far more glamorous from our side of the footlights than from theirs.

The specific world of a Marsh novel, carefully and elaborately drawn, is used at first to draw the reader in; the milieu of the story is quickly established and certain expectations about characters and events to come are raised. Whatever the realm, its activities define the routines of daily life that will be disrupted by murder, and the murder will be so much a part of this world that some feature or detail (seemingly just part of the background) will be closely connected to the murder itself and to the success of the investigation. These closed, somewhat isolated worlds often give the appearance of being calm, well-ordered and decent; the murder comes as a shattering intrusion into a safe realm. But as Alleyn, Fox and the others do their patient work, it becomes apparent that these worlds were not well ordered, not even at the beginning of the story. The very bonds which unify the group – friendship, propinquity, enterprise or accidental circumstance – can be the cause of violence, and the protection that the group finds in isolation is converted, under the pressure of the murder, into alienation and suspicion, which can be resolved only when the group comes to grips with the fact of homicide. This it does not want to do, and often in a Marsh novel some natural event occurs which forces the issues to a crisis: the dense fog that surrounds the boat in *A Clutch of Constables*, the snow that locks in the guests in *Death and the Dancing Footman*, the storm that cuts off the island in *Dead Water* – these are the coincidental events that assist Alleyn in leading the group to a confrontation with the dangerous forces and feelings that were developing below the surface of the world before we entered it.

The seemingly healthy world which presents itself to the reader contains a criminal who acts as an infectious agent. The body of characters – ranging from five or six people in an isolated place to the whole of London Society in *Death in a White Tie* – is unknowingly invaded by someone who feeds on, threatens or directly endangers the group. The murder or murders are the violent symptoms of an established disease, and Alleyn, Fox and their investigations are the physic that must be endured. The treatment has unpleasant side-effects: past crimes, petty or otherwise, are brought to light; established relationships are damaged; the comfortable are afflicted. But once the cure is begun, it must be suffered to the end. As Alleyn puts it, 'Do you realise you're starting something you may want to stop and – not be able to stop?...I think I ought to warn you. I'm a bit of state machinery. Anyone can start me up but only the state can switch me off.'

It is, of course, the working of the 'machinery' as the mystery is solved that provides the chief pleasure of detective fiction. Marsh's puzzles are elegant and stimulating, never bizarre or rococo. The problems of murder and detection she works out for us are dependent on an ordinary world which has gone slightly awry, and part of the pleasure the mind feels in her books results from our own exploration of the ways in which the pattern of the murder twists the pattern of ordinary life for the characters. The chief pleasure lies in discovering how we come to know who did the killing; for the Marsh reader, the identity of the murderer is less important than the pattern of detection. As Alleyn brings himself and the reader to an understanding of the puzzle, the pattern becomes a perfect, complete whole.

However, Marsh does not settle for single puzzles. Many of her novels contain secondary or supplementary problems which the reader can enjoy solving along the way. The supplementary puzzles, like the half-burned note whose message we decipher (or misdecipher) in *Death in Ecstasy*, do not further the main investigation, and can send us down a blind alley or after a red herring. The secondary puzzles, like the blotting-paper traces that must be deciphered in *False Scent* or Rory's half-waking dream of a spiralling stretch of railway in *Vintage Murder*, are subordinate to the major puzzle, but must be solved correctly to reach the right conclusion to it. For these smaller mysteries, as for the large ones, Marsh provides enough data for us to work with.

Critical pieces of evidence are always made available in a

Marsh mystery. Most of the time Alleyn discovers, identifies and describes ample clues right before our eyes; his author is scrupulously fair in posing her puzzles. We have enough information – even excluding matters of motive or character – to solve the crime, if we are smart enough. Alleyn works with the same information we have, but his analysis is maddeningly swift and clear; and it is this analysis that Marsh withholds from us, or renders only in tantalising fragments. We are told that Alleyn explains his thoughts to Fox, but the explanation itself is passed over by the narration:

> 'This inference is strongly supported [says Alleyn to Fox] by the fact that I saw an envelope with a wad of typescript inside, addressed in the Colonel's hand to Mr Phinn, on Mr Phinn's desk. So what, my old Foxkin, are we to conclude?'
> 'About Chapter 7?'
> 'About Chapter 7'.
> 'You tell me', said Fox with a stately smile. Alleyn told him.
> 'Well, sir', Fox said, 'it's possible. . . '.   (*Scales of Justice*)

> 'We're in for a reconstruction, my boy, and I'll tell you why. Now, listen'. [End of chapter!]   (*Death of a Fool*)

At such points the reader is left to his own devices, and a second or third reading confirms that Marsh has given enough information for us to guess Alleyn's thoughts accurately. On a first reading, we must do what Alleyn does – separate the important clues from the irrelevancies. We go through all the phases of his investigation with him; we hear the interviews; we get the medical report; we see the fingerprint evidence developed, and so on. Sometimes in mid-story a local superintendent, a chief constable, or other intelligent character will present us with a list of suspects or an outline of the case; these are either misleading or oblivious to some crucial aspect of the crime, and if we are clever enough we will see this. Thus we get a chance to outsmart somebody – we cannot be as brilliant as Alleyn, who is always ahead of us, but at least we can be better detectives than the character who sums up. Our own interest in solving the case is sustained by our faith in a principle rigorously adhered to by Alleyn and his creator: *the evidence is always present*.

Sure in this conviction, Alleyn begins his tasks. He may enter the novel on the first page or two-thirds of the way through, but his approach is almost always the same. The reader who takes up Marsh's works chronologically soon learns the intricacies of CID procedures, procedures that are so firmly established that when Alleyn takes a chance and flushes out a fact with bold tactics, psychological pressure or low cunning, Marsh sardonically informs us that 'Alleyn clearly exceeded his duty.' The steps are familiar enough: keep the scene of the crime undisturbed; get the medical evidence; interview everybody who might be connected with the victim; build a dossier on the victim's habits and movements; think, probe, wait; increase the pressure, even to the point of holding a reconstruction of the crime; fit in the last piece of the puzzle and make the arrest. To say only this is to suggest a mechanical or formulaic approach to the mystery novel which Marsh almost never falls into. She has her habits as a writer, but even these allow for so many possibilities of development that the reader will always be delightfully misled.

Of the classic three elements in crime detection – means, motive and opportunity – Alleyn usually concentrates on opportunity. In a few cases, such as *Death at the Bar*, he might agree with Lord Peter Wimsey: 'If you know how, you know who' – but in a Marsh novel the place for the reader to look and think is opportunity in all its guises (access to the victim, access to the means of murder, time enough to commit the crime, and so on). Alleyn's interrogations move towards establishing a minute-by-minute account of who was where at the time of the murder; often the opportunity timetable must be refined to minutes or even seconds, though sometimes, as in *Artists in Crime* and *A Clutch of Constables*, it is a matter of hours. Usually there is physical evidence that assists in filling in the timetable – a sequence of footprints, the condition of the corpse, an unusual means of conveyance, or the impossibility of covering a certain distance in the required time, for example. Since plentiful physical evidence makes for effective prosecutions, Alleyn tries to base his map of movements and times on the kinds of facts that will serve in court.

But physical evidence of motives is less likely to appear, and such evidence is difficult to interpret correctly. Most murder cases are rife with motive, and Alleyn avoids thinking about it as much as he can. As he bursts out in *Death of a Fool*, 'I *despise* motive. ...The case is lousy with motive...it won't bring home the

bacon, Brer Fox. Opportunity's the word, my boy. Opportunity.'
He never changes his opinion. A preoccupation with motives is
the sign of the amateur; the professional investigator cannot find
much good in studying impulses that leave such problematical
evidence, if any. In a Marsh mystery, we have the problems of
how and *when* the crime took place laid out and solved – and all the
while, of course, we want to know *why*: the inner workings of the
murderer's mind are the ultimate mystery for the reader. Marsh
obliges us to a degree. Many of the novels conclude with Alleyn
explaining the whole case – motives, emotions and all – to Troy,
or Nigel Bathgate the journalist, or to one of the exonerated
suspects. For the most part, however, analysis of the killer's mind
is left to the reader.

The means and cause of death leave plentiful evidence in most
cases, and Marsh enjoys making the question of means a
complicated secondary puzzle for the reader. She has a taste for
the complex means, from the classic pistol-rigged piano (with a
few new tricks) in *Overture to Death* to the deadly spray of *False
Scent*; her murderers contrive fiendishly complicated and
intricate death-dealing devices from the most ordinary objects.
One tends not to find in Marsh the exotic South American
poisons (cyanide does the job well enough), the Indian throwing
sticks, or Chinese death-needles; she is fascinated by the potential
deadliness of the most commonplace things. The murderer acts
under rapidly accumulating, desperate compulsions; the killing is
planned at the last minute and executed with the materials at
hand. In *Death and the Dancing Footman*, the murderer creates
a seemingly insoluble closed-room mystery by using fishing tackle
and drawing pins to remove himself from the scene. The killing in
Vintage Murder is witnessed by Alleyn himself, and it has been
accomplished by a clever rearrangement of the ropes, pulleys and
weights used to move theatrical sets. Having trained her faithful
audience to expect this sort of thing, Marsh proceeds to double-
cross us. In a *Wreath for Rivera* she sets up the possibility of a
nicely complicated means of murder (one which throws all
suspicion on one character) and allows us to blind ourselves to the
plain but critical piece of evidence that proves the murder was
done simply, directly and by somebody else entirely.

The prime fact of murder – the corpse itself – is not only
present, but graphically described in grisly detail:

Roberta saw inside the lift. Lord Wutherwood was sitting in there. A ray of light from the roof of the lift-well had caught the side of his head. For the fraction of a second she had an impression that in his left eye he wore a glass with a dark ribbon that clung to the contours of his face. Then she saw that the thing she had mistaken for a glass was well out in front of his eye. . . . His mouth and his right eye were wide open and inside his mouth the sound of gargling grew louder, and still Roberta could not move. *(Death of a Peer)*

Hazel Rickerby-Carrick's face, idiotically bloated, looked up: not at Troy, not at anything. Her mouth, drawn into an outlandish rictus, grinned through discoloured froth. She bobbed and bumped against the starboard side. And what terrible disaster had corrupted her river-weed hair and distended her blown cheeks? *(A Clutch of Constables)*

The sharp beam of light ran from the torch to the table. It ended in the man's face. It was the face of a gargoyle. The eyeballs started from their sockets, the protruding tongue was sulphur yellow. The face was yellow and blue. . . . Not without an effort he examined the terrible face. There were yellow spots on the jaw amongst the half-grown beard. The mouth was torn, and a glance at the finger-nails showed by what means. *(Artists in Crime)*

The Sommita lay spread-eagled on her back across a red counterpane. The bosom of her biblical dress had been torn down to the waist and under her left breast, irrelevantly, unbelievably, the haft of a knife stuck out. . . . a thin trace of blood had slid down toward naked ribs like a thread of red cotton. The Sommita's face, as seen from the room, was upside-down. Its eyes bulged and its mouth was wide open. The tongue protruded as if at the moment of death she had pulled a gargoyle's grimace at her killer. The right arm, rigid as a branch, was raised in the fascist salute. *(Photo Finish)*

The slow tour of the victim's desecrated body is a literary shock tactic at least as old as Euripides; plenty of writers, great and small, have specialised in such pictures of the results of violence.

At its basest, such writing is mere sensationalism, pitched at our lower instincts and our undeniable curiosity about things most of us have been fortunate enough not to see. Marsh's use of the grisly corpse has a higher purpose than this. She wants to show us forcefully that the consequence of an acted-out urge to kill is not only a puzzle for the detective; the result of murder is a loathsome corpse, the corrupted, degraded husk of a human being who was even now alive. Some characters in the novels get shielded from these ghastly sights, but the reader is not:

> This grotesque shell, seconds before its destruction, had been the proper and appropriate expression of a living woman. Whether here, singly, or multiplied to the monstrous litter of a battlefield, or strewn idiotically about the wake of a nuclear explosion or dangling with a white cap over a cyanosed, tongue-protruding mask – the destruction of one human being by another was the unique offence. It was the final outrage.
>
> (*Dead Water*)

That sense of outrage is what propels Alleyn over the decades, and perhaps Marsh's graphic descriptions of the murdered are intended to evoke the same emotion in her readers. Certainly she means to show the wild desperation and hatred in the murderer, who is often flailing out in terror, in a twisted version of self-defence. Murder is an extreme crime which requires in the killer a wilful turning away from his own humanity. Murder assaults human weakness and violates our sense of the need for mutual aid. It is not surprising, given Marsh's views, that there are so few easeful deaths in her novels. The victims suffer poisoning (frequent), stabbing (several), strangling or smothering (several), beating or clubbing (several), gunshot wounds (three) – all with ghastly results described in relentless detail. Rereading one of these descriptions does not lessen its shock value.

While they live, Marsh's murder victims are a varied lot. Frequently we do not know much about them, or have only a distant view of their behaviour. In the majority of cases there is something distinctly unlikeable about the victim, ranging from having an offensive manner (not a capital crime, though powerful in its effect on the reader's own motivations) to being utterly despicable, mean, cruel, vicious and dangerous. Of the entire list of victims, we know the least about Cara Quayne, who meets a violent end on page 12 of *Death in Ecstasy*. When alive, Quayne is known to us only as a frenzied member of a grotesque religious cult. Alleyn must put together a picture of her life from the remnants of evidence she has left behind, and thus the reader must solve an intermediate problem: 'Who was this woman, and what in her life made her a target for murder?' At the other extreme is Luke Watchman, the victim in *Death at the Bar*, about whom we know a great deal; in fact, the opening chapters of the novel are narrated with Watchman as the centre of consciousness, in a bold and successful experiment by Marsh. Surely the most hateful victims in Marsh's canon must be Idris Campanula, the old dragon of *Overture to Death*, and Lord Wutherwood, the heartless, coarse uncle in *Death of a Peer*. Various likeable characters are subjected to insults, humiliations, threats and punishments by these two worthy victims, and consequently their cases are all the more complex. The plethora of suspects in each novel must be scrutinised in the light of mixed feelings: some decent character may have done the world a favour in knocking off one of these two. And surely the most likeable victim in all of Marsh is Bunchy Gospell in *Death in a White Tie*. Not only do we see parts of the novel through his eyes; not only do all who know him declare Bunchy to be the kindest of men; not only is he charming, helpful and sweet-tempered – he is also a friend of Roderick Alleyn. Making the victim in a murder mystery a fully developed character is risky and unusual, and creating a sympathetic and lovable victim is downright daring. Neither Alleyn nor the reader can effect a professional detachment from this case. One has been touched – even betrayed – and one willingly joins in the relentless hunt for the killer of a good man.

The murderers themselves are less various in temper, behaviour and complexity than their victims. All but a few of the killers are criminals of some kind before they descend to murder, and only a few times does Marsh have recourse to that old standby, the homicidal maniac. Most frequently the prior crimes involve money – an inheritance, a theft, extortion, blackmail or embezzlement – and usually the victim has found out something about the earlier crime. The most powerful motive for murder in Marsh's novels is not hatred or jealousy or even greed, but the fear of discovery. The actual workings of the murderer's mind are closed to us; only in *Overture to Death* do we see briefly into the thoughts and emotions of the killer, and this is well before the crime occurs. Still, we are often able to feel some degree of sympathy for the murderer; Kitty Cartarette, the coarse and uncultivated outsider who marries into the closed little society of *Scales of Justice* is a case in point. We dislike her, and yet we feel sorry for her; her murderous acts are an outgrowth of her social isolation and her wish for love and status. Especially in those cases where the victim is thoroughly hateful, Rory Alleyn, like Lord Peter Wimsey, sometimes wonders whether the crime might better be left unsolved and whether the murderer might· not deserve as much sympathy as condemnation. These reservations, however, are never so strong as to deter him from his detections, unpleasant though they may be.

The side-effects of a murder investigation are numerous, and most of them are unsettling to some or all of the innocent characters. To uncover the pattern which will lead to the murderer, Alleyn must uncover painful matters that people in the case would rather keep hidden. Though he continuously assures people that anything which is found to be irrelevant to the murder case will be buried again and forgotten, he often takes himself and the reader down blind alleys created by someone's desire to prevent the disclosure of a bad act or secret totally unrelated to the murder. All must come out, and what comes out is a pattern in which the murder is embedded. Murder is the crime of crimes, and the worlds which seemed to be sound and healthy at their first appearance turn out to be laced with wrongdoing. Someone has betrayed another; someone is blackmailing; another is working a swindle or angling for a fortune; others are involved in illicit sexual adventures, and so on. Some are fools, and others are knaves; one is a murderer, and many will suffer before he is found out.

In a few cases, the side-effects of this painful process are quite desirable. Some innocent person will discover a falsity about his or her past life and make a change for the better. The more admirable of Marsh's characters find that the ordeal of the murder investigation calls forth reserves of strength neither they nor their closest friends knew they had. An example of this is Carolyn Dacres in *Vintage Murder*, who loses a husband she truly loves (in a limited way), but is able to accept both that loss and the love of a long-time friend and pursuer without allowing feelings of guilt to dominate her life and destroy her chances for happiness. Sometimes a fortune or a piece of property falls unexpectedly into the hands of someone who actually deserves it. Perhaps an artist will have a success, or a precious artefact will be preserved, as in *Killer Dolphin*. And often in Marsh's novels some people will find love in the midst of the disaster. The young lovers (a frequent feature) may well be in the stories as merely part of a successful formula, but they also provide a counterflow to the murder-and-detection plot; as the detectives close in, the lives of the lovers open up with new possibilities for private happiness. In *Artists in Crime* and *Death in a White Tie*, the love affair is Roderick Alleyn's own: in the first he meets Agatha Troy and is drawn to her, only to be severed from her by murder among her students; in the second, the London Season provides a backdrop for the incidental meetings that gradually lead them to love. Marsh's handling of this particular romance is brittle and mannered; the gulf that yawns between Alleyn and Troy is too artificial and smells too much of 'biology is destiny' for current tastes. Nevertheless, the relationship itself is interesting; as Troy and Rory gradually age through the novels (at something less than the normal rate), they move with their culture into a much warmer and more realistic marriage. For Marsh, human beings are such that even out of the deepest possible horror, a degree of understanding and compassion can emerge. The end of the ordeal of finding the killer leaves people free to begin again.

In Marsh's earlier novels especially, more than individuals benefit from the catching of the criminal. The world of each novel is restored to equilibrium and bettered as a whole. The village of Ottercombe in *Death at the Bar* is rid not only of a murderer, but of an embezzler whose secret dealings, affecting a local organisation, led directly to the killing. With the exposure of the murderer in *Death in Ecstasy*, London has one less gang of con artists fleecing the public through bogus religion. The London Society in *Death in a White Tie* is hardly an ideal world – lots of people are committing mild wrongs in it, such as gambling or womanising – but the deeper problem is the presence of a blackmailer, a parasite who feeds on indiscretions and little sins, magnifying them into a society-wide disorder. These and other earlier novels are informed by a powerful conviction that it is possible, through the efforts of such as Roderick Alleyn, to serve the cause of order and goodness. The solution of a murder and its associated crimes, then, leads not so much to the punishment of a single criminal (this is never shown) as to an affirmation that it is possible to decrease the sum of evil in the world. Destruction, death, the painful search for truth, retribution – these are necessary parts of human existence; by coming to grips with them, by combating them and by comprehending them, we can find meaning in them and place ourselves within a universal order.

Gradually, after the second world war, Marsh's views begin to darken. By the time of *Scales of Justice*, she has begun to brood about just how much good Alleyn's solving of a murder or two can do. And the deeper question she poses is whether or not the worlds of the novels are worth saving. The village of Swevenings in *Scales of Justice* is populated by a collection of eccentrics, has-beens, posturers and upstarts, who collectively stand for (according to the nurse who is a major centre of consciousness) the good old ways of doing things in a proper English country district. South Mardian in *Death of a Fool* (another novel about the survival of the old ways) is presided over by a degenerate aristocratic family and looks to be staggering toward an end to its pointless existence. Even the seemingly safe, ideal world of a vacation cruise in *Singing in the Shrouds* is infected with jealousy, rivalries and the presence of a perverted homicidal maniac. *Tied up in Tinsel* represents an ironic return to the country-house murder tale, now headed by a rather repellent host with a household of convicted murderers as his servants. He and his cohorts are not representatives of a fine old tradition; they are restorers and collectors – ghouls of a sort, who feed upon old traditions but don't uphold them. Such are the worlds and the people Roderick Alleyn now must protect and cure.

In the still later *Black as He's Painted*, there is little or no suggestion that Alleyn's detection of the murderer makes a significant difference to the community (now a confused international mélange), or even satisfies Alleyn personally. In this novel Alleyn's values and methods come into direct conflict with those of a friend from school days who is now the despotic president of an African republic. In the end, though our initial, civilised sympathies lie with Alleyn and the Yard, the value system of the African, marked as it is by loyalty, dedication and high purpose, becomes a kind of heroic force. Like Alleyn, we are forced to accept a value system we cannot wholly condone. No real justice, legal or rough, has been done; Alleyn has suffered a painful betrayal, and murder has been officially overlooked. *Black as He's Painted* takes place in a world of political intrigue which extends beyond Alleyn's reach. Similarly, other late novels transmit a sense of a global web of criminality through repeated references to the international drug trade. When Alleyn deals with the violence of drug-traffickers in *When in Rome* and *Spinsters in Jeopardy*, he faces a destructive force that no legal power can control, a force that infects minds and feeds on that infection. Murders – once the shocking event at the centre of evil – seem to be mere symptoms of an epidemic disease. In Marsh's last novel, *Photo Finish*, another kind of widespread criminal network is presented: the mafia vendetta stretches across decades and continents to strike down the prima donna. Alleyn finds out the secrets and nabs the murderers in these novels, as he always has, but the reader knows that the imperative battle of the forces of order against the chaos of evil is ultimately futile.

Yet still we read, and reread, as we always will with a classic author. For entertainment value, for the intellectual stimulation of a new puzzle and a range of new issues, for the pleasure of meeting old friends – Rory, Troy, Fox, Bailey, Thompson and the others – again in a new setting, for her more probing meditations on evil and for her other literary excellences, three generations of readers eagerly awaited the next Ngaio Marsh novel. The thirty-one she gave us over nearly forty years have aged well, and rereading them gives ample proof that Ngaio Marsh was not only a master of her craft, but a fine and thoughtful artist as well.

NOTE

1. We have dealt very little in this essay with the details of Roderick Alleyn's life and personality, preferring to direct the reader to the excellent 'biography' by Earl F. Bargainnier, 'Roderick Alleyn: Ngaio Marsh's Oxonian Superintendent', *Armchair Detective*, 11:1 (Jan. 1978) pp. 63–71.

CHRONOLOGY

Publication data are given for the earliest imprint of each work, and the current American paperback publisher is indicated by [B] (Berkley Publishing Company, New York) or [J] (Jove Publications division of Harcourt Brace Jovanovich, New York).

1934 – *A Man Lay Dead* (London: Geoffrey Bles [J].)
1935 – *Enter a Murderer* (London: Geoffrey Bles [B].)

1935 – *The Nursing Home Murder* (London: Geoffrey Bles [J].)

1936 – *Death in Ecstasy* (London: Geoffrey Bles [B].)

1937 – *Vintage Murder* (London: Geoffrey Bles [J].)

1937 – *Artists in Crime* (London: Geoffrey Bles [J].)

1938 – *Death in a White Tie* (London: Geoffrey Bles [J].)

1939 – *Overture to Death* (London: Collins [J].)

1940 – *Death at the Bar* (London: Collins [B].)

1940 – *Death of a Peer* [alternative title: *Surfeit of Lampreys*] (Boston: Little, Brown [J].)

1941 – *Death and the Dancing Footman* (Boston: Little, Brown [J].)

1943 – *Colour Scheme* (London: Collins [B].)

1945 – *Died in the Wool* (London: Collins [B].)

1947 – *Final Curtain* (London: Collins [B].)

1949 – *A Wreath for Rivera* [alternative title: *Swing, Brother, Swing*] (London: Collins [B].)

1951 – *Night at the Vulcan* [alternative title: *Opening Night*] (London: Collins [J].)

1953 – *Spinsters in Jeopardy* (Boston: Little, Brown [B].)

1955 – *Scales of Justice* (London: Collins [B].)

1956 – *Death of a Fool* [alternative title: *Off with His Head*] (Boston: Little, Brown [J].)

1958 – *Singing in the Shrouds* (Boston: Little, Brown [J].)

1959 – *False Scent* (Boston: Little, Brown [B].)

1962 – *Hand in Glove* (London: Collins [J].)

1963 – *Dead Water* (Boston: Little, Brown [B].)

1966 – *Killer Dolphin* [alternative title: *Death at the Dolphin*] (Boston: Little, Brown [B].)

1968 – *A Clutch of Constables* (London: Collins [B].)

1970 – *When in Rome* (London: Collins [B].)

1972 – *Tied up in Tinsel* (London: Collins [J].)

1974 – *Black as He's Painted* (London: Collins [J].)

1977 – *Last Ditch* (Boston: Little, Brown [B].)

1980 – *Photo Finish* (Boston: Little, Brown [B].)

1982 – *Light Thickens* (Boston: Little, Brown.)

4 Dashiell Hammett and the Poetics of Hard-Boiled Detection

JAMES NAREMORE

I

Dashiell Hammett is a profoundly romantic figure, and the most important writer of detective fiction in America after Edgar Allan Poe. During the years when he was doing his best work – chiefly the late 1920s – he managed to reconcile some of the deepest contradictions in his culture. He was a man of action and a man of sensibility, an ex-private-eye who looked like an aristocrat; he wrote five novels and a few dozen stories which provided material for scores of film, radio and television adaptations, but at the same time he evolved one of the most subtle and influential prose styles of his generation. Unfortunately Hammett was an alcoholic in an era when alcoholic authors were glamorous, and this helped cut his work short. In other ways, too, he was a deeply symptomatic writer of the twenties, and his career seems to have ended with the historical conditions that had sustained it. Afterwards, according to Stephen Marcus, 'His politics go in one direction; the way he made his living went in another – he became a hack writer, and then finally no writer at all.'[1]

There is, however, an admirable integrity about Hammett's behaviour in those later years. He worked in Hollywood for a while, but he did not neurotically dramatise himself in the manner of Fitzgerald, nor did he try to write a Hollywood novel. He was not suicidal like Hemingway (whom he resembles in so many other ways), and when a doctor told him he would have to quit drinking or die, he quit. In the fifties he was imprisoned and then blacklisted for his Marxist political sympathies, but unlike many others he did not complain publicly and refused to make himself a martyr. *Tulip*, the unfinished autobiographical novel he worked on when he left prison, is touchingly pastoral and a fascinating account of his attitude towards his work: 'When you write,' his protagonist says at one point,

> you want fame, fortune and personal satisfaction. You want to write what you want to write and to feel it's good, and you want this to go on for hundreds of years. You're not likely ever to get all these things, and you're not likely to give up writing and commit suicide if you don't, but that is – and should be – your goal. Anything else is kind of piddling.[2]

Such behaviour indicates that Hammett was probably as strong as any of his heroes, who are all to some extent like him. The Continental Op has a job similar to the one Hammett once had with the Pinkerton Detective Agency; Sam Spade has Hammett's first name (Samuel Dashiell Hammett); Ned Beaumont resembles Hammett physically; and Nick Charles's life with Nora is based on the one Hammett shared with Lillian Hellman in the early thirties. More importantly, all these characters speak with what might be called the Hammett voice, which can be heard in the passage quoted above. Its diction is homely; its syntax mainly declarative statements strung together with conjunctions. It has a fine rhythm which depends on the rather calculated run-on syntax, the driving repetition of certain words and the variation between long and short periods; nevertheless, this rhythm is meant to seem more instinctive than eloquent. It is a transparent language, of the sort that wants to cut through the crap and get down to truths so basic to the culture that they seem like natural laws. It sometimes makes an appeal to commonplace notions of behaviour, trying to sweep away lies and rationalisations. For example, here is Ned Beaumont speaking to Janet Henry in *The Glass Key* (1931), when she tells him about one of her dreams: 'I think you made that up. It starts out to be a nightmare and ends up something else and all the dreams I ever had about food ended before I ever got a chance to do any actual eating.'[3] And here is Nick Charles telling Nora what will happen to all the characters in *The Thin Man* (1938) after the murder has been solved: 'Nothing new. They'll go on being Mimi and Dorothy and Gilbert just as you and I will go on being us and the Quinns will go on being the Quinns. Murder doesn't round out anybody's life except the murdered's and sometimes the murderer's.'[4]

This less deceived language is always placed in the dialogue of the detective or in his first-person narration, rather than in the neutral, third-person descriptions, where Hammett's prose is much more ambiguous and stylised. It is a dramatised voice, taking the form of a virile man talking to women, children or mendacious crooks. It isn't quite the voice of Reason, as with Dupin or Holmes, because it has less to do with solving puzzles than with exposing various kinds of falsehood or naïveté. Nor is it quite the voice of Metaphysics or Morality, as with Father Brown (even though in a general sense any fictional detective becomes the story's omniscient narrator and hence a type of God), because Hammett is sceptical of absolutes and his heroes are not virtuous. It is more like the voice of Male Experience, and it usually speaks with brutal frankness after a period of reticence or silent knowingness. In *Red Harvest* (1929), when the ageing capitalist tells the Continental Op that he wants a 'man' to 'clean this pig-sty of a Poisonville for me, and to smoke out the rats, little and big', the Op replies, 'What's the use of getting poetic about it? If you've got a fairly honest piece of work to be done in my line, and you want to pay a decent price, maybe I'll take it on.'[5] In *The Maltese Falcon* (1929), when Brigid argues that Spade can't turn her over to the police because he loves her, he comments, 'But I don't know what that amounts to. Does anyone ever? But suppose I do? What of it? Maybe next month I won't. . . . Then I'll think I played the sap.'[6] Clearly it is a voice which cannot be taken in by abstract appeals to morality or even love, and while it situates itself on the right side of the law, it is too honest to give the usual reasons for being there. As Ned Beaumont says, 'I don't believe in anything.'

The sceptical, unpretentious honesty of Hammett's various spokesmen is one of the things that marks him as a writer with serious aspirations. But because he is a writer of detective stories, and because he is such a classic instance of the literary tough guy, he presents special problems for the critic who wants to take him seriously. His fiction is a rare combination of light entertainment and radical intelligence. He challenges the easy distinctions between popular and high art, and the critical language that normally sustains those divisions; any critical approach to him is likely to go awry if it becomes too serious, too sociological or too frivolous. A much greater problem is that the toughness of his characteristic voice is sexualised, linked to fantasies of male power, and nowadays especially it invites an easy clinical interpretation. Even Neil Simon has been able to joke about Sam

Spade, in *Murder by Death*, where the private eye is revealed as a closet gay. Hence the sexual case against Hammett needs to be acknowledged at the outset, in order to get at the complexities beyond it.

The pen may not always be a substitute penis, but with Hammett it often seems to be. His best prose has a Parnassian hardness, a lack of 'feminine' adornment, and many of his titles have a phallic quality. He writes about strong, silent men who have an acute sense of discipline, and about predatory women who have to be sent off to prison. His detectives are usually bachelors, but unlike their nineteenth-century predecessors they are loners, eating meals in various restaurants or hotel rooms, living as far from domesticity as a frontier scout. They are somewhat homophobic – see, for example, the Continental Op's reaction to Burke Pangborne in 'The Girl with the Silver Eyes', or Sam Spade's reaction to Cairo and Wilmer in *The Maltese Falcon* – and although they are attracted to the sexy females they encounter, the only women they trust are the ones who behave like boy scouts. Thus Nora Charles is described by a veteran cop as a lady with 'hair on her chest', and Sam Spade compliments Effie Perine, his 'boyish' secretary, by saying 'You're a demned good man, sister.' Of course Hammett wrote charmingly about married life in *The Thin Man*, but Nick and Nora Charles are only buddies compared to Ned Beaumont and Paul Madvig, the male couple of *The Glass Key*, who have an intense, passionate, sometimes violent relationship that feels more like love.

Hammett was fond of blood sports and military camaraderie, and he wrote fiction in which women are always 'other' to a central male consciousness. It would be meaningless to call him a latent homosexual because everyone is always potentially another sex; nevertheless his work speaks a masculine ideology, generally portraying women as naïve students of male wisdom or as dangerously amoral creatures. What redeems Hammett is that his protagonists never become proto-fascist supermen of the James Bond variety. His novels are written in an impersonal, detached style that sometimes allows the male ethos to undermine itself, and his readers are not allowed to settle into a comfortable identification with characters like Sam Spade. The sparse autobiographical evidence indicates that Hammett *was* tough, in a way that goes far deeper than braggadocio or sportsmanship. His temperament was egalitarian, and his later work, no doubt tempered by his relationship with Lillian Hellman, shows that he was somewhat dissatisfied with the figure of the phallic detective; the autobiographical protagonist of *Tulip* even jokes about homophobic 'he-men'. In any case, a properly useful analysis of Hammett's sexual politics should avoid glib ego-psychology; it should focus on Hammett's language rather than his 'personality', partly because he was always deeply concerned with problems of literary form, and partly because his style was an historical phenomenon.

American literature of the twenties was generally hard-boiled, and if Hammett had not become the 'father' of the tough detective, someone else probably would have. Actually his attraction to the detective story is as much a sign of his aestheticism as of his love of male action. Like Chandler, he began by writing verse, and like the other aesthetes of his period he found his true vocation by reacting against the genteel, prettified, vaguely homosexual tone of the nineties. (Dupin and Holmes were of course nineteenth-century aesthetic types.) In the teens the manner of Pater and Wilde had given way to the manner of T. E. Hulme, and metaphors of sculpture began to replace metaphors of music in poetic theory. Pound, Yeats and the early Imagists had tried to purge poetic language of 'rhetoric' and beauty, a project later supported by the writers who experienced the first world war. The 'little magazine' became a vehicle for most of these authors, but Hammett's distinction is that he applied the new literary sensibility to the pulps, attacking bourgeois values from below rather than from above. In fact, *Black Mask*, where his hard-boiled stories first appeared, was begun by H. L. Menken as a way of supporting *The Smart Set*, a little magazine which published some of the early modernists. Hammett was therefore very much a part of the literary atmosphere of his period, and it is no accident that he and Hemingway became popular at virtually the same moment.

Hammett's writing, like Hemingway's, is an especially clear instance of the irony and suspicion of noble language which can be found everywhere in post-war literature, a phenomenon admirably documented by Paul Fussell in *The Great War and Modern Memory*.[7] Indeed Hammett was a veteran of the war, which left him with a serious respiratory ailment, and all his life he was fascinated with combat. Among the other extra-literary influences on his work, his experience as a Pinkerton agent in the years before and after the war is obviously of major importance. San Francisco, where he worked in the early twenties, was the most aesthetically pleasing of American cities, but it was also the home of the Hearst Press, the Barbary Coast and the most famous of Chinatowns. It had some of the feel of the wild west, and Hammett lived there during one of the most brutal phases of the national history – a period of unrestrained capitalism and vicious labour struggles, of official corruption in the White House and of legal hypocrisies spawned by Prohibition. In America in those days, as Sam Spade says, you could 'take the lid off' life, in much the same way as the war had taken the lid off European civilisation. Nevertheless, the Depression had not yet arrived, and it was still possible to view it all in terms of rather detached, cynical adventure stories. Hammett was in a good position to become the Flaubert of detective fiction.

II

The reputation Hammett ultimately achieved is succinctly stated by his current paperback publishers, who describe him as the 'creator of the modern, realistic crime novel'.[8] We should remember, however, that the origin of any literary form is impossible to establish, and as Hammett's protagonist in *Tulip* says, 'Realistic is one of those words when it comes up in conversation sensible people put on their hats and go home.' Hammett's work seems real in the sense that it constructs a relevant model of his society, but also in the sense that it never departs truly from the realist conventions of the nineteenth century. He was a key practitioner of what was immediately named a 'modern' style, but much of his early work was geared to the demands of pulp fantasy. Before examining some of the more unusual aspects of his fiction, therefore, it may be useful to emphasise the typical fantasies he offers his readers.

One of his stories, 'The Gutting of Couffignal', has an amusing self-reflexive moment which alludes to his function as an entertainer. The Continental Op has been hired to guard some expensive wedding presents at a reception on the island of Couffignal, just off the California coast. After the guests have left and the owners of the house have gone up to bed, he pulls up a chair beside the mound of gifts and decides to pass the time by burning a few Fatimas and reading a book:

The book was called *The Lord of the Sea*, and it had to do with a strong, tough, and violent fellow named Hogarth, whose modest plan was to hold the world in one hand. There were plots and counterplots, kidnappings, murders, prison-breakings, forgeries and burglaries, diamonds large as hats and floating forts larger than Couffignal. It sounds dizzy here, but in the book it was as real as a dime.

With a few qualifications, this is a good description of the story Hammett is writing, which suddenly turns into a tale of bombings, burglaries and conspiracies, peopled with Russian emigré crooks, a femme fatale, and assorted thugs who plan to loot the entire island. Like all of Hammett's work, the story contains elements of mystery, including an ending in which the detective uncovers a killer we had not expected. Nevertheless, Hammett is writing adventures as much as puzzles, so he keeps his detective in physical danger, transforming the intellectual quest into an actual chase, with bullets flying through the air. The audience for *Black Mask* seems to have expected such plots, and Hammett gave them true thrillers, stories that are still interesting for the way they subordinate everything to flat, paratactic statements of action.[9]

But if, as Graham Greene once suggested, the key to the modern thriller lies in the formula, 'adventure happening to unadventurous men', then Hammett's work is more modern than *The Lord of the Sea*. Certainly his hero is no Hogarth. All his early fiction concerns a short, fat, fortyish man with no name and no life beyond his job with the San Francisco branch of the Continental Detective Agency. He is an unglamorous and hence 'realistic' creation who, in terms of his general social status, probably resembles the majority of Hammett's first readers. There is in fact a potentially Walter-Mittyesque comedy (which Hammett takes care not to exploit) in the disparity between the Op's appearance and his physical powers. For example, in a quasi-Western story called 'Corkscrew', involving murder in an Arizona mining town, the Op rides a bucking bronco which tosses him four times; on the last try he punches out a cowboy who wants to restrain him from remounting. A bit later in the same story, the Op has a street fight with an ex-boxer, who breaks his fist on the Op's jaw. In *Red Harvest* he spends all night drinking gin with a blonde, takes a cold bath, and has a fight with a killer, whom he overpowers and hauls to the police; he then takes another cold bath and has another battle with *two* killers, knocking one out and beating the other to the draw; finally, having been grazed on the wrist with a stray bullet, and without even the benefit of another cold bath, he captures an escaped convict in a dark alley and solves a murder mystery that has had the local police fooled for years.

True, during all this the Op complains about being old and out of shape, and after the events in *Red Harvest* he needs a good twelve hours of sleep. Nevertheless, to borrow one of Hammett's similes, he is as tough as a bag of nails. He resembles the other great detective heroes in being improbably heroic and a bit eccentric – outwardly the quintessential company man, he seems to love his rough life for its own sake. He is an effective instrument of fantasy precisely because he does not encourage readers to imagine that they are handsomer, younger or richer (W. H. Auden's test for 'escapist' literature); instead he encourages the notion that such things do not matter, given courage, stamina and a certain hard-edged view of life.

The Op needs these last qualities because he inhabits a world of almost cataclysmic violence; some of his longer adventures have as much action as a Keystone cops film and more corpses than an Elizabethan revenge tragedy. It is difficult to keep count of the dead in 'The Big Knockover', '$106,000 Blood Money', 'Corkscrew', *Red Harvest* and *The Dain Curse* (1929), all of which have plots that leap from one killing to another and scenes of pitched battle that portray a society literally at war. Hammett published this longer fiction serially in *Black Mask*, making each instalment build to a violent climax or to the solution of a mystery, then having the story continue because the ultimate resolution was not at hand. Even granting the demands of their form, however, the Op stories contain an extraordinary amount of death and destruction. In 'The Big Knockover', an army of crooks invades the San Francisco financial district, loots the two largest banks and has a shoot-out with the entire police department; they escape with the bank money, but their greed makes them begin killing one another, so that the Op's pursuit of them leads to whole rooms full of dead bodies. A comment the Op makes during one of the brawls in the story is an apt description of Hammett's work as a whole during this period:

Swing right, swing left, kick, swing right, swing left, kick. Don't hesitate, don't look for targets. God will see that there's always a mug there for your gun or blackjack to sock, a belly for your foot.

Sometimes this delirious violence freezes into a tableau, as if Hammett were providing material for the pulp illustrations. In *Red Harvest* a prize-fighter wins a match, and as his hand is raised in victory a knife comes whistling out of the audience, its 'silvery streak' ending as the blade plunges into the figher's neck. In *The Dain Curse* the crazed leader of a religious cult attempts ritual murder on a crystal altar illuminated by a beam of blue light, his carving knife poised over the body of a semi-nude woman who is bound head and foot. In 'The Girl with the Silver Eyes', a crook named Porky Grout stands in the middle of a roadway, 'the dull metal of an automatic in each hand', and blasts away at an automobile which is rushing towards him like a 'metal comet'. In 'Dead Yellow Women' the Op is trapped on a stairway in the secret passageway of a house in Chinatown; below him is a beautiful girl with a 'red flower of a mouth' and four Tong-warriors reaching for their automatics; above him is a big Chinese wrestler with a 'foot of thin steel in his paw'.

It is difficult to tell how much burlesque is intended in these over-heated visions – although Hammett seems to me to have a greater sense of humour in the Op stories than is usually recognised. The Op recounts everything in deadpan fashion, as if he were making raw reports under pressure. The style gives him a plausible character, and it suggests that Hammett himself has the same values as his protagonist, doing a quick professional job in a relatively disreputable but adventurous trade, with a minimum of fuss and a single-minded determination to get the story told. In a sense, the plainness of the language contributes to the illusion of realism and honesty, especially when Hammett combines the spectacular events with documentary detail or accounts of the more quotidian aspects of the Op's job. He fills the stories with precise, almost city-map-style references to San Francisco street and place names, and he likes to include bits of information about the 'inside' of professional detective work. In this regard it is worth noting that the self-reflexive passage quoted earlier from 'The Gutting of Couffignal' has a double function: at the same time that it declares an affinity between Hammett and the traditional romancers, it also contrasts the Op's workaday world with that of literature. Hammett may have been writing melodramas, but he knew how to make them as real as a dime.

III

Hammett soon abandoned the Op and began to write more subtle, complex fictions, but even at the first it was clear that his work was as much about language as about toughness and mystery. Although much of his early prose seems to have been hastily composed, it inevitably contains moments of wordplay and lapidary stylisation. Sometimes the clipped, stark language seems pushed toward a kind of self-parody. Here, for example, is an excerpt from the opening of a piece called 'The Farewell Murder':

> I was the only one who left the train at Farewell.
>
> A man came through the rain from the passenger shed. He was a small man. His face was dark and flat. He wore a gray waterproof cap and a gray coat cut in military style.
>
> He didn't look at me. He looked at the valise and gladstone bag in my hands. He came forward quickly, walking with short, choppy steps.
>
> He didn't say anything when he took the bags from me. I asked:
>
> 'Kavalov's?'
>
> He had already turned his back to me and was carrying my bags towards a tan Stutz coach that stood in the roadway beside the gravel station platform. In answer to my question he bowed twice at the Stutz without looking around or checking his jerky half-trot.
>
> I followed him to the car.
>
> Three minutes of riding carried us through the village. We took a road that climbed westward into the hills. The road looked like a seal's back in the rain. . . .
>
> Presently we left the shiny black road for a paler one curving south to run along a hill's wooded crest. Now and then this road, for a hundred feet or more at a stretch, was turned into a tunnel by tall trees' heavily leafed boughs interlocking overhead. . . .
>
> The flat-faced man switched on the lights, and increased our speed.

He sat rigidly erect at the wheel. I sat behind him. Above his military collar, among the hairs that were clipped short on the nape of his neck, globules of moisture made tiny shining points. The moisture could have been rain. It could have been sweat.

We were in the middle of one of the tunnels.

The flat-faced man's head jerked to the left, and he screamed.

In terms of 'content' this is nothing more than the ordinary paraphernalia of Gothic melodrama. The language, however, is more interesting. There is first the play on the name 'Farewell', which suggests that Hammett is interested in something more than pure representation. Then there is the narrator's style, which is so curt that it vaguely resembles free verse, given a kind of significance by all the empty white space around the lines. The language is radically simple, but it can't be described as telegraphic because it contains several deliberate repetitions, little jerking points of emphasis which create a nervous rhythm in keeping with the chauffeur's 'short, choppy' steps: 'A man came through the rain from the passenger shed. He was a small man'; 'He didn't look at me. He looked at the valise and gladstone bag.' Everything has been reduced to a series of bald, brief statements, so that even the simplest figures of speech or variations of syntax are foregrounded. For example, once the car speeds away from the station and into the woods, a complex, alliterative cadence asserts itself: the road 'was turned into a tunnel by tall trees' heavily leafed boughs interlocking overhead'. The imagery works along similar lines, confining itself to a few notes of colour or references to the chauffeur's 'flat face',[10] until a single, vivid simile appears: 'The road looked like a seal's back in the rain.'

In keeping with the demands of a journal like *Black Mask*, the opening of 'The Farewell Murder' is designed to get the story underway as quickly as possible, without windy exposition or authorial promises of dangers to come, offering what the pulp writers used to call narrative 'hooks' to keep the reader turning pages. Hammett conveys everything in dramatic form, but even though he tells everything from the Op's point of view, he has been selective about how much subjectivity he allows us to see. The Op is a sort of *camera obscura*; if he is fatigued by his journey, baffled by his reception, fearful of the speed of the car or the sudden scream, he does not say so. This was a style much admired by the French existentialists in the forties and fifties, who gave it a sort of philosophic interpretation; to them it was a 'zero degree' prose suggesting a mind living completely in the present, in touch with an imminent reality. The cerebral French in those days had a tendency to romanticise the physical Americans, but there is some truth to what they believed. One of the deepest pleasures of reading Hammett may come from the illusion he creates of a mind which never seems alienated, uncertain or even seriously troubled. It isn't a primitive consciousness because it registers things with a certain aesthetic grace; if the world it describes is violent, it responds to that violence by simply attending to the business at hand.

Hammett's later novels use an even more neutral technique, a third-person narration which presents everything from the detective's point of view without ever telling us what the detective is thinking. The narrator stands outside the character, like a camera watching an actor, describing only his movements. But it is typical of Hammett that this language of pure action sometimes calls attention to itself *as* language. Here, for example, is a scene from *The Maltese Falcon*, just after Spade has received a phone call telling him that his partner has been murdered:

Spade's thick fingers made a cigarette with deliberate care, sifting a measured quantity of tan flakes down into curved paper, spreading the flakes so that they lay equal at the ends with a slight depression in the middle, thumbs rolling the paper's inner edge down and up under the outer edge as forefingers pressed it over, thumbs and fingers sliding to the paper cylinder's ends to hold it even while tongue licked the flap, left forefinger and thumb pinching their end while right forefinger and thumb smoothed the damp seam, right forefinger and thumb twisting their end and lifting the other to Spade's mouth. He picked up the pigskin and nickel lighter that had fallen to the floor, manipulated it, and with the cigarette burning in a corner of his mouth stood up. He took off his pyjamas. The smooth thickness of his arms, legs, and body, the sag of his big rounded shoulders, made his body like a bear's. It was like a shaved bear's: his chest was hairless. His skin was childishly soft and pink.

In part, this technique serves the interest of the mystery story, characterising Spade in terms of the objects around him, but keeping his chain of thought a secret until he solves the crime. By withholding information, Hammett gives the plot tension, investing the simplest movements with the importance that gunshots and fistfights had in the earlier fiction. As in the Op stories, the method suggests a world where actions are more important than thoughts; it portrays Spade as a sort of latter-day cowboy, rolling a cigarette while he ponders his next move. In other ways, however, the technique is less 'organic'. Except for the phrase, 'made a cigarette with deliberate care', the description of Spade rolling a cigarette is almost as defamiliarised as the pseudo-scientific account of Bloom returning home in the penultimate chapter of *Ulysses*. It makes Spade a technician, brooding on the fine points of a problem, but it also displaces the traditional ratiocinative values of detective fiction in favour of another quality that was always inherent in the form – a representation of the surfaces of things. Detective stories are the most fetishistic of literary genres because the trivial objects of the investigation – the 'clues' – function like the overdetermined symbols of dreams. But in Hammett's work this overdetermination extends to everything: the reader, confronted with impersonality and a cool, objective description, is invited to interpret the meaning of images. At one point the narrator himself seems almost surprised, or perhaps hypnotised, by these ambiguous surfaces, so that he repeats himself: 'like a bear's. It was like a shaved bear's.'

This is a very different style from Raymond Chandler's, and I think it is closer to the spirit of literary modernism. I make this point because Chandler is normally regarded as a man who polished Hammett's relatively crude innovations, bringing them to their full literary potential. But consider this play with the word order of a descriptive sentence in *The Glass Key*:

> He found and lit a cigar then and, with it between his teeth burning, stood by the table and squinted down through smoke at the front page of the *Observer* lying there.

Again the effect is rather Joycean, and it is the opposite of Chandler, who played syntactical tricks only with the dialogue.[11] Hammett now and then makes the third-person narration rather strange, calling attention to his artifice in a more basic way.

Of course Hammett was conservative in other respects, and was easily adapted to the movies. Hollywood never accurately reproduced the trenchant social observation or the moral ambiguity of his best work, but they took the melodrama and much of the dialogue straight from his pages. A brilliant dramatist, Hammett wrote effective speeches for his characters, but like a film-maker he also used what I have described as a *camera obscura* narration, and he paid close attention to clothing and décor. His most specialised vocabulary refers to colours and fabrics, and he carefully documents popular tunes, slang and hair styles.[12] Sometimes it is hard to tell how much he influenced the movies and how much he was influenced by them. Notice, for example, this description of Janet Henry in *The Glass Key*:

> She turned on a lamp beside the piano and sat down there with her back to the keyboard, her head between Ned Beaumont and the lamp. Her blond hair caught lamplight and held it in a nimbus around her head. Her black gown was of some suedelike material that reflected no light and she wore no jewellery.

The passage seems to have come straight from a Hollywood photographer of the period, complete with backlighting and black-and-white composition – although it suggests that Janet herself has been watching movies and has arranged her own lighting. In any case it shows how much Hammett's prose sometimes aspired to the condition of cinema, and why his novels made some of the best American films.

IV

Hammett was no avant-gardist, but the impersonal, ironic technique of his novels grows out of a deeply critical and sceptical attitude towards American society, a view of life that affects the form of his fiction in other important ways. The endings of his novels are always bleak, even in the early work where there is somewhat less emphasis on characterisaton: in *Red Harvest* the Op solves the mysteries in a technical sense, but nothing has fundamentally changed at the conclusion, and the Op himself has barely survived with his job intact. In *The Dain Curse* the killer Fitzstephan is captured, but he spends only a year in an insane asylum before being set free; most of his body has been destroyed by one of his own bombs, and Hammett's understated description of his insane egotism haunts the end of the story, like an evil that cannot be exorcised. Always Hammett threatens to undermine the authority of the detective and the neat closure of the typical mystery plot; even the tough-guy ideology and the love of adventure which defines his heroes show signs of strain. The following brief review of his later work should indicate the delicate balance he sustained between popular forms and the deep questioning of those forms.

From the first Hammett was admired by critics who did not particularly like the detective-story formula, because in his novels the crimes were messy, the chase circuitous, the solution to the murder less important than the depiction of a *milieu*. To slightly revise Edmund Wilson's famous question, Who cares who killed Miles Archer? In one sense nobody, and that is the whole point of *The Maltese Falcon*. Archer's murder has a crucial function in the plot, and is part of a whole chain of enigmas; nevertheless, we and Spade soon become distracted by the search for the falcon, and one of Hammett's deepest ironies is that Spade himself has a possible motive and the right temperament to have committed the crime. Archer is an unpleasant fellow whom we meet only once, when he crudely looks Brigid up and down and pockets her money. He has been cheating on his wife, who in turn has been having an affair with Spade, and he is not particularly clever or trustworthy as a detective. Spade thinks he is a 'louse' and has been planning to sever the partnership anyway, by legal means. He tells Brigid that she has done him a kind of favour by killing Archer, and when he turns her over to the police the seven reasons he gives have nothing to do with revenge, justice or law and order. Commentators on his long speech usually claim that it shows a 'code' which sustains Hammett's heroes; looked at closely, however, the speech is about nothing more than self-preservation. Spade knows that somebody has to 'take the fall' for the murder, and that Brigid is likely to get a 'better break' from the police. 'When a man's partner is killed', he says, 'he's supposed to do something about it'; in other words he is *expected* to do something about it, and if he did not obey the conventional social ethic, his business would suffer. People would assume he is either incompetent or a killer himself. At the level of Nature rather than Culture, Spade says that he is instinctively a hunter, and that letting his quarry go wouldn't be the 'natural thing'. He admits that this rule has its exceptions, but in this case too much is at stake: his entire position has been compromised by the death of his partner. Brigid obviously can't be trusted anyway, and if he did not turn her over he would have no job or anything else.

Spade's climactic speech indicates that Hammett isn't writing about guilt or innocence, or even about professional ethics, but about what he regards as a bewildering, predatory struggle beneath civilisation. Civilisation makes everyone, including the detective, an impostor. 'Don't be too sure I'm as crooked as I'm supposed to be', Spade tells Brigid. 'That kind of reputation might be good for business.' This remark may serve to reassure the reader about Spade's intentions, but it is a more ambiguous reassurance than we are usually given. It tends to mock the idea of a 'just solution' to murder, just as the Maltese Falcon itself mocks the idea of ownership or private property. Born out of a colossal hypocrisy – a 'Holy War' which, as Gutman says, 'was largely a matter of loot', the Falcon does not rightly belong to anyone. To quote Gutman again, 'An article of that value passed from hand to hand by such means is clearly the property of whoever can get hold of it.' The final irony, as Stephen Marcus has pointed out, is that the *rara avis* turns out to be as bogus as everyone else; a disguised (but rather phallic) signifier, it is supposed to have value beneath its skin, giving a meaning to the frantic, violent activity of the novel.[13] But when the skin is peeled away, there is only a lead shape, an empty object of exchange.

Spade is the hero of this potentially anarchistic world, but he is a hero of an unusual kind. Morally he is hardly any better than his dead partner, and there is nothing particularly likeable about him. Physically and emotionally he is somewhat frightening, a very different character from the one created by Humphrey Bogart in John Huston's film version of the novel.[14] Spade is a big 'bear' of a man with thick fingers and a face described in the first paragraph as 'rather pleasantly like a blond Satan'. He has a nasty temper and an animal quality which Hammett repeatedly emphasises ('Spade grinned wolfishly, showing the edges of his teeth far back in his jaw'). His 'glowing' eyes are contrasted with Brigid's 'velvet' gaze, and this contrast is given meaning by one of his own similes: 'expecting me to run criminals down and then let them go free is like asking a dog to catch a rabbit and let it go.' He seems as potentially cruel as any of his adversaries –

particularly so in the scene where the dying Captain Jacobi delivers him the Falcon: in one hand Spade grasps the statuary, his fingers showing 'ownership in their curving'; with his free arm he grips Effie Perine so strongly that she cries out in pain; and with his left foot he inadvertently steps on the dead Jacobi's hand, 'pinching a quarter-inch of flesh at a side of the palm between heel and floor'.

The novel makes us respect Spade in a complex, qualified way, chiefly because of his intelligence and ability to master his own sometimes ugly instincts. His behaviour suggests that he has a heightened sense of the danger lying in wait for him should he try to join Brigid or Gutman. In the first chapter he is vividly contrasted with Archer, who serves as his foil. Spade has a suspicion of easy sex and money, a reserve that ultimately keeps him alive. He tells Brigid that life is not a 'clean orderly sane responsible affair', and what is especially interesting about this philosophy is that it means that he might as well be a crook as a cop. At some point he has become neither, operating a private practice in a legally indeterminate region between. Ultimately he serves the interests of official society, but not out of any faith in its justice. His job satisfies his taste for hunting and adventure, and he can survive best on the right side of the law.

It is almost a rule of Hammett's novels that at some point the detective's ambiguous position must be tested by a bribe. If he passes this test, his victory is mainly personal, a kind of survival of the fittest. There is no question of returning the society to some kind of order; if decent people exist in that society, they are always rather naïve, like Effie Perine and her family, or like the 'liberal' Donald Willsson, the first murder victim in *Red Harvest*. The only alternative to such innocence is the stoic, isolated intelligence of the detective, who is affected in various ways by the world he investigates. Thus another rule of Hammett's novels is that the detective is always personally involved in some basic betrayal of trust. In *Red Harvest* the Op complains that the violence of Personville (the most obviously symbolic of Hammett's names) is making him 'blood simple', and he feels vaguely responsible for the murder of Dinah Brand, the amoral lady who has been a sort of friend to him; in fact at one point he thinks he might have stabbed her while he was drunk or drugged. In *The Dain Curse* the Op's friend and only confidant turns out to be the killer. In *The Maltese Falcon* Spade must betray Brigid, just as she has betrayed him, and just as he has betrayed his partner and his partner's wife. In *The Glass Key* Ned Beaumont spends the entire novel trying to save his closest friend, only to end up leaving town with the woman his friend loves. In *The Thin Man* the killer is revealed to be an old wartime companion of Nick Charles, a man whose life Charles once saved in the trenches in Europe.

The best example of this troubling, pessimistic quality of Hammett's work is *The Glass Key*, which gives such a detached, accurate picture of the politics of a moderately large American city that the detective story elements – a set of clues involving a hat and a fancy walking stick, a denouement in which an amateur detective forces a confession out of a killer – become somewhat obtrusive. To his credit, however, Hammett treats these elements ironically and makes them thematically functional. For example, the clue of the hat, emphasised throughout, is finally dismissed as 'unimportant'. The detective doesn't believe the confession, calling it a 'campaign speech' and leaving us in doubt as to what actually happened. As in *Falcon*, the victim deserved to die, and the detective says that the killer performed a 'favour'. Also as in *Falcon*, the only truly innocent characters are naïve females who live under the protection of corrupt men. Paul Madvig, the wrongly accused suspect, is a political boss who collects graft and intimidates the nominal leaders of the community into following his orders. He is a likeable enough fellow, with a sweet old mother and a certain working-class directness, and Ned Beaumont says he 'never had anybody killed'; nevertheless he is as crooked as anyone else.

The murder in the novel is interesting, given the city's strongman politics. It is an Oedipal anxiety made real; a state senator murders his own son – with a walking stick, no less – in order to preserve his reputation and rule. This phallic imagery is carried over into the book's title; the glass key is identified ultimately as a symbol from Janet Henry's dream – a key which unlocks a door and then breaks, releasing chaos. At one level the symbol describes Hammett's ironic solution to the murder story: there is a 'key' to the mystery, but its discovery results in an end to the friendship between Beaumont and Madvig. At other levels the failed key is an appropriate image for a novel that seems preoccupied with symbolic castrations – for example, Ned Beaumont coolly seduces a newspaper publisher's wife, thus driving the publisher to suicide. In the last scene, Paul Madvig suffers one of these castrations, losing the woman he loves to his best friend. It is as though the tough-guy ethos were unleashing a horror, even though the novel as a whole makes toughness a value.

In keeping with this atmosphere, *The Glass Key* contains Hammett's darkest treatment of violence and sexuality, particularly in the extended, sado-masochistic torture scenes of chapter 4, where the thug Jeff keeps calling Beaumont 'sweetheart', and where the symbolic castrations threaten to become real:

'I got something to try.' He scooped Ned Beaumont's legs and tumbled them on the bed. He leaned over Ned Beaumont, his hands busy on Ned Beaumont's body.

Ned Beaumont's body and arms and legs jerked convulsively and three times he groaned. After that he lay still.

Even conventional relations between men and women are ambivalent – as between Beaumont and Janet Henry – or drained of passion. For example, here is a scene describing the aftermath of a night at a speakeasy:

The remaining girl took Ned Beaumont, who called her Fednik, to an apartment on Seventy-third Street. The apartment was very warm. When she opened the door warm air came out to meet them. When she was three steps inside the living-room she sighed and fell down on the floor.

Ned Beaumont shut the door and tried to awaken her, but she would not wake. He carried and dragged her difficultly into the next room and put her on a chintz-covered day-bed. He took off part of her clothing and opened a window. Then he went into the bathroom and was sick. After that he returned to the living-room, lay down on the sofa in all his clothes, and went to sleep.

Such prose resembles Hemingway at his best, but *The Glass Key* is better described as Hammett's *The Waste Land*. He had been reading Eliot at about the time he wrote the novel (Lillian Hellman says that she and Hammett discussed the poet for hours when they first met in 1930),[15] and he has named one of the streets in his fictional city 'upper Thames Street' (cf. *The Waste Land*, line 260). Ned Beaumont, the professional gambler momentarily turned detective, is vaguely implicated in the corruption of the city, but he has aristocratic looks and a certain sensibility that suggests an Eliot-like cultural nostalgia. His rooms are decorated 'in the old manner, high of ceiling and wide of window', and when Janet Henry first sees them she remarks, 'I didn't think there could be any of these left in a city as horribly up to date as ours has become.' She thinks Beaumont is a 'gentleman', although he sneers at the word, knowing that Janet's father, the other gentleman of the novel, is capable of any crime.

Actually *The Glass Key* has a good deal in common with modernist literature in general, chiefly because it refuses to give the reader any comfortable position from which to judge the events it depicts. The crooked politicians, the sadistic gangsters, the criminally naïve females, the cruelly detached gambler-detective are all recognisable stereotypes from familiar cultural or literary 'texts', but they are presented without any narrative commentary and without any character (like Chandler's Marlowe) who could act as a moral norm. *The Glass Key* has all the adventure and heroics of a normal melodrama and much of the social detail of a muck-raking naturalist novel, but it presents this material neutrally What, finally, are we to think of Beaumont and Madvig? How are we to judge the city without feeling like the 'respectable element' of comfortable bourgeois citizens whom Beaumont mocks? Perhaps the deepest reason why we feel Hammett is tough is that his commonplace, clear language is destructive of any liberal complacency.

After this impressive novel, however, Hammett seems to have become cautious. *The Thin Man*, written two years later when he was out of money, strongly resembles the classic detective story form. Nick Charles, the hero, is a retired detective who has married a rich young woman; she becomes his Watson, eager to go slumming in the New York underworld. The murder plot is elaborately complicated and more like a puzzle than Hammett's other work. The setting is a glamorous one, and the tone is largely comic – perfect and harmless escapism for the years of the Depression. Even so, Hammett's attitude is much more satiric than the immensely popular series of *Thin Man* films derived from the book:[16]

We went into the living room for a drink. Some more people came in. I spoke to them. Harrison Quinn left the sofa where he had been sitting with Margot Innes and said: 'Now ping-pong.' Asta jumped up and punched me in the belly with her front feet. I shut off the radio and poured a cocktail. The man whose name I had not caught was saying: 'Comes the revolution and we'll all be lined up against the wall – first thing'. He seemed to think it was a good idea.

Clearly this is a dark, absurd comedy, and Nick Charles seems to be using liquor mainly as an anaesthetic. In fact his alcoholism becomes the sign of a man who feels slightly guilty and emasculated. Much as he and Nora like one another, he is a potential *Doppelgänger* of Jorgenson, the gigolo who has married Mimi Wynant, and the only point when he briefly stops drinking is when he becomes a detective again.

With only a slight turn of the screw *The Thin Man* could have been as unsettling as any of Hammett's other works. The chief metaphor of the novel is cannibalism, established in the long quotation from Duke's *Criminal Cases of America* in chapter 13.[17] And like the previous books, it returns us at the end to a world where nothing has fundamentally changed – as the Continental Op says to his client in *Red Harvest*, the city is 'all nice and clean and ready to go to the dogs again'. Hammett again calls the solution to the crime into slight question: in the last chapter Nick explains everything to Nora, acting the role of the typical omniscient detective. Normally in such scenes the detective is a privileged narrator, but this novel is comic and Nora Charles is no passive Watson. Her questions continually upset our expectations by exposing the holes in Nick's story. 'But this is just a theory, isn't it?' she asks. Nick says he is only trying to describe what is most probable, and reaches for a drink. At the end Nora complains, 'it's all pretty unsatisfactory.'

Of course Nora's words actually function as Hammett's defence; by satirising his form he allows it to work. Nevertheless, it is interesting that these are his last words as a novelist, and it may be significant that he gave them to a woman.

No one can say exactly why Hammett stopped writing, but there is a theory, as tentative as Nick Charles's account of a crime, that offers one reason: the detective novel had become unsatisfactory to him. During his long silence he once complained, 'it is impossible to write anything without taking some sort of stand on political issues.'[18] Throughout the 'committed' thirties Hammett was too good a writer not to realise that the form of writing is itself political; he seems to have been reluctant to use language in a completely transparent, authoritarian way, and the reactionary fifties silenced him altogether. He could not become a demagogue or a party hack, and his one surviving fragment is *Tulip*, a novel about the problem of writing a novel. This problem is not expressed as a matter of content, but as a matter of form. 'Where in the name of God', says his exasperated protagonist at one point, invoking the name that stands behind most of the supposedly 'realistic' uses of language, 'do you get the notion that writers go around looking for things to write about? Organising material is the problem, not getting it.'

In the long view, and given the particular historical context of Hammett's work, this emphasis on the problem of form has important political implications. It suggests that Hammett had become philosophical about the relation between language and ideology. Thus his central character in *Tulip* has been experimenting with the sort of language games that would appeal to the post-Wittgenstein theorists – including writing a story on paper shaped into a Möbius strip, in such a way that the reader can start at any point. He is critical of any philosophy of language or science that is based on a notion of ultimate reality or metaphysical presence, and he wonders 'what arrangements would be necessary in mathematics if one, the unit, the single item, were not considered a number at all, except perhaps as a convenience in calculating'. He tries to write a story about a friend named Tulip, who represents a facet of himself:

> His being a side of me was all right, of course, since everybody is in some degree an aspect of everybody else or how would anybody ever hope to understand anything about anybody else? But representations seemed to me – at least they seem now . . . devices of the old and tired . . . like conscious symbolism, or graven images. If you are old and tired you ought to rest, I think, and not try to fool yourself or your customers with coloured bubbles.

Hammett never solved his problem, but his attempt was

leading him in characteristically radical directions. He could no longer figure out a way to be a popular writer, and, as he says, he was feeling old and tired. In any case the novels he did write need no apology. They are a remarkable achievement, a moment when melodrama becomes indistinguishable from literature.

NOTES AND REFERENCES

1. Stephen Marcus, 'Introduction' to the *The Continental Op*, by Dashiell Hammett (Random House, 1974), p. xxviii. After 1930 Hammett worked mainly as a screenwriter, and until more research is done into this period, it may be an exaggeration to call him a 'hack'. His best-known scripts are *City Streets* (1933), for which he is credited as the author of the 'original story', and *Watch on the Rhine* (1943), an adaptation of Lillian Hellman's play, which won him an academy award nomination.
2. *The Big Knockover* (New York: Vintage Books, Random House, 1956).
3. *The Glass Key* (New York: Vintage Books, Random House, 1972).
4. *The Thin Man* (New York: Vintage Books, Random House, 1972).
5. *Red Harvest* (London: Pan Books, 1975).
6. *The Maltese Falcon* (New York: Vintage Books, Random House, 1957).
7. (New York: Oxford University Press, 1975).
8. *The Thin Man.*
9. A brief history of *Black Mask* and its publishers is in Frank MacShane's *The Life of Raymond Chandler* (New York: E. P. Dutton, 1976), pp. 44–50.
10. Hammett liked to describe his crooks in terms of some simple deformity, and in the Op stories he sometimes creates the feeling of a cartoon. In 'The Big Knockover', the Op walks into a speakeasy full of thugs: 'Men – rat-faced men, hatchet-faced men, square-jawed men, slack-chinned men, pale men, scrawny men, funny-looking men'.
11. See *The Life of Raymond Chandler*, p. 58. Chandler's brilliant essay, 'The Simple Art of Murder', originally published in *The Atlantic Monthly*, Dec. 1944, may be chiefly responsible for Hammett's reputation as a kind of primitive. Chandler also implicitly argued that Hammett never showed a world of official corruption, where 'gangsters could rule cities'. This is an odd notion, given *Red Harvest* and *The Glass Key*.
12. The slang in Hammett's work is interesting because so much of it is no longer in use, and it is difficult to say how accurate it might be. Some of his characters like to speak in Pig-Latin, as in 'the big umpchay', or 'unkdray'. Sometimes they sound like Jazz-Age college boys: 'What's the proposish', or 'What's the diffugalty?' Other terms, especially in the Op stories, are more obscure. 'To get a rear out of' means to enjoy. 'Let's screw' means let's get out of here. 'Give me your sig' means give me your signature. 'For fair' means for sure. 'Swing the play' means do the job. I am uncertain what 'It's one underdish' might mean.
13. 'Introduction' to *The Continental Op*, p. xxv. See also Roland Barthes's commentary, 'From Sculpture to Painting', in *S/Z* (New York: Hill & Wang, 1974) pp. 207–8.

14. See James Naremore, 'John Huston and *The Maltese Falcon*', *Literature/Film Quarterly*, Summer, 1973, pp. 239–49.

15. 'Introduction' to *The Big Knockover*.

16. The thin man in the novel is of course the victim, not the detective popularised by the series of films. However, I cannot resist praising William Powell's beautiful performance as an elegant, graceful drunkard.

17. This book, published in San Francisco by J. H. Barry Publishers, 1910, appears to have been a personal favourite of Hammett's. My thanks to Chris Anderson for locating bibliographic information about the book for me.

18. Quoted by Martin Seymour-Smith, *Who's Who in Twentieth-Century Literature* (New York: McGraw-Hill, 1977), p. 148.

5 A Knock at the Backdoor of Art: The Entrance of Raymond Chandler

LEON ARDEN

'I tried to explain to them that I was just a beat-up pulp writer and that in the USA I ranked slightly above the mulatto.'[1]

Such was his response upon learning that he had become the darling of the British intellectuals, that all the poets raved about his work and that Edith Sitwell read him with passion. Moreover, W. H. Auden, J. B. Priestley and Cyril Connolly had praised him in print and he was made the guest of honour at London parties. Never the most self-confident of men, Raymond Chandler suspected condescension. He was rapidly won over.

'A thriller writer in England', he wrote in 1955, 'if he is good enough is just as good as anyone else. There is none of that snobbishness which makes a fourth-rate serious novelist, without style or any talent, superior by definition to a mystery writer who might have helped create a whole literature.'[2] But as Chandler well knew, for he had been educated in England, a rigid class structure can be difficult to alter; no less so was the class system of American literature. There, where popularity is highly suspect, a writer who finds himself read by 'everyone' can be sure that 'respectable' critics and professors of literature will start edging toward the door. Parvenu insecurity was how Chandler saw it. And, indeed, while this American Spartacus had fought his way out of the rock quarry of pulp fiction to be accepted in the English drawing-room of art, at home he was still in the pit. While the revolution abroad seemed all but triumphant, in the States few even noticed that one was being fought.

Raymond Thornton Chandler was born in Chicago on 23 July 1888 and from the start it appeared that destiny had singled him out to be almost anything but a writer. His mother, Florence Thornton, was born in Waterford, about 100 miles east of Cork, and his father, Maurice Chandler of Philadelphia, was descended from Irish Quakers; he became a drunk and a wastrel and eventually disappeared, leaving his family without support. This was an act of betrayal for which his son would never forgive him. The seven-year-old boy and his distraught mother had to travel to London to be rescued by relatives. But life in the house where they were forced to live was tense and lonely. He was surrounded by snobbish women (there were no older men), and he became fiercely loyal to his mother as she suffered the petty humiliations of her now lowly social position. A profound hatred of injustice grew out of this boyhood trauma, and something of the English sense that adhering to a code of correct behaviour was the touchstone of decency. He also developed the idea that women were frail creatures in need of man's protection. When this proved otherwise, then it was man who needed protection against them. Events in his stories demonstrated this danger again and again.

Chandler's formal education, steeped in the classics, was superb. But the English public-school system left him sexually repressed. 'I never masturbated, thinking it dirty,' he wrote. He had formed a 'curious idea in his head' that the practice involved the fantasising of beautiful, unattainable women which, later in life, made actual love affairs with such ladies 'very disappointing'.[3] When it came to sex, nothing but the unattainable was ever really good enough. Most of his life he was a knight unhappy inside his shining armour, yet afraid to climb out.

After leaving school, knowing his relatives would not support him while he tried his hand at writing, he considered becoming a barrister, but was sent instead, and meekly went, into the civil service. Without really trying, he was placed third in a class of 600 and first in maths and the classics. Six months later he enraged his entire family by resigning.

In 1912, when he was twenty-three, having by then proved himself a failed poet, a failed journalist and, as was increasingly obvious, a failed expatriate, he borrowed £500 and went to the States, where he drifted, lived with his relatives, was joined by his mother, and a year later entered the Canadian Army to fight in the Great War. His experiences in France were so brutal that he blocked out most of his memories of them. The climax came when an artillery barrage concussed him and wiped out his entire outfit. Chandler, who was given to writing almost endless letters about everything to do with his life, rarely referred to this horrifying episode. Ironically, the man who was to make his name in the hard-boiled school of crime writing, full of gunfire and dead bodies, chose to leave untouched the one area of violence he knew first-hand.

Back in the United States again, Chandler met and eventually married Cissy Pascal. Much has been made of this union, and the facts are indeed overripe for conjecture: he was thirty-six, she fifty-three. The marriage, disapproved of by his mother with whom he was living, was delayed for some years, and then took place two weeks after she died. Cissy looked years younger than her age. She had been a photo and artists' model, was a fine pianist, an excellent cook. With her exceptional beauty she must have seemed, to the highly romantic and still relatively innocent Chandler, the unobtainable vision possessed at last. They, as he put it, 'just seemed to melt into each other's hearts without the need for words'.[4] Cissy's maturity and her many accomplishments very likely filled yet another need: paradoxically she became the immediate subconscious replacement for the mother he had worshipped. It was this element that helped hold the marriage together in the face of what was to come.

At this time Chandler was employed by a small oil company and soon rose to become vice-president. He was skilled at this job, the best he ever held, and with his many responsibilities, a good income and a newly acquired wife, he was totally respectable at last. It was then that things went awry. As the disparity in their ages became an ever-widening division, Chandler turned to adultery and heavy drinking. Cissy, after all, was approaching sixty, while he was still in his thirties. Her beauty faded and despite desperate, often pitiful, efforts to maintain a girlish appearance, she was frequently mistaken for his mother. Increasingly they stayed at home. Unlike his father before him, he dedicated himself, if not with loyalty, at least with care and consideration, to this at times almost untenable union. The price was high. His drinking got completely out of hand and he lost his job. At forty-four he had hit bottom; no hope of employment, no prospects whatever.

The urge to write had always been there like so much kindling. The spark of good fortune was the ironic discovery, by this man so steeped in the classics, of pulp fiction. Chandler saw almost at once the enormous possibilities hidden in this 'lowly' genre. Never an admirer of the mystery story as practised by Dorothy L. Sayers and Agatha Christie, he made a study of the work of Dashiell Hammett who, Chandler wrote, 'gave murder back to the kind of people who committed it for reasons, not just to provide a corpse'.[5] He believed he could do better than Hammett, in whose hands the American language 'had no overtones, left no echo, evoked no image beyond the distant hill'.[6] But his debt to his predecessor was gladly conceded: '*The Maltese Falcon* may or may not be a work of genius, but an art which is capable of it is not "by hypothesis" incapable of anything. Once the detective story can be as good as this only the pedant will deny that it *could* be even better'.[7] There are many reasons why Chandler settled on the detective story for his medium: one of them was the striking clarity with which he saw into the future. In 1944 he spoke of a

world in which gangsters can rule nations and almost rule cities . . . and the nice man down the hall is a boss of the numbers racket. . . . where no man can walk down a dark street in safety because law and order are things we talk about but refrain from practicing; a world where you may witness a hold-up in broad daylight and see who did it, but fade quickly back into the crowd rather than tell anyone, because the hold-up men may have friends with long guns.[8]

Chandler apprenticed himself to pulp fiction, rewrote tirelessly, worked five months on a story called 'Blackmailers Don't Shoot' and sold it for $180. He had hit the ground running. Later he said about these earlier stories that they had 'the smell of fear. Their characters lived in a world gone wrong'.[9] Quickly his skill grew, his style developed, and by 1938, after five years of labouring over these short works which were really truncated novels, Chandler 'cannibalised' several of them, combining their plots and characters, and the expanded result was his first novel, *The Big Sleep*. If the average full-length mystery of that time had a sale of about 2500 copies, as has been claimed, then the sale of 10,000 was remarkable. The book itself, despite its faults, was more remarkable still.

Although Chandler was to better this effort in his later works, no detective writer, and remarkably few American fiction writers of any sort, have reached this level of literary artistry. More than anything else, it is the first-person voice of Philip Marlowe, perfected in the early stories, that gives the book its mesmeric tone. 'To me Marlowe is the American mind,' Chandler wrote in his notebooks,

> a heavy portion of rugged realism, a dash of good hard vulgarity, a strong overtone of strident wit, an equally strong overtone of pure sentimentalism, an ocean of slang, and an utterly unexpected range of sensitivity.

One might add to this list a touch of self-absorption, moments of self-pity, a streak of cynicism, signs of racial prejudice, anti-homosexuality, anti-intellectuality, a tendency to view women as a threat, and a tendency toward self-deprecation.

This last is central, for Marlowe is made to seem very human in his concern for his safety and his willingness to depict himself as the comic anti-hero. Here he is getting physically attacked by a woman: 'The blonde was strong with the madness of love or fear, or a mixture of both, or maybe she was just strong.' Or these:

> I wasn't scared. I was a full-sized man and I had a gun in my hand. But the blond man back in the other cabin had been a full-sized man with a gun in his hand, too. And he had a wall to hide behind. I wasn't scared though. I was just thoughtful about little things. I thought Barron was breathing too loud, but I thought I would make more noise telling him he was breathing too loud than he was making breathing. That's the way I was, very thoughtful about little things.

> A good man had a chance now. He would fall quickly to the ground, do a back flip from a kneeling position, and come up with his gun blazing in his hand. It would happen very fast. The good man would take the little man with glasses the way a dowager takes her teeth out, in one smooth motion. I somehow didn't think I was that good.

Another demonstration of Chandler's art is the way his descriptive detail conveys the drama to come before the scene begins or anyone has entered the stage. Early in *The Big Sleep*, as Marlowe enters the rich mansion of General Sternwood, we sense that something is terribly wrong:

This room was too big, the ceiling was too high, the doors were too tall, and the white carpet that went from wall to wall looked like a fresh fall of snow at Lake Arrowhead. . . . The ivory furniture had chromium on it and the enormous ivory drapes lay tumbled on the white carpet a yard from the windows. The white made the ivory look dirty and the ivory made the white look bled out. The windows stared toward the darkening foothills. It was going to rain soon. There was pressure in the air already.

Chandler's descriptions are often symbolic and comic at the same time, as on the first page of the novel when we are told that over the Sternwood mansion entrance, 'which would have let in a troop of Indian elephants', there was a stained glass panel

showing a knight in dark armor rescuing a lady who was tied to a tree and didn't have any clothes on but some very long and convenient hair. The knight had pushed the visor of his helmet back to be sociable, and he was fiddling with the knots on the rope that tied the lady to the tree and not getting anywhere. I stood there and thought that if I lived in the house, I would sooner or later have to climb up there and help him. He didn't seem to be really trying.

This last is particularly ironic because of the three women in the book with whom Marlowe comes into close contact: one saves his life, another tries to take it, and the third, rescued by the detective from a mugging, displays such unrestrained gratitude that to avoid seduction he is forced to such extremities as rude behaviour and bad dialogue. Staving off lovely women who keep running at him is one of Marlowe's avocations, since the un-obtainable is apparently his goal as well as Chandler's. One of the flaws of *The Big Sleep*, and many of his other works, is that Chandler rarely handles these episodes with charm or wit. A testy and impeccably moral side to Marlowe, or his creator, comes out whenever women display overt sexuality. At such moments these otherwise marvellously comic novels become strident. 'The first time we met I told you I was a detective,' Marlowe barks at Vivian Regan. 'Get it through your lovely head. I work at it, lady. I don't play at it.' After getting rid of her he drives home only to find Carmen Sternwood, Vivian's sister, waiting naked in his bed. Marlowe ejects her as well, and then in a bizarre episode, referred to by more than one critic, he notices the imprint of her head on the pillow and that of 'her small corrupt body' on the sheets, and he tears 'the bed to pieces savagely'.

Michael Mason, in his incisive article, 'Marlowe, Men and Women',[10] argues that this extreme repugnance is one of the many clues in Chandler's fiction that reveals a repressed homosexuality. Mason's detailed thesis is difficult to refute. The truth is that Chandler could very easily have arranged for Marlowe to avoid the physical offerings of both ladies by a logical adjustment of the plot to bring about a promising scene in which the detective takes one eager sister home to his apartment only to find the other eager sister waiting expectantly. This humorous confrontation, which might have appealed to Dashiell Hammett (*The Maltese Falcon* abounds in three-way conflicts), would not have revealed Marlowe's code of ethics, so important to his creator, nor would it have uncovered quite so blatantly, to us at least, Chandler's sexual conflicts.

The Big Sleep begins as superbly as any of Chandler's novels and the early scene where General Sternwood receives Marlowe in the steaming greenhouse is as memorable as any in American fiction:

> The air was thick, wet, steamy and larded with the cloying smell of tropical orchids in bloom. The glass walls and roof were heavily misted and big drops of moisture splashed down on the plants. The light had an unreal greenish color, like light filtered through an aquarium tank. The plants filled the place, a forest of them, with nasty meaty leaves and stalks like the newly washed fingers of dead men.

Unfortunately the novel does have 'pulpy' elements not found in the later books. For example, Marlowe's arms are immobilised by an inner tube brought down suddenly over his shoulders, and only then, as could easily have been done earlier, is he struck on the head from behind; or the obligatory shoot-out towards the end; or that final confrontation with the semi-retarded Carmen Sternwood, she of the 'little sharp predatory teeth'. Finally, there is an overuse of coincidence to propel the story.

Otherwise, the vividness and variety of characterisation, the poetic descriptions, the all-pervasive sharp edge of Marlowe's wit, the encyclopaedic knowledge of Los Angeles, the evocation of its climate and the diverse elements of its society are all so excellently drawn, including the bright and the stupid members of the underworld and the bright and the stupid officers of the law, that the publication of this book should have emphatically announced the arrival of a major new talent, not just in the mystery genre, but in the mainstream of American fiction.

And the novel that was to follow should have established this fact beyond doubt, for it is Chandler's masterpiece. Indeed, the reviewers were favourably disposed, yet few understood the uniqueness of the writer they were asked to assess. One came close: Morton Thompson wrote in the *Hollywood Citizen-News*:

> I am perfectly willing to stake whatever critical reputation I possess today or may possess tomorrow on the literary future of this author. Chandler writes with amazing absorption in the tasks of craftsmanship. He tries never to miss a trick. His sentences, all of them, show intense effort, constant editing, polishing, never-ending creative activity. His construction is a paradox of smoothness and abruptness of technic. He has a fine taste in story, in drama and comedy. He employs this sense constantly and he tells his story as well as he possibly can. His book and himself are ornaments to his profession. Lord, but it is good to see honesty and pains and fine impulses again. It's been months.

Farewell, My Lovely displayed all this and more. Oddly enough, it was written and rewritten in fits and starts along with two other novels, until it dominated Chandler's imagination and he concentrated on it to the exclusion of all else. Almost everything went right. The characters are believable and memorable with an assortment of society's law-abiding and criminal elements, each member comprising more or less an equal balance of both good and bad motives. One of Chandler's favourite themes is here given full play: a hatred of the rich, and the influence they exert on the police to enforce not the law but the ground rules of special privilege. The brutality that corruption eventually leads to is chillingly depicted in the behaviour of the Santa Monica (here called Bay City) Police Force. And yet Chandler allows one of these villainous sergeants to speak convincingly in his own defence:

Okay, how many cops do you find living on a street even as good as this, with lawns and flowers? ... Cops like me live in itty-bitty frame houses on the wrong side of town. ... Cops don't go crooked for money. Not always, not even often. They get caught in the system. ... You know what's the matter with this country, baby? ... A guy can't stay honest if he wants to. ... You got to play the game dirty or you don't eat.

This was written in 1939 and prophetically Chandler has the sergeant add:

A lot of bastards thinks all you need is ninety FBI men in clean collars and brief cases. The percentages would get them just the way it does the rest of us. You know what I think? I think we gotta make this little world all over again.

The plot of the book is purposely complex to help create an atmosphere of the tangled urban jungle into which Philip Marlowe is drawn. He meets a cast of about twenty characters, who represent a gamut of the social order starting at the bottom with the ex-con Moose Malloy, searching for his working-class girlfriend in a now black neighbourhood, and ending in the upper reaches of privilege. The story involves someone's desperate effort to keep the past a secret so that newly acquired wealth and status will remain unthreatened. This attempt brings about something far worse than that which was meant to be hidden. The ending is grim and poignant, for the struggle brings only desolation. And all this springs from an opening that is the funniest Chandler ever wrote, as Marlowe, against his will, is literally lifted into the story:

A hand I could have sat in came out of the dimness and took hold of my shoulder and squashed it to a pulp. Then the hand moved me through the door and casually lifted me up a step.
. . .

'All right', I yelled, 'I'll go up with you. Just lay off carrying me. Let me walk. I'm fine. I'm all grown up. I go to the bathroom alone and everything. Just don't carry me'.

'Little Velma used to work here', he said gently. He wasn't listening to me.

We went up the stairs. He let me walk. My shoulder ached. The back of my neck was wet.

There is always that sense in Chandler of time slowly altering things. The very opening sentence of the novel touches upon this: 'It was one of the mixed blocks over on Central Avenue, the blocks that are not yet all negro.' This motif of change and of the past is suggested in the first description of Moose Malloy who is released from prison after eight years and who, looking for his girlfriend, goes to a dance hall where she once worked. He eyes the place 'like a hunky immigrant catching his first sight of the Statue of Liberty'. At the end of the book when the girl is finally tracked down, Marlowe thinks:

> Suddenly without any real change in her she ceased to be beautiful. She looked merely like a woman who would have been dangerous a hundred years ago, and twenty years ago daring, but who today was just Grade B Hollywood.

The enormous size and gaudy dress of Malloy is summed up this way: 'Even on Central Avenue, not the quietest dressed street in the world, he looked about as inconspicuous as a tarantula on a slice of angel food.' This simile also suggests an ironic reversal of the old stereotype. Central Avenue 'not yet all negro' is therefore mostly black. But this great white man is described as a black spider against a white background, as if to stress that in America the dangerous ingredient is the white attitude towards, and treatment of, minorities, which is soon to be demonstrated by the ignorant Malloy freely savaging one black man and killing another. All this in search of a woman who is suggested by the image of the Statue of Liberty.

Binding the novel together, as always, is Marlowe's wry, distinctive voice. Here he is entering the world of the rich: 'A man in a striped vest and gilt buttons opened the door, bowed, took my hat and was through for the day.' Later Marlowe's thinking process, after a blow on the head, is understandably confused: 'Time passes very slowly when you are actually doing something. I mean, you can go through a lot of movement in a very few minutes. Is that what I mean? What the hell do I care what I mean. Okay, better men than me have meant less.' And, as always, danger for Marlowe is painfully real: 'A motor throbbed above the rim of the bush. I didn't jump more than a foot. . . . A gun slid into my hand all by itself.' Marlowe, of course, has an eye for young women: 'It was a blonde. A blonde to make a bishop kick a hole in a stained glass window.' But he is equally observant of the aged: 'a dry withered smile that would turn to powder if you touched it'.

The High Window, published next, was in Chandler's opinion his least successful novel. It is extremely sentimental and coincidence repeatedly rears its lazy head. Marlowe hears a key dialogue while standing behind a curtain; a link in a chain of events owes its existence solely to the fact that an otherwise incompetent detective recognises Marlowe's face from out of the past; and the solution to the mystery is based on a photograph having been taken at a very unlikely moment. Finally, the cast of characters represent a throwback to those oddities and eccentrics that populate his first novel. Here they approach caricature.

If *The High Window* is the weakest of the first five novels, it is by no means less enthralling page by page. The theme centres on the need by the powerful to control the weak and to maintain the status quo. Chandler's interest in this stems from those days when he and his mother had to suffer the begrudging generosity of insensitive relatives. At the opening of the book we again find Marlowe at the front door of a wealthy home. As he waits to be let in, a Good Humor truck goes by in wry contrast with the ill-humoured people he will meet inside. Toward the end of the novel we again wait with him at this same door:

A mockingbird sang in a dark tree nearby. A car tore down the street much too fast and skidded around the next corner. The thin shreds of a girl's laughter came back along the dark street as if the car had spilled them out in its rush.

This symbolic incident delivers a last laugh at Marlowe's expense, due to his inability to bring to justice the one woman in the book who deserves it and, added to this, because, in an excessive display of gallantry, he will drive the sad, semi-helpless, pseudo-heroine all the way back to the safety of her parents' home in Wichita, Kansas. This rather flamboyant good deed leaves depleted not only his bank account but his spirit as well: 'I had a funny feeling when I saw the house disappear, as though I had written a poem and it was very good and I had lost it and would never remember it again.'

Some of the best moments in the book are when Chandler

burlesques melodrama, as he does in a tense scene in a rooming house when Marlowe and the 'carroty faced' manager knock on a door behind which is heard loud dance music and a woman screaming hysterically. The door is opened by a blonde 'with sultry eyes one of which was puffed and the other had been socked several days ago'. When told to pipe down, the girl looked back over her shoulder and screamed against the noise of the radio: 'Hey, Dell! The guy says to pipe down! You want to sock him?' He does. But after a losing struggle the man, whose name is Hench, runs to the bed and thrusts his hand under a pillow. Marlowe says, 'Look out – a gun.'

'I can fade that too', the carroty man said between his teeth and slid his right hand, empty now, under his open vest.

Hench was down on both knees. He came up on one and turned and there was a short black gun in his hand and he was staring down at it, not holding it by the grip at all, holding it flat on his palm.

'Drop it!' the carroty man's voice said tightly and he went on into the room.

The blonde promptly jumped on his back and wound her long green arms around his neck, yelling lustily. The carroty man staggered and swore and waved his gun around.

'Get him, Dell!' the blonde screamed. 'Get him good!'

Hench, one hand on the bed and one foot on the floor, both knees doubled, right hand holding the black gun flat on his palm, eyes staring down at it, pushed himself slowly to his feet and growled deep in his throat: 'This ain't my gun'.

While Chandler was writing this book, his least successful one to date, he was at the same time, in one of those mysteries of the creative process, at work on what some consider his best novel ever. *The Lady in the Lake* took him four years to complete and was finally published in 1943, twelve months after *The High Window*. The writing is especially elegant and controlled, and it is a better balanced and more subtle work than any of his others. Nothing obtrudes, and the plot, though it builds slowly, is continually engrossing. Philip Marlowe is here highly skilled, even brilliant, as he snares his prey through a logical process of detective work that at no time forces the reader to suspend disbelief. A nice touch of realism at the end is when Marlowe, without a gun, is forced to rely on others to apprehend the killer. The story begins in the reception room of a cosmetic firm:

> There were perfumes in tall thin bottles that looked as if a breath would blow them over and perfumes in thin pastel phials with ducky satin bows, like little girls at a dancing class. The cream of the crop seemed to be something very small and simple in a squat amber bottle. . . . It was definitely the stuff to get. One drop of that in the hollow of your throat and the matched pink pearls started falling on you like summer rain.

Then, seven chapters later:

> There was a horrible, sickening smell in the air. Bill Chess didn't seem to notice it, nor Patton nor the doctor. The man called Andy got a dusty brown blanket out of the car and threw it over the body. Then without a word he went and vomited under a pine tree.

The head of this cosmetic firm wants his missing wife found. Marlowe is hired, persists in the investigation and, when he starts getting close to the truth, is brutalised by the Bay City police who play a major role in this book. They are portrayed both as comically incompetent and highly dangerous when thwarted. Since one of their members is the murderer, the final confrontation between three licensed but vastly different representatives of separate branches of the law is comic and chilling. Providing a distant backdrop for this story is the second world war, which can be seen as a tragic enlargement on the very theme of the book: that one corrupt man in an organisation can, if no one stops him, corrupt the entire organisation.

Not for another ten years would Chandler come closer to writing a story about a detective rather than a detective story. It is not perhaps his conscious goal in this book, but the possibility of elevating the genre by moving it closer to the straight novel was never far from his mind. There are no blondes, for example, vamping Marlowe at every opportunity, and the dialogue is all the better for it. We are given the usual detailed portrait of Los Angeles, as well as that of a rustic mountain resort with its collection of unsophisticated locals. The villainous big city police are contrasted with one of Chandler's best creations, Jim Patton, town constable:

> I lit a cigarette and looked for an ash tray.
> 'Try the floor, son', the large friendly man said.
> 'Are you Sheriff Patton?'
> 'Constable and deputy sheriff. What law we got to have around here I'm it. Come election anyways. There's a couple good boys running against me this time and I might get whupped. Job pays eighty a month, cabin, firewood and electricity. That ain't hay in these little old mountains'.
> 'Nobody's going to whip you', I said. 'You're going to get a lot of publicity'.
> 'That so?' he asked indifferently and ruined the spittoon again.
> 'That is if your jurisdiction extends over to Little Fawn Lake'.
> 'Kingsley's place. Sure. Something bothering you over there, son?'
> 'There's a dead woman in the lake'.
> That shook him to the core. He unclasped his hands and scratched one ear. He got to his feet by grasping the arms of his chair and deftly kicking it back from under him. Standing up he was a big man and hard. The fat was just cheerfulness.
> 'Anybody I know?' he enquired uneasily.

Frank MacShane wrote in his excellent *The Life of Raymond Chandler* that this novel 'is a somber book because it concentrates on those who are caught up in the system of Southern California instead of those who direct it. They are the foot soldiers of society rather than the picturesque eccentrics of *The High Window* to whom the system belongs.' [11] Surprisingly, MacShane has his doubts about this novel. He mistakes its quiet poetry and subtle comedy as a signal that Chandler was depressed when he wrote it (which he was) and thus below form artistically (which he wasn't). Actually the novel is an almost perfect blend of style, characterisation, theme and plot, and it seems to reach in and touch the very core of our violent society. In the book's defence, I will let Michael Gilbert, crime novelist and London solicitor, deliver the final summation:

In my view *The Lady in the Lake* is, by a short head, the finest of Chandler's books. There is no physical violence in the first hundred pages of any sort, yet the whole thing crackles with that inimitable Chandler electricity; every sentence a tiny spark, every paragraph craftily put together by a literary electronics engineer.[12]

In 1943, when Chandler was fifty-five, he was summoned to Hollywood to write film scripts; he went, as many did, for the money. Leaving the cloistered home life he shared with Cissy was traumatic. The numerous attractive young secretaries who worked in the Writers Building at Paramount disturbed him considerably, especially when he learned that the younger writers were often sleeping with these secretaries. His acerbic personality, which came to the surface whenever he was unsure of himself, irritated many people on the lot and eventually, for one reason or another, brought an end to his tenure there.

He first collaborated on film work with Billy Wilder. Although their teamwork resulted in personal conflicts, nothing could dim the young man's admiration for Chandler's novels. 'They were no great structural things,' Wilder said.

They had nothing to do with the Conan Doyle and Agatha Christie type of superb plotting. They weren't even as well plotted as Dashiell Hammett; but, God, a kind of lightning struck on every page. How often do you read a description of a character who says that he had hair growing out of his ear long enough to catch a moth? Not many write like that; and the dialogue was good, and the dialogue was sharp.[13]

Some time later he went even further, saying that Chandler was 'one of the greatest creative minds' he had encountered.[14]

As expected, Chandler had his own views on the subject of writing for Hollywood. In June of 1957 in a letter to Edgar Carter he said, 'I'd never be a good TV writer for the same reason I was never a really good screenwriter. I love words.' Though he often gently deprecated himself to give others a chance to contradict, here he came close to the truth. To a magazine editor he wrote: 'In the long run . . . the most durable thing in writing is style, and style is the most valuable investment a writer can make with his time.'[15] An investment that understandably, on a Paramount lot, failed to accrue its best returns.

It was no great surprise that Chandler's next book, *The Little Sister*, was set in the film capital. MacShane is of the opinion that the Hollywood material is 'decorative', yet the central female character is a working actress and the many scenes that involve the film world are funnier, more vivid and convincing than in any novel I can remember on the subject. Though the book has been called over-ripe, and it represents no advance over the previous one, in fact it crackles with wit and good writing, and it indeed goes beyond Chandler's other works in its experimentation with mood description, such as that long drive Marlowe takes while alone in his car, a scene which occupies all of chapter 13. In a bitter and cynical mood he ruminates about his problems, makes passing comments on the California social scene, describes the countryside and the sea and the terrible steak he ate in a diner:

> I paid off and stopped in a bar to drop a brandy on top of the New York cut. Why New York, I thought. It was Detroit where they make machine tools. I stepped into the night air that nobody had yet found out how to option. But a lot of people were probably trying. They'd get around to it.

The reason why many critics felt that *The Little Sister* seems not to reach the level of Chandler's best, despite a demonstration of his usual energy, humour and inventiveness, is that in this case, by keeping to his usual method of creating plot as he went along, Chandler went astray (his dislike of deductive detective fiction made him underestimate the need for tight plots), and the story is needlessly complicated, ending in a series of semi-climaxes instead of one satisfying culmination. After a hiatus from his usual sexual wrangling, Marlowe is back at it again. Still the important thing, as always with Chandler, is how much is captured *en passant*. J. B. Priestley said this about the book:

> To read him is like cutting into an over-ripe melon and discovering that it has a rare astringent flavour. He reduces the bright California scene to an empty despair, dead bottles and a heap of cigarette butts under the meaningless neon lights, much more adroitly than Aldous Huxley and the rest can do; and suggests, to my mind, almost better than anyone else the failure of a life that is somehow short of a dimension, with

everybody either wistfully wondering what is wrong or taking short cuts to nowhere.[16]

Jacques Barzun, however, in his essay 'The Illusion of the Real', claims that

> there is no warrant for the commonly held belief that the tough
> detective tale yields greater truth than the gentler classical
> form and marks a forward step toward 'the real novel'. The
> 'soft' genteel story, in which the corpse is found in a library by
> the butler, may be a period piece, but is in itself neither truer
> nor falser than the story set in the back alleys of Glasgow or Los
> Angeles. Butlers may be an anachronism, but so are boot-
> leggers.[17]

There is, I think, a determination on Mr Barzun's part to miss the point. In the 'gentler classical form' to which he refers, one learns little about the world we are introduced to because usually the characters suffer as much from *rigor mortis* as does the corpse; the dialogue is wooden enough to be thrown on the drawing-room fire; everyone's motivation is as hard to take as the prose style; and what passes for a logical explanation as to why and how the killer produced that corpse in the first place is usually nothing more than an intricately concocted absurdity. What truth lies hidden here would take a Sherlock Holmes to uncover. And whether or not bootleggers are an anachronism, the point is that real crime, in whatever form, is not. Barzun stands on somewhat thicker ice when he complains that the modern fictional detective as he has evolved is not believable either. He is poor, heroic, 'slugged, drugged, shot at' and 'never down for long'[18] – in short, indestructible. But what Chandler has written, as Edmund Wilson points out, is not so much a detective story as 'a novel of adventure'.[19] Philip Marlowe is an adventurer as much as is Robinson Crusoe or Ulysses or Ishmael, those battered examples of man's ingenuity, wisdom or endurance. With each new trial or tribulation, yet another of life's absurdities is revealed, an opportunity to triumph demonstrated.

In seven novels Marlowe gets knocked unconscious five times in over ten years as a detective, is shot at on only two occasions early in his career, and kills one man in self-defence. In *The Big Sleep* he is thirty-three years old; in *The Little Sister* he's thirty-eight; and he's forty-two in *The Long Goodbye*, where he says, 'I feel old and tired.' At another point in that novel, when he comes awake after having had too much to drink:

> I got to my feet and it took character. It took will power. It took a lot out of me, and there wasn't as much to spare as there once had been. The hard, heavy years had worked me over.

Chandler was getting on in years himself and his hope was that his next effort, *The Long Goodbye*, would be his masterpiece. He was sixty-four when he wrote it, but the energy was beginning to ebb from his prose. To prove that detective fiction, at its best, could be called literature (which he had already demonstrated), he decided, at last, to alter the form and bring it closer to the serious novel. It took Chandler this long to make such an attempt because, I think, at least part of him felt the attempt unnecessary. In a letter in 1945 he wrote, 'What greater prestige can a man like me . . . have than to have taken a cheap, shoddy, and utterly lost kind of writing, and have made of it something that intellectuals claw each other about.'[20] But the imitators, he felt, were closing in, and 'so you have to go where they can't follow you'.[21] More to the point, when a book of his received a poor review, the experience often shook his faith and once even provoked him into complaining 'that the better you write a mystery, the more clearly you demonstrate that the mystery is not worth writing'.[22] A few months earlier he had expressed just the opposite feeling:

> I am not satisfied that the thing can't be done, nor that sometime, somewhere, perhaps not now nor by me, a novel cannot be written which, ostensibly a mystery and keeping the spirit of mystery, will actually be a novel of characterization and atmosphere.[23]

In *The Long Goodbye* he attempted just that; sadly, it comes close to floundering due to Chandler's belief that by deepening the relationship between his hero and some of the major characters, the book itself would deepen. It might have had he not blocked his own intention. To begin with, it is the friendship Marlowe feels for Terry Lennox, an extremely charming upper-class alcoholic, which is the crux of the story. We are frequently informed of but rarely witness this charm, and Lennox, partly because he is in Mexico and thus off stage through most of the book, is as thin as air-mail paper. The necessary demonstration of rapport or camaraderie is missing. This vacancy leaves Marlowe's loyalty and bruised feelings for the elusive Lennox more like those of a rejected lover. There are other problems, too. The beautiful Eileen Wade, whose first appearance prompts Marlowe to remark, 'and right then a dream walked in', is presented with romantic soft focus and consistently maintains all the depth of a thimble. Her husband, an alcoholic author of trash fiction, has real, though abrasive, substance. But here Chandler's old habit of having two characters 'snot at each other' to keep the scene alive, deprives each confrontation from developing significant dimensions. The same is true in the exchanges between Marlowe and his love interest, the rich Linda Loring whom the detective meets, sleeps with and rejects in *The Long Goodbye*, becomes engaged to in *Playback*, Chandler's next novel, and is married to at the beginning of *The Poodle Springs Mystery*, the book that was left unfinished at the author's death. Mrs Loring is as prone as Marlowe to needless needling, which leaves the two of them endlessly bantering at the shallow end of things. Though in every other way this book is more fleshed out than any of the others, these errors, by design or execution, cause *The Long Goodbye*, if not to run aground then frequently to scrape the bottom with that grating noise of sterile fiction.

There are, as usual, many who place the novel among its author's finest. This, I suspect, is due at least in part to the belief that more is better. The descriptions, however many, are not as sharp as in his earlier books; the irony is heavy-handed; the cynical asides lack subtlety or comic inspiration; and the sentimentality threatens the book's edifice like an advanced case of rising damp.

There are, even so, memorable set-pieces: the opening, for example, when it is discovered in a night-club car park that the wealthy Terry Lennox is actually broke. ('The attendent had the white-haired boy right where he could reach him – in a low-income bracket.') Marlowe, speaking through Chandler's personal experience, gives Lennox advice on the difficulty of curing alcoholism:

'It takes about three years'.
'Three years?' He looked shocked.

'Usually it does. It's a different world. You have to get used to a paler set of colours, a quieter set of sounds. You have to allow for relapses. All the people you used to know well will get to be just a little strange. You won't even like most of them, and they won't like you too well'.

'That wouldn't be much of a change', he said.

Scenes in which Marlowe, in handcuffs, is grilled by the police or is left alone in his jail cell, and the climactic confrontation, with its surprise ending, when he is trapped by thugs in his own house, are all excellent. The final chapters, also containing a surprise at the end, and the denouement are well done. All the same, these high points cannot save the day, and the sex scene Marlowe has with the edgy and difficult Mrs Loring convinces us how right Chandler was to leave bedroom manoeuvring out of Marlowe's earlier adventures.

An added burden for the author during the writing of this novel was his wife's long terminal illness. Cissy died at eighty-four, after the book was published. 'She was the beat of my heart for thirty years', he wrote afterwards.[24] That her loss should have deeply affected the sixty-six-year-old Chandler is understandable: but his reaction to her death was more like that of a morbidly loving son for an overly possessive and protective mother. Indeed, for a time Chandler went off the rails. It happened mostly when he was in London, there to find a much needed change of scene and, to his surprise, to be lionised. Those who at first gladly received him soon found themselves engulfed by an exhausting and apparently endless responsibility. His insecurity, bad temper, flamboyant play-acting, insistence on being the centre of attention, imagined throat cancer, repeated drunkenness, sudden depressions and not infrequent suicide threats made him, at the very least, a nerve-racking companion. He also developed a penchant for sending his long-suffering lady acquaintances what Dilys Powell described as

tiny sketches of sexual encounters which at the time seemed dimly pornographic. I had a little packet of them, long since lost . . . and I fancy that after a while I stopped acknowledging them. I was obscurely aware that Raymond was in need of some sort of help.[25]

That he did not suffer a complete breakdown was probably due to a creative agility that enabled him to take on and throw off a series of protective personas, sometimes witty and engaging, sometimes effusive with boyish fantasies which he offered up as real, and at all times demanding from others a selfless and motherly attention.

He survived this period and even disgorged another novel. *Playback*, his last completed work, is almost totally unrecognisable as the product of Raymond Chandler. Early we have this description of Marlowe waking up after having been knocked unconscious:

> The first sensation was that if anyone spoke to me harshly I should burst out crying. The second, that the room was too small for my head. The front of the head was a long way from the back, the sides were an enormous distance apart, in spite of which a dull throbbing beat from temple to temple. Distance means nothing nowadays.

And much later there is this: 'Jovanen smiled – very slightly. Call it a down payment on a smile.' Only these are reminiscent of the old energy; the rest suffers from an almost total power shortage.

But seven novels, of which many, if not most, are classics, is achievement enough, especially for a man whose first book appeared when he was fifty. To list all seven in order of merit is to invite dispute, at least from his devotees. Actually Chandler, quite unconsciously, did the listing for us. As mentioned earlier, he had remarked how his earlier stories had the smell of fear. 'It's not a very fragrant world,' he wrote in *The Simple Art of Murder*.[26] And 'It's a smelly business,' says Marlowe about his poorly paid occupation. As if to italicise his hero's reaction to the tawdry world around him and to a society whose morals are often rank, Chandler gave his alter ego a most highly developed olfactory sense. Here are a few examples:

> The coffeeshop smell was strong enough to build a garage on.

> The corridor . . . had a smell of old carpet and furniture oil and the drab anonymity of a thousand shabby lives.

He had a nice breath. Haig and Haig at least.

The Indian smelled. Even the elevator operator noticed it. . . . the office breathed air and the smell of dust.

It had an elderly perfume . . . like three widows drinking tea.

The breath of the garage was sweet and sinister with the smell of hot pyroxlin paint.

The perfume had an elegant something or other, not strong, not decisive.

I knew he was breathing. I could smell it.

Perhaps there was a drifting smell of man on the air. And perhaps I was just on edge.

I smelled of gin. Not just casually, as if I had taken four or five drinks on a winter morning . . . but as if the Pacific Ocean was pure gin and I nosedived off the deck.

Adding up all the references to odour in the novels gives us this listing:

(1) *Farewell, My Lovely*   =   47
(2) *The Big Sleep*   =   27
(3) *The Lady in the Lake*   =   25
(4) *The Little Sister*   =   23
(5) *The Long Goodbye*   =   18
(6) *The High Window*   =   16
(7) *Playback*   =   6

If we reverse the positions of *The High Window* and *The Long Goodbye*, whose length alone enables it to nose out its nearest rival, the list is reasonably accurate. It was as though the repressive effect of Chandler's upbringing strengthened his defences, including his awareness of smell, and as this awareness heightened or diminished, so did his talent.

Evaluating his works, one to another, is relatively easier than the task of determining how his corpus ranks with the best American fiction of this century. Placed beside the novels of Ernest Hemingway, to make an arbitrary comparison, Chandler's excel in the vividness and variety of characterisation, in wit, in believable dialogue and in demonstrating the author's grasp of the many rungs of the social ladder. The two men are equal as prose stylists and in conjuring up a sense of place. Hemingway's world is wider geographically; Chandler's concentrates on the smaller canvas of Los Angeles and environs. Of these two Illinois-born writers even some of their shortcomings match: sentimentality, a certain woodenness in romantic confrontations, plus an over-reliance on death and violence and manly adventure. Chandler's adherence to the detective story presented hurdles he did not always surmount. Yet it offered dramatic opportunities the so-called serious novel lacked. For all this, the Nobel Prize-winning Hemingway is ranked (or was) among America's best, while Chandler is directed to the service entrance.

'Raymond Chandler is not just one more detective writer,' Elizabeth Bowen wrote; 'he is a craftsman so brilliant, he has an imagination so wholly original, that no consideration of modern American literature ought, I think, to exclude him.'[27]

The real mystery concerning this mystery writer is why his exclusion shows every sign of continuing; why he is condemned for his flaws while 'serious' writers are forgiven theirs. One long-range factor in Chandler's favour, of course, is that for an artist of such attainment his novels are extremely popular. In time, he might, like Dickens, simply outlast those forces of evaluation who finally became aware that they were trying to suppress a reputation that had climbed permanently beyond their reach.

NOTES AND REFERENCES

1. RC to Hamish Hamilton, 27 Apr. 1955.
2. RC to Hillary Waugh, Oct. 1955.
3. RC to Helga Greene, 28 Apr. 1957.
4. RC to Deirdre Gartrell, 23 Apr. 1957.
5. RC, 'The Simple Art of Murder', *Atlantic Monthly*, Dec. 1944; reprinted in RC's *Pearls Are a Nuisance* (London: Penguin Crime, 1969), p. 195.
6. Ibid.
7. RC, ibid., p. 196.
8. RC, ibid., p. 197.
9. RC's introduction to *Pearls Are a Nuisance*.
10. Michael Mason, 'Marlowe, Men and Women', in Miriam Gross (ed.), *The World of Raymond Chandler* (London: Weidenfeld & Nicolson, 1977).
11. Frank MacShane, *The Life of Raymond Chandler* (London: Jonathan Cape, 1976), p. 102.
12. Michael Gilbert, 'Autumn in London', *The World of Raymond Chandler*, p. 104.

13. 'On the Fourth Floor of Paramount' (interview with Billy Wilder by Ivan Moffat), *The World of Raymond Chandler*, p. 47.
14. Quoted in press release of Mystery Writers of America after Chandler's death, March 1959; RC Files.
15. RC to Mrs Robert J. Hogan, 7 Mar. 1949.
16. J. B. Priestley, *New Statesman*, 9 Apr. 1949.
17. Jacques Barzun, 'Illusion of the Real', *The World of Raymond Chandler*, p. 160.
18. Ibid., p. 161.
19. Edmund Wilson, 'Who Cares Who Killed Roger Ackroyd?', *The New Yorker* (1945).
20. RC to Charles Morton, 21 Jan. 1945.
21. RC to Bernice Baumgarten, 14 May 1952.
22. RC to Hamilton, 5 Oct. 1949.
23. RC to Baumgarten, 21 Apr. 1949.
24. RC to Leonard Russell, Jan. 1955.
25. Dilys Powell, 'Ray and Cissy', *The World of Raymond Chandler*, p. 87.
26. RC, 'The Simple Art of Murder', p. 198.
27. 1972 Penguin edn of *Lady in the Lake*, back cover.

CHRONOLOGY

1939 – *The Big Sleep* (New York: Alfred A. Knopf; London: Hamish Hamilton).

1940 – *Farewell, My Lovely* (New York: Alfred A. Knopf; London: Hamish Hamilton).

1942 – *The High Window* (New York: Alfred A. Knopf; London: Hamish Hamilton, 1943).

1943 – *The Lady in the Lake* (New York: Alfred A. Knopf; London: Hamish Hamilton, 1944).

1949 – *The Little Sister* (London: Hamish Hamilton; Boston: Houghton Mifflin).

1953 – *The Long Goodbye* (London: Hamish Hamilton; Boston: Houghton Mifflin, 1954).

1958 – *Playback* (London: Hamish Hamilton; Boston: Houghton Mifflin).

6 Ross Macdonald and the Past of a Formula

ERIC MOTTRAM

> Their obligations are there and they see to it. If in obliging
> themselves to do so to discharge their obligations there are no
> complications and no further pleasures, farther and farther
> and then in no wise and then as to the way of spending them-
> selves, they spend themselves repeatedly.
>
> (Gertrude Stein, 'Subject-Cases:
> The Background of a Detective')

The turning point is Mark Twain's detectives who parody the
unsubtle methods of both Pinkerton's Agency and the private eye,
in a burlesque of disguised surveillance, the amassing of
voluminous information, and the elaborate manoeuvring to gain
a suspect's confidence to betray it. *The Amateur Detective* (1877)
is a poor play, and Twain is not all that alert to the invasion of
privacy, the false arrests and police harassment, and the Agency's
notorious aggression against suspects and innocents alike. His
farce is directed against detective methods. Every fictioneer who
employs withheld and discharged information techniques might
well feel the urge to attack a genre, an agency, which pro-
fessionalises investigation and detection plots, the stock-in-trade
of most nineteenth-century fiction to the point of stereotype. 'We
ought never to do wrong when people are looking,' mocks the
epigraph to *A Double-Barrelled Detective Story* (1902), a
multiple ironic warning against the mixture of spying and
vengeance barely hidden in the genre. Twain demolishes the
man-hunt plot and the Sherlock Holmes plot of aristocratic
ratiocinative powers, derived from Poe's Chevalier Auguste
Dupin. Archie is a superior detective–tracker because his violent
birth has conferred on him a psychic 'birthmark' : 'the gift of the
blood-hound is in him!' He becomes a wandering avenger–dick
with 'just a grand natural talent . . . but no intellect in it'.

Holmes's intervention among the silver miners is exposed by his nephew Fetlock Jones: 'Anybody that knows him as I do knows he can't detect a crime except when he plans it all out beforehand and arranges the clews and hires some fellow to commit it according to his instructions.'

The ambiguous twentieth-century development of the genre is overshadowed by Twain's joke. By 1975, in Arthur Penn's *Night Moves*, the detective's motives move him into self-investigations which come too late. He is a revealer, a psychopathic unraveller, moving towards death rather than the solution of a death. The supersleuth is analysed in the manner of the less destructive Robert Altman film of *The Long Goodbye* (1973), in which Chandler's Marlowe becomes a bewildered decoration of his original. *Night Moves* interprets 'private eye' as an eye turned inward towards motive, too late. So that the plot of investigation only scaffolds a story of bankrupt resources which cannot be renewed by habitual search for information about other people, habits falsely believed to be for truth and to help people involved. The detective resorts to a gun. He discovers that the world *is* deception and lies, and *therefore* resists investigation. The old probity reliant on 'our best self' is no longer valid.

The earlier Lew Archer is late in the line of the old guard; he finally sees the genre into impossibility, moving into fictions of self-deception and self-expenditure rather than ratiocination at the pure disposal of law. The site of Macdonald's series – a long first-person novel in fact – focuses the problems a distinguished formula writer may encounter as his skill moves him towards decisions which break the stereotype – a form already an interface between pure detection of the Dupin kind and the thriller. In the former, cerebrations celebrate a post-violence situation. The dick is one step behind murder, and then catches up. His apartness is relatively gentlemanly. The thriller involves him in violence, which he sometimes commits himself. Macdonald's hero is ex-police and still calls his terrain a beat (the Continental Op operates anywhere). He needs his clients' fees for a living. This local boy knows the social scene, Macdonald's California site, but as late as *The Blue Hammer*, in 1976, is still learning the ambiguity of his own place in it. (Pudd'nhead Wilson, in 1894, was helpless against both the aristocratism of America and its absurdly vicious racism, until he discovered fingerprints.) John Skow's review of *Sleeping Beauty* questioned Archer's age,

physical condition, inadequate salary and problematic retirement
funds – 'It's time for him to marry a rich, pretty widow and
retire.'[1] But in fact the Archer novel does not need to retire
because its active elements – Archer and the Californian site –
constitute an American epitome, rooted in continual tensions
within capitalist democracy run on certain violent ambiguities of
law. As early as 1954, in *Find a Victim*, Archer gives Sheriff
Brand Church a compact description which will carry him
through to the 1970s:

> I understand this. I'm trying to solve two homicides, and
> something is trying to stop me. Something that looks like law
> and talks like law but doesn't smell like law. Not in my nostrils.
> It smells like zombie meat. A zombie that takes the public
> money and sits behind a courthouse desk pretending to be an
> officer.

The re-opened and re-closed formula is: a *personal* collection
of information which increases Archer's vulnerability – an
archaic involvement, it might be argued, in a world controlled by
the electric assemblages of computer data. The reader can, if he
wishes, assemble the data, but Macdonald is interested more in
the detective-society interaction than in preventing the reader
from detecting the villain. In fact he sometimes says openly who is
lying. Working efficiently back from the solutionary area (in the
spatiality Dickens showed Poe he knew from Godwin, and which
Twain parodies), the author presents the hero plunged into the
inefficiencies of law and order. His imagination injects energy
into what could become a moribund systematic. Ishmael Reed
invents Papa LeBas as a HooDoo-empowered dick whose Agency
is magic as law. In *L'Emploi du Temps* (1956), Michel Butor's
Jacques Revel is, like Oedipus, looking for a murderer and trying
to answer enigmatic questions. He sees a stained glass window
depicting the murder of Abel. He assumes the detective role 'to
unveil and to unmask'. In Robbe-Grillet's *Les Gommes* (1953),
the Oedipus elements are parodies by being everywhere obses-
sively imaged in the city location. Up to *The Blue Hammer*,
Macdonald largely suppresses such myth mystique and its usages,
parodied or not, or the implications of Robbe-Grillet's *Le Voyeur*
(1955), which announces a murder and requires the reader to
reconstitute a criminal event from an inventory of effects. In the

year after *The Blue Hammer*, Thomas Berger's *Who Is Teddy
Villanova?* (1977) brings Twain's parodic revenges *and* the
'nouvelle roman''s parodic detective assumptions together into
high farce. Russel Wren, dumb ex-English-literature teacher and
failed playwright turned private eye in New York, finds he has to
prove he is not himself the archfiend and international criminal
he is paid to track down. Berger's style system is itself horribly
literary and heavily coherent in the manner of the more arty
examples of the genre, and packed with opinionated pseudo-
analysis and *Reader's Digest* data. Borges, too, parodies the
deadly urge to epic coherence – an impulse Macdonald admits in
On Crime Writing[2] – which denies luck among the detective's
choices by insisting on some tidy 'all' in 'the world'. In 'Death and
the Compass' (1942), the criminal traps the detective in his own
desire to investigate an assumed totality, a labyrinthine puzzle
which, because it is man-made, must be solvable. But it is in fact
composed for him by the villain, the author's alter ego.

The questions inside every detective fiction are: who made the
location and its information, and who made the fiction of its
making? Borges' Red Scharlach is anyone who cares to challenge
the grotesque need to believe in, and even enact, complete
Control. In 'On Chesterton', Borges writes: 'He speaks of a jail of
mirrors; of a labyrinth without a centre; of a man devoured by
metal automatons. . . . Something in the makeup of his
personality leaned toward the nightmarish, something secret, and
blind, and central.'[3] Lew Archer is a writer in a room, writing up
his formulaic experience – as L.A. Murillo observes of Borges,
'what the reader has before him as he goes through the narrative
in the first person is a representation, a polarized account, of the
occurring consciousness of the character.'[4] Archer needs his interventions and needs to narrate, a pseudo-autobiographer
justifying his position, addictively, and the sheer number of books
in the total somewhat Proustian novel suggests that this, like the
high incidence of crime, is normality. Self-irony therefore
emerges where fallibility works in tension with skill: some of 'the'
solution is out there to be discovered and reported to gain a
double livelihood as a detective and a writer. As Macdonald tells
us, 'I wasn't Archer, exactly, but Archer was me.'[5] Enough said:
total analysis of the elements of the writing situation would
probably ruin the formula-genre's useful limitations. But it is
undoubtedly a strength in Macdonald that it is not pretentious to

consider him in the context laid out preliminarily here. As Murillo remarks: 'the archetypal detective mystery is the predicament of the human intellect committed to deciphering the enigmatic and ultimately elusive order of the universe. The predicament and its human reality is the mystery'.[6]

At the end of DePalma's *Sisters* (1972), the detective is literally and mentally up the pole – a telegraph pole, archly exemplary of the fact that studying at a school of modern methods has rendered him incapable of communication. He remains peripheral to the actual reasons for both heroines' neurotic or murderous behaviour. *The Way Some People Die* establishes, in 1951, a key Macdonald formula: the missing girl; and Archer intervenes at this crux of young female sexual and financial vulnerability and of the parents' responsibility or its reverse. The bourgeois parents initiate the search. They can afford Archer but do not want police publicity and such immediate legality. Archer comes forward as repairman-observer in the social breakdown, but in the narrative itself a consistent use of animal images for human action undermines any depth of humanism. An archer is a killer and hunter of killers. This one left official bureaucracy. At one point he observes 'I am God' but immediately checks this hubris. He enters a chain of biographies in a series of locations, shaped largely through descriptions and metaphors of decay, set in California as Nature, unchanging in itself, changing under human pollution.

> Romanticism
> soughed in her voice
>
> like a loosely strung
> Aeolian harp.

The text mostly avoids the kind of 'style' Jonathan Williams's poem – entitled 'Lew Archer Hits a Really Heavy Note' – parodies.[7] But it can serve to remind us that Macdonald moves in Fitzgerald's Keatsian ore and 'blue lawn' country. The community operates without rooted morality, a class system liable to break into overt violence, its climactic norm. The plot is a close metonymy of a society which regards itself as a tried formula, and Macdonald relies on this to let Archer deduce *his* plot from discoveries. The police are mostly ciphers of order within chaos, part of a continuous mopping-up action Archer shares, in a rule by money, drugs and guns, and uncertain family emotional holds and inheritances. The actual explanation of the case of Galatea Lawrence is frequently written in rapid journalistic prose, the least interesting passages in the book. Macdonald is already engaged in defeating the detective-mystery structure in order to sustain it, in using an addictive formula to expose an addictive society of 'possessive individualism'. The reader expects a formulaic injection – the elements reactivated by literary skills.

Archer is based on excellent detectives Macdonald had seen at work.[8] His hero, traditionally, 'represents his creator and carries his values into action in society'. The series is therefore the production of Macdonald's ratiocination and physical presence in his society – in Poe's terms, reason versus the ape in 'unstable balance'.[9] But the traditional detective dream of bringing apparent mysteries and irrational behaviour into rational accessibility, under one man's perspicacity, wanes within the Archer series. All is not lost, as John Milton might say, but increasingly the dream of control of all within law – to justify the ways of man to man – by a man whose legal agency is subordinate to police, is eroded. The advantages of single intelligence go towards the 'betrayal' of a complex clientele to fixed and simple law. The state moves in where it has belonged and controlled all the time. Archer is not a radical, but as he lives into the 1970s, he becomes a severe critic whose belief in law, as distinct from a very few policemen, and in American society, crumbles irrevocably.

The Macdonald narrative is not split into narrator *and* detective hero, as in Poe's and Conan Doyle's 'narcissistic fantasy'.[10] Nor is Archer neurotically friendless or bound to one associate or to drugs. Byronic self-regard is invaded by a wry noting of repeated faults. Macdonald notes Conan Doyle's satisfaction with privilege in the British class system – obvious, too, in Buchan, Sayers and Christie. But Archer does need a terminal society for his gaze to penetrate the gaps in coherence. Hammett and Chandler were openly against a corrupt triadic system of police, criminal and plutocrat. The resultant continental op or private eye was, Macdonald believes, 'the classless, restless man of American democracy, who spoke the language of the street'.[11] For 'democracy' we really should read 'American capitalist democracy', and then remember how, in *Red Harvest* (1929), the Continental Op writes, like an Army general: 'I spent most of my week in Ogden trying to fix up my reports so they would not read as if I had broken as many Agency rules, state laws, and human bones as I had.' Nor is he entirely released from Holmesian addiction: 'I encouraged my brain with two Fatimas.' His arrogance is fairly complete: 'I juggled death and destruction,' he reports, and: 'They own the courts, and, besides, the courts are too slow for us now. I've got myself tangled up in something.' The incorruptible Old Man of the Agency will have to be deceived. Chandler's detective writes: 'Down these mean streets a man must go who is not himself mean, who is neither tarnished nor afraid',[12] but he is not, in practice, 'sea-green incorruptible'. Detective-story writers, Macdonald not excepted, tend to idealise their heroes in order to excuse liability for violence traded off against violence. The lone anarchist is his own justification. (T.S. Eliot and Graham Greene naturally had a soft spot for the genre because its moral world could all too easily be converted into a simplistic battlefield for Christian dogma: those not for me are against man, as the man said, threateningly.) But the lone Archer becomes lonely, and his sympathy repeatedly reaches out to the lonely American, worried about ageing and money, or to youthful isolation in a non-supportive society. Macdonald often moves immediately from the existential bleakness of his towns-people to the indifferent Ocean, 'the image of Eternity – the throne of the Invincible', as it is given as the end of *Childe Harold's Pilgrimage*.

For Macdonald, Archer is not the 'emotional centre' of the books but the indicator of 'the main thing', the people in his beat. But these we know only through Archer (and the range is relatively small) and through his reporting style as novelist–detective. But Macdonald is accurate in his belief[13] that Archer's innovation in the genre is his questioning conscience – the concealed motive in his obsessive story-telling, part of the cultic power taken up by a readership which constitutes a following. A convention is a ritual. Fictive ritual enables subversive and irrational material to be offered in apparent confrontation. Guilt for the ambivalence of a self-styled peaceful society enjoys such circumscribed darkness, such danger theatricalised – in the sense Barthes uses in *Sade/Fourier/Loyola*: 'What is theatricalization? It is not designing a setting for representation, but unlimiting language.'[14] Barthes reminds us that 'the pleasure of the Text also includes the amicable return of the author' – a return, in Macdonald's sense, to a similar site of similar events, a return which makes crime in the state of the nation, imaged as part of California, familiar without the necessity for breeding either contempt or revolution.

The Ocean, 'the blue eternity at the far edge of my life'[15] contributes to 'the epic impulse which almost all writers of fiction try to serve in some degree'[16] The Oedipus system which structures *The Galton Case* (1959) – the concealed or overt assault on parents – is an epic constant in the Archer fictions, useful in their account of generations lost in the past three decades of American domestic and overseas conflict. Archer does not renounce technology in the epic manner of Ike McCaslin in the Mississippi wilderness, but restricts himself to the late-nineteenth-century inventions of the telephone, the car and the revolver: the Hemingway stoic code still roughly holds, and the feats are not super-human as in Superman. But the archaic hunter does enjoy tracking a quarry. The hard-boiled Op vanishes, and has vanished in the fictions of the late 1970s. Already in 1951, in *The Way Some People Die*, we read:

> I needed food, sleep, shave, and shower. Most of all I needed a talk with or even a look at somebody who was happy, prosperous, and virtuous, or any one of the three.

Archer is far less a victim of official and unofficial brutality than Sam Spade, and less sacrificial, mutilated and masochistic than Philip Marlowe. For him, as for William Thompson, California exists 'at the edge of history', with 'Ronald Reagan and the hippies [as] a joint persuasion that a new exchange between myth and history was taking place at the edge of America'.[17] Archer's beat is the beat of *The Day of the Locust* and *The Crying of Lot 49*, where families fall apart, youngsters break from the parent generation, the inheritance, and end up in experimental disasters and revenge. His girls are Patty Hearsts before the event. The twenty-five-year-old Galatea Lawrence '*always* came home for Christmas'. Now her mother spends Christmas alone and calls Archer to rescue her daughter from 'how evil men can be'. Then Archer looks at her photograph in nurse's uniform: 'With her fierce curled lip, black eyes and clean angry bones she must have stood out in her graduating class like a chicken hawk in a flock of pullets.' In Pacific Point, 'divided neatly into social tiers, like something a sociologist had built to prove a theory', Archer encounters men who carry a gun because they work for a pinball company, and hysterical car-lemmings, one half 'rushing down to the sea and the other half had been there and decided not to get wet.' He recalls 'a brigadier I'd known in Colòn during the war', who hunted sharks with a mask and a knife: 'It gave him background for dealing with human beings.' The retainer from a thug client 'twisted in my hand like a fat green tomato-worm', kept separate from his other money, to be bet on horses 'at the earliest opportunity'. And back inside the contemporary scene, the 'desert outpost' of the recent past.

In page after page of ostensible tracing story appears the plot of social lacks — a thug afraid to be left alone, another thug's 'tarnished gold Christ writhing on a dark wood cross', a cormorant flying over the Pacific 'like a sharp black soul hell-bent'. The epic impulse verges on cliché melodrama exactly as it does in life. Hell in California is actual: 'The metal fist came down across his face' — 'A part of her left arm was pitted like ancient marble by hypo marks.' Arnold's merman emerges from the Pacific for an addicted girl who remembers studying the poem 'in English last year'. Swimming in that Ocean, Archer is stopped by kelp beds: 'I hated the touch of underwater life.' The young are sucked into a despairing violence Archer barely resists himself:

It was depressing not to be able to hit him again because he was younger and softer and too easy. . . . There was really nothing to be done about Ronnie, at least that I could do. He would go on turning a dollar in one way or another until he ended up in Folsom or a mortuary or a house with a swimming pool on top of a hill. There were thousands like him in my ten-thousand-square-mile beat: boys who had lost their futures, their parents and themselves in the shallow jerry-built streets of the coastal cities; boys with hot-rod bowels, comic-book imaginations, daring that grew up too late for one war, too early for another.

Macdonald inherits Gatsby–Carraway nostalgia as he negotiates Archer in heavy traffic between oilfield derricks in 'suburban wilderness': 'I felt as if I were passing through dream country, trying to remember the dream that went along with the landscape and not being able to'. Since his divorce — his wife claimed 'extreme mental cruelty' — he returns to his middle-class mortgaged home, between Hollywood and Los Angeles, only to sleep. War and the police are his official past – 'Intelligence' and leaving the Long Beach force for refusing 'Sam Schneider's monthly cut': 'Most good policemen have a public conscience and a private conscience. I just have the private conscience; a poor thing, but my own.'

The Way Some People Die is a classic part of the American fiction of controlled hysteria: from Twain to West and into what has recently been termed 'the American Nightmare' of the 1960s and 1970s. At times Archer moves almost as if he were in limbo: 'The sun and the other stars had burned out long ago, and Mosquito and I were journeying for our sins through a purgatory of grey space'. He sees himself as a police-trained fall-guy with a series of Virgils, all treacherous ('all that energy and ingenuity wasted'), proceeding through purgatorial pocket biographies in exhausting locations. The tone is melancholy because he expects to find no community of mutual aid. Money, gangsters, guns, bewildered people, and some corrupt cops, control. He is expected to demonstrate moral altruism where it has died. So the novel becomes a formula for a formulaic society, an addictive genre for an addictive society, living in series, hoping for examples of lone moral responsibility on the edge of exile, at the edge of history, looking for a hero. By the 1970s the series turns increasingly towards the psyche beneath predatory games and inside the tracker. The Sophoclean Freud told Theodor Reik, in 1913, that rather than be compared to Holmes, he would prefer Giovanni Morelli, a nineteenth-century art scholar who specialised in fakes.[18] But, he remarked, 'I shall have to bear it.'

'What is the analyst's desire?' Archer is part of what Jacques Lacan calls 'the analytic Great Work', which cannot end.[19] The desire to track is in itself an object, and the tracker–analyst's desire is, in Lacan's words:

> a desire to obtain absolute difference, a desire which intervenes when, confronted with the primary signifier, the subject is, for the first time, in a position to subject himself to it. Then only may the signification of limitless love emerge, because it is outside the limits of the law, where alone it may live.[20]

Crime needs beating but Archer must maintain 'absolute difference', which is the significance of a well-known passage in

The Drowning Pool (1950), whose elements will reappear during the next twenty-five years or more: 'There had to be a difference between me and the opposition, or I'd have to take the mirror out of my bathroom. It was the only mirror in the house, and I needed it for shaving.' But Archer does harden: 'wild cats terrify me, but people are worse' – 'sex and money: the forked root of evil' – 'the soul-destroying monotony of phonies' – 'for an instant I was the man in the mirror, the shadow-figure without a life of his own who peered with one large eye and one small eye through dirty glass and the dirty lives of people in a very dirty world' – 'he moved like a man whose conscience is clear, or lacking' – 'her atmosphere was like pure oxygen; if you breathed it deep it would make you dizzy and gay, or poison you' – 'I kissed her, felt her toes on my instep, her hand move on my body. I drew back from the whirling vortex that had opened, the drowning pool' – 'she fed the quarters one by one into a machine near the door. Somebody phoning long-distance to somebody else who had been dead for years'. That is the internal plot of *The Drowning Pool*, its infrastructure or, if you will, 'the unconscious of the work'.[21]

Within such a system, Archer has to manufacture his morality. In *The Zebra-Striped Hearse* (1963), a father hiring him to stop his rich daughter's marriage to a young painter, asks him: 'You feel you can afford to lay down terms to your prospective clients?' Archer replies: 'Certain terms are always implied. . . . I have a license to lose, and a reputation.' Such are the legal and moral limits of his employment, out of which his involvement and withdrawal succeeds:

> 'Young people never seem to learn from their parents' experience. It's a tragic waste. . . . ' Blackwell was a sad and troubled man, hardly competent to play God with anybody's life. But the sadder and more troubled they were, the more they yearned for omnipotence. The really troubled ones believed they had it.

In fact, Blackwell takes his daughter as his 'most treasured possession'; the alienation of 'the holy family', to use Marx and Engels' exemplary terms, is the critical presence once again. Inheritance and possession, the core issues of modern societies – too often swept into a false arrangement called 'the generation gap' – also appear in the function of gambling (a mainstay of nineteenth-century fiction, too), the convulsive hand-pulling at one-armed bandits, through which gamblers pathetically, faintly echo the Declaration of Independence: 'Am I getting old? Have I failed? Am I immature? Does she love me? Why does he hate me? Hit me, jackpot, flood me with life and liberty and happiness.' And at the same time, and not for the only time, Archer identifies himself with a myth of the early days of the Republic, Natty Bumppo, 'a great rifleman and a great tracker'. If the Mohicans are the good cops (with 'an inflexible mind'), the hostile Indians are the murderers defined in chapter 21:

> Most of them were acting out a fantasy which they couldn't explain themselves: destroying an unlamented past which seemed to bar them from the brave new world, erasing the fear of death by inflicting death, or burying an old malignant grief where it would sprout and multiply and end by destroying the destroyer.

The tone hovers characteristically between neutrality and sympathy, an ambivalence which replaces ideology, or even an ideological tendency. The colon does not lead to the murderers' un-selfexplained fantasy but to Archer's unexplainable prognosis of murder psychology in social terms. 'Brave new world' carries both Marina and Huxley, and the whole passage rests in the sacrificial continuities of *The Golden Bough*, while remaining tentative in its paradoxes, nearly as reluctant to admit commitment to its myths as *The Waste Land*. The bleached surfers in their striped hearse, in chapter 8, are, in contrast, an epitome of clear vision, a 'platoon' with a tribe's identity in unison action, and Colonel Blackwell's erotic military dream actions with his daughter appear even more pathological, a ghastly epitome of all training of the young by their elders:

> . . . a puppet, a kind of zombie. He supervised her reading, her games, her friends, even her thoughts. He made her keep a diary which he read. . . . He got her so confused that she did not know whether she was a girl or a boy, or if he was her father or her lover. . . . He taught her to shoot and climb mountains and play polo. He even took to calling her Harry.

Since his wife could not afford a court battle, he won. As Archer observes in classic despair: 'People start out young on the road to becoming murderers. They start out equally young on the road to becoming victims. When the two roads intersect, you have a violent crime.' Life is therefore a fixed field of tracks, as it is in *Our Mutual Friend* and *Daniel Deronda*, novels of concealed destiny. Macdonald's moral schematic has to become the detective desire to alleviate destiny rather than initiate social change. Archer's gloom is deeply bourgeois, deeply American and alienated. His last comment on Blackwell's daughter is: 'I had nothing to give Harriet.' He has less and less to give as the series continues.

Ambivalences of parent–child relationship, as the child grows into an adult world of war and competition, are openly stated in *The Underground Man* – but what else could an honest writer do in 1971? (Nicholas Ray's *Rebel without a Cause* had appeared as long ago as 1955, but it is regularly reshown on television).

'We're losing a whole generation. They're punishing us for bringing them into the world.'

'There are dozens of missing young people every week. But I never thought my daughter would be one of them. Susan had a really good life. We've given her every advantage.'

It was often the same problem – an unreality so bland and smothering that the children tore loose and impaled themselves on the spikes of any reality that offered. Or made their own unreality with drugs.

'I asked him in a friendly way what he planned to do with himself, and he said all he wanted was just to get by. I didn't think that was a satisfactory answer, and I asked him what would happen to the country if everybody took that attitude. He said it had already happened to the country. . . . I told him if that was his philosophy of life he could leave home and not bother coming back.'

Archer's interventions for money have become even more awkward: 'I took the money, since I needed it for expenses, but I felt vaguely declassed by the transaction, like a repossession man.' And later he gives it to a woman who needs to get away: 'I was sort of glad to get rid of it, though here again I was conscious of buying and being sold at the same time.' He also now openly admits himself as a cause: 'I sometimes served as a catalyst for trouble, not unwillingly.' The earlier 'drowning pool' becomes a woman 'who had drowned herself in her own life'. Addictive drugs are not only commonplace, but the 'Einstein trip' is a common necessary – 'where you go all the way out, past the last star, and space loops back on you'. The romantic language carries the *Gatsby* load again but Archer's despair is nearer to Monroe Stahr's, as he watches the jays in his yard:

> . . . like watching a flashing blue explosion-in-reverse that put the morning world together again.
> But the central piece was missing.

The investigation can never find that completion. A sports meeting 'resembles a staging area just back of the lines in a major battle. On the grass oval inside the cinder track, bubble 'copters were landing and taking off with reinforcement.' A victim's convertible is 'a relic of an ancient civilization, ruined and diminished by the passage of centuries, already half buried among their droppings'.

The Underground Man accumulates into an archaeology of America beneath its vanishing detective plot. The biographical studies are now necessarily longer. A woman writes of her grandfather, Robert Driscoll Falconer – 'son of a Massachusetts scholar and businessman and a student and disciple of Louis Agassiz', who, to recuperate from 1863 wounds, reaches the Pacific and a ranch 'originally part of the Mission Lands, secularized in 1834 and becoming part of the Mexican Land Grant'. His son compiles 'the first checklist of native [ornithological] species in the Santa Teresa region', and his collection becomes 'the nucleus of the bird collection' of the local museum. His daughter writes that he was 'a god come down to earth in human guise', as her handwriting breaks up, 'like a defeated army', under Archer's gaze. Consequently the present-day plot is a subdued, appalled account of behaviour since those impossible combinations in the past. Mrs Snow's biographical narrative takes up two chapters of weary bewilderment. Even when criminal or criminally bewildered, the characters retain certain human vestiges the Californian scene works to deny: 'The moveable lettering on the marquee in front offered "Steak, Lobster and Continuous Entertainment". When I parked in front of the office, I could hear western music like the last wail of a dying frontier'. The pelicans diving in Dunes Bay are the last: 'their bodies are poisoned with DDT, and it makes their eggs all break.' Discontinuity in ecology parallels and exemplifies the carelessness of Californian, American society. Archer's bleakly terse comment on the adolescent kidnappers follows: 'I wanted to end their wild flight, not only for the child's sake but for their own.' A hotel clerk cares about one of them: 'I never had a daughter.' The girl's father refuses police help: 'They shoot first and ask questions afterwards.' Archer: 'I couldn't help agreeing with him.' And then: 'I had no children, but I had given up envying people who had.' When he promises the girl standing suicidally on the edge of the bridge to take her to 'a safer place', she calls him 'a dirty filthy liar' and he recognises 'the depth of my lying and the terrible depth of her rage'. Given her life in the adult world since the age of three, she is, quite simply, accurate. The summary of the whole situation places the other young kidnapper: 'He belonged to a generation whose elders had been poisoned, like the pelicans, with a kind of moral DDT that damaged the lives of their young.'

A little heavy-handed? Perhaps, but accurate; Archer can now only manage a holding stance against social corruption and his own weariness: 'I liked the woman. I almost trusted her. But I was already working deep in her life. I didn't want to buy a piece of it or commit myself to her until I knew what the consequences would be.' What can a private eye do in a society where a child cannot believe it is his mother on the phone? – 'I thought maybe it was taped' – and where he himself concludes that the kidnappers were in fact 'a pair of alienated adolescents. They seem to have thought they were rescuing Ronny from the adult world. To a certain extent it was true.' And in prison, boys are subjected to 'dreadful cruelties and wickedness'. The law is illegal. Archer is pinned to a dilemma:

> I had no overriding desire to pin her husband's murder on Mrs. Broadhurst. The hot breath of vengeance was growing cold in my nostrils as I grew older. I had more concern for a kind of economy in life that would help to preserve the things that were worth preserving. . . . I told myself I didn't care who killed them. But I cared.

That 'economy' is Thoreau's sense of economy, an ecology of both human and non-human life. When the murderer claims moral motivation against wickedness, cheating and fornication, Archer is defeated: this kind of paranoid clear conscience, 'blaming everything on other people' is characteristic of the whole society's refusal to act out of radical diagnosis. All Archer can wish for the kidnapped boy is what thousands of 'other people' wish: 'a benign failure of memory'.

The Underground Man signals the end of a genre, the death of the detective's moral security in self-righteous investigation. Like the hero of *Tristes Tropiques*, Archer has to reconstitute a society in which he is irrevocably involved: 'the most august of investigations is surely that which reveals what comes before, dictated, and in large measure explains all the others.'[22] He tries, like Lévi-Strauss's *bricoleur*, to be a liberator confronting 'a collection of oddments left over from human endeavours',[23] and like this anthropologist he 'never can feel himself "at home" anywhere; he will always be, psychologically speaking, an amputee'.[24] So he really engages in 'entropology', 'the discipline that devotes itself to the study of the process of disintegration in its most highly evolved forms'. Archer must refuse broadly traditional definitions of villainy. The outlaw has never been, by crude definition, either good or bad; it is the myth-makers and myth-repeaters who categorise him morally. Archer becomes not so much the victim of his own complex relativism as part of the increasing impossibility of equating law with accurate moral judgement. In 1963 he could confidently define the qualities of 'a first-rate detective' as 'honesty, imagination, curiosity, and a love of people' (*The Zebra-Striped Hearse*). There was no danger, then, that Lew Archer could, like the Op in *Red Harvest*, 'go blood simple like the natives', but he was certainly trapped in the Fitzgerald dream: 'Now we were stuck with the dream without meaning. It had become the nightmare we live in' (*The Barbarous Coast*, 1956).

The Blue Hammer (1976) therefore deepens the sense of archetype within the local and the contemporary. The problematic daughter appears here in a context comprising the painting market, veterans of 'the war', rising prices, and campus 'unrest'. She identifies Archer immediately between cop and shrink: 'I can smell the dirt on you, from other people's secrets'. And in an exchange with another girl: 'You don't smell like a painter' – 'What do I smell like?' – 'A cop, maybe.' (Smell, in fact, reaches hyperaesthetic intensity in this part of the series – for example: 'I could smell the sour animal anger of their bodies, and hear them breathing quickly, out of phase'). The pressures now shift Archer into a third confessional investigative role, always incipiently there:

> There were times when I almost wished I was a priest. I was growing weary of other people's pain and wondered if a black suit and a white collar might serve as armour against it. I'd never know. My grandmother in Contra Costa had marked me for the priesthood, but I had slipped away under the fence.

For one thing, his feminism, always strong, if considerably armoured, in the St George manner, is liable to intervene: 'the grief you shared with women was most always partly desire. At least sometimes you could take them to bed, I thought, and exchange a temporary kindness, which priests were denied.' His weariness can have no uniform, therefore, even if something of his Catholic rearing sustains him. And love is too dangerous a commitment. When his girlfriend Betty provokes him to sign a letter 'Love, Lew', he has 'a sudden cold urge to recall it and cross out the word I had added. So far as I could remember, I hadn't written the word, or spoken it, to a woman in some years. But now it was in my mind, like a twinge of pain or hope.'

Painting as creation and money, copper as private wealth, is the double focus of power within which the stability of 'family' is confused, as parents remarry, move apart, change names, until their children hardly know who they are. Wars create more gaps in relationship in 'a world where money talked, or bought silence'. The priest–cop–shrink elements of authority have become virtually invalid. Archer has to – Macdonald has to – recognise the facts: 'Perhaps, after all, the truth I was looking for couldn't be found in the world. You had to go up on a mountain and wait for it, or find it in yourself.' But the Bartleby in him curtails the implications of such radical self-analysis:

> Like other lost and foolish souls, Fred had an urge to help people, to give them psychotherapy even if it wrecked them. When he was probably the one who needed it most. Watch it, I said to myself, or you'll be trying to help Fred in that way. Take a look at your own life, Archer.

But I preferred not to. My chosen study was other men, hunted men in rented rooms, ageing boys clutching at manhood before night fell and they grew suddenly old. If you were a therapist, how could you need therapy? If you were the hunter, you couldn't be the hunted. Or could you?

But the habit of investigation continues through *Night Moves* into that 'connectedness' which obsesses him, that epic impulse again, and he recognises his privilege:

> I lived at the intersection of two worlds. One was the actual world where danger was seldom far from people's lives, where reality threatened them with its cutting edge. The other was the world where [police captain] Mackendrick had to operate in a maze of tradition and a grid of rules – a world where nothing officially happened until it was reported through channels.

In the former, a lost son can 'father his father' and Archer can say to a nurse who recognises a fellow professional: 'I chose this job, or it chose me. There's a lot of human pain involved in it, but I'm not looking for another job.' Archer's nervous vulnerability, in 1976, repeatedly breaks his armour. When a woman mentions leaving her Denver family at fourteen, he observes: 'She may have been feeling what I felt, the subterranean jolt as the case moved once again, with enough force to throw a dead man out of his grave.' Investigation leads down dark routes to the primal place where half-brothers, one 'illegitimate', struggle for power; the surface is pecuniary; the interior is, in the fullest sense, erotic. As David Brion Davis states:

> In American literature, the theme of alienation from a central human family was often expressed as the struggle between virtuous and evil brothers for the possession of lands or women in the situation where symbols of paternal authority were either weakened or totally lacking.[25]

As one of Macdonald's brothers leeches the other dry, the plot enacts a primary scene, and Archer is drawn into the one which immediately precedes it:

'God and Archer', she said bitterly, 'they know everything. Don't you and God ever make a mistake?'

'God did. He left off Eve's testicles.'

Betty let out a cry of pure sharp female rage, which somehow diminuendoed into mirth.

Such atavistic myth-mongering would be ludicrous, except that Macdonald's pessimism is strong enough to afford it. The title of this novel is a clue to an adoration, an example of love penetrating a cynicism on which myths thrive, and which is given an ultimate report in the final pages. The DA tells Archer, 'you're probably not as familiar as some of us with recent developments in psychology' – with 'an edge on his smile'. Since Archer needs information, he replies: 'It's true I never went to law school.' Law, psychology, the police: one of Macdonald's strengths in *The Blue Hammer* lies in his dramatisation of their contemporary malign interaction in repetitions of primal scenes. Courthouse proceedings remind Archer of 'the initiation rite into a tribe of aborigines', and the closing line of the whole book re-enacts a primary emotional drive, warped once again into the corruptions of inheritance. Overt political diagnosis is circumvented, as if such investigative documentary patterns as this might be spoiled by theoretical or revolutionary weapons of analysis. Macdonald is a characteristically mid-century American author, humane but locked into the entropy of a refusal to cut to the core of the social structure he diagnoses. Unlike Kafka and Borges, who create anxieties of interpretation for the reader at the centre of their works, Macdonald creates anxieties as a scaffolding for watching Archer in his routines. But he has certainly moved away from single-solution formulas to the multiple motivation plot in which 'all explanation is superfluous.'[26] Betty's suspicions about Lew's self-aggrandisement are historical. The idea of a singular moral authority is finished, and in fiction the *coup de grâce* was delivered by, among other things, Robbe-Grillet's statements in *For a New Novel* – 'God alone can profess to be objective'[27] – and in the structure of *Le Voyeur*, where the reader has to be the analyst of the protagonist, the detector of a psyche, a process which, in *La Jalousie*, extends to the whole text and the method required to read it.

The American private eye, and especially one as conscience-stricken as Archer, fights a nostalgic rearguard action, whereas Robbe-Grillet operates from another basis altogether, as Europeans must: 'We had thought to control the [world] by assigning it a meaning, and the entire art of the world, in particular, seemed dedicated to this enterprise.' So that the revolution was precise: 'not only do we no longer consider the world as our own private property, designed according to our needs and readily domesticated, but we no longer even believe in its "depth".' In the space left by God and his apes, the investigative fictioneers of nineteenth-century tradition, grows a rankly luxuriant nostalgia for order as a hegemony controlled by law, psychiatry and money, and for the charisma of some lone authority, civilian or otherwise. The spy novel now interests everyone, therefore, and, as Aryeh Neier reminded us not long ago, 'according to a 1937 report of the U.S. Senate's La Follette Civil Liberties Committee, Pinkerton, Burns and a few other agencies furnished 3,871 spies and provocateurs to corporations during the preceding three years.'[28] The continental op was never a democrat, and Lew Archer left the police but still necessarily hands over his investigated criminals, his victims, to the law. Even if society is part of the blame. He never joined an agency. The formula series begins on these premises, and there is a good deal in Tzvetan Todorov's observation that 'detective fiction has its norms; to "develop" them is to disappoint them: to "improve" upon detective fiction is to write "literature", not detective fiction.' Furthermore, 'a rule of the genre postulates the detective's immunity.'[29] Hammett, Chandler and Macdonald in their several ways erode the genre under pressures from the nature of law in the American power structure, and Billy Wilder's *The Private Life of Sherlock Holmes* (1970) put the finishing touches to the undermining suspicion that the detective's ratiocinations were in any case written up into fiction from fiction.

Ross Macdonald accepts the consequences of Todorov's characteristic twentieth-century commonplaces: 'no observation exists without an observer; the author cannot, by definition, be omniscient as he was in the classical novel.' When law itself is an agency in the preservation of the status quo, in the last years of the twentieth century the private eye becomes pure form. Lew Archer is a writer. Ross Macdonald breaks the mould.

. . . luck, chance, and talent are of no avail, and the man who wishes to wrest something from Destiny must venture into that perilous margin-country where the norms of Society count for nothing and the demands and guarantees of the group are no longer valid. He must travel to where the police have no sway, to the limits of physical resistance and the far-point of physical and moral suffering. Once in this unpredictable borderland a man may vanish, never to return; or he may acquire for himself, from among the immense repertory of unexploited forces which surrounds any well-regulated society, some personal provision of power; and when this happens an otherwise inflexible social order may be cancelled in favour of the man who has risked everything.[30]

NOTES AND REFERENCES

1. *Time*, 14 May 1973.
2. Ross Macdonald, *On Crime Writing* (Santa Barbara, Calif.: Capra Press, 1973).
3. Jorge Luis Borges, 'On Chesterton', in *Other Inquisitions 1937–1952* (University of Texas Press, 1965), p.83.
4. L.A. Murillo, *The Cyclical Night* (Cambridge, Mass.: Harvard University Press, 1968), p.126.
5. *On Crime Writing*, p.192.
6. *The Cyclical Night*, p.192.
7. Jonathan Williams, *Glees . . . Swarthy Monotonies . . . Rince Cochon . . . & Chozzerai for Simon* . . . (New Mexico: DBA Editions, 1980).
8. *On Crime Writing*, p.9.
9. Ibid., p.11.
10. Ibid., p.12.
11. Ibid.
12. Raymond Chandler, 'The Simple Art of Murder', *Atlantic Monthly*, Dec. 1944; reprinted in Chandler's *Pearls Are a Nuisance* (London: Penguin Crime, 1969), p.195.
13. Ibid.
14. Roland Barthes, *Sade/Fourier/Loyola* (New York: Hill & Wang, 1976), p.5.
15. *On Crime Writing*, p.28.
16. Ibid., p.31.
17. William Thompson, *At the Edge of History* (New York: Harper & Row, 1971), p.8.
18. S.E. Hyman, *The Tangled Bank* (New York: Atheneum, 1962), p.313.
19. Jacques Lacan, *The Four Fundamental Concepts of Psychoanalysis* (Harmondsworth: Penguin, 1979), p.9.

20. Ibid., p.276.
21. Pierre Macherey, *A Theory of Literary Production* (London: Routledge & Kegan Paul, 1978), p.92.
22. Claude Lévi-Strauss, *Tristes Tropiques* (New York: Atheneum, 1964), p.60.
23. Claude Lévi-Strauss, *The Savage Mind* (London: Weidenfeld & Nicholson, 1966), p.19.
24. E.N. and T. Hayes (eds), *The Anthropologist as Hero* (Cambridge, Mass.: MIT Press, 1970), p.189.
25. David Brion Davis, *Homicide in American Fiction 1798–1860* (Ithaca, NY: Cornell University Press, 1968), p.xv.
26. *A Theory of Literary Production*, p.253.
27. Alain Robbe-Grillet, *For a New Novel* (New York: Grove Press, 1975), p.23.
28. Aryeh Neier, 'Mouchards and Provocateurs', *The Nation*, 13 Sept. 1980.
29. Tzvetan Todorov, *The Poetics of Prose* (Ithaca, NY: Cornell University Press, 1977), pp.42–52.
30. *Tristes Tropiques*, p.41.

CHRONOLOGY

Dates of first publication:

1949 – *The Moving Target* (New York: Alfred A. Knopf; London: Cassell)
1950 – *The Drowning Pool* (New York: Alfred A. Knopf; London: Fontana)
1951 – *The Way Some People Die* (New York: Alfred A. Knopf; London: Fontana)
1952 – *The Ivory Grin* (London: Collins)
1954 – *Find a Victim* (London: Collins)
1955 – *The Name Is Archer* (London: Bantam; London: Collins)

1961 – *The Wycherly Woman* (London: Fontana)
1963 – *The Zebra-Striped Hearse* (London: Fontana)
1964 – *The Chill* (London: Fontana)
1965 – *The Far Side of the Dallar* (London: Fontana)
1966 – *Black Money* (London: Fontana)
1968 – *The Instant Enemy* (London: Fontana; Collins)
1969 – *The Goodbye Look* (London: Fontana; Collins)
1971 – *The Underground Man* (London: Fontana; Collins)
1973 – *Sleeping Beauty* (London: Fontana; Collins)
1976 – *The Blue Hammer* (London: Fontana; Collins)
1977 – *Lew Archer, Private Investigator*
1980 – *The Dark Tunnel*

7 P. D. James

BRUCE HARKNESS

I

The classic murder of the classic detection novel was committed, of course, by Raymond Chandler; it appears that the classic obituary was pronounced by Julian Symons.[1] The genre is dead; but not only will it not lie down – it's all alive again and doing very well indeed. P. D. James is by no means the only writer to be living disproof to Symons, but she is clearly one of the most interesting practitioners of the classic genre.

Mrs James specifically identifies herself with the genre, in different terms: 'I have never felt that a crime novelist is barred from exploration of the realities of the human condition merely because, as in *The Black Tower*, she is working within the constraints of the classical English detective story,' she said in the introduction to *Murder in Triplicate*. Or, similarly in the introdution to *Crime Times Three*, she sketches her concept of the classical tradition:

> The old conventions may still be retained. There will be a violent death; a limited circle of suspects all with motives, means, and opportunity; false clues; and a tenable ending with a solution to the mystery which both author and reader hope will be a satisfying consummation of suspense and excitement but which the reader could himself arrive at by a process of logical deduction from revealed facts with the aid of no more luck or intuition than it is reasonable to permit to the detective himself.

Hence, like every new woman writer, such as Ruth Rendell, Mrs James was immediately compared to Dorothy L. Sayers, Agatha Christie, Margery Allingham, and pronounced the new High Priestess or Crown Princess of the form. (It is clear that her affinities are greatest with Dorothy L. Sayers in her use of literary

119

characters, literary epigraphs and allusions, her Anglican interests.)

It appears that the death of the classical English detective novel has been pronounced, like the death of books themselves, prematurely. For most critics, the detective novel is specifically a form of popular literature, a literature for relaxation and often valued most highly for that very reason – the last form that an academic can read without a pencil in his hand. Perhaps Jacques Barzun was right in finding the distinctiveness of the detective story in *story* itself. As so many have said, the novel, while certainly a higher literary form, has to a great extent ceased to tell stories. It lacks the 'and then, and then' quality regretted by E. M. Forster and many another modern critic. The novel now foregoes the suspense of Scheherazade, Dickens and the whodunit-spinner.

Doubtless the classic form is difficult to define just as is the 'crime novel' or the 'sensation novel' or 'thriller' – and definition shall not be attempted here. Mrs James's description above is quite sufficient, though other topics might be listed as well: the classic detective story is not only one of puzzle, it is often self-consciously literary and witty. The closed society contains many an eccentric character, overseen by a series detective who is the most fully characterised of all. The background and locale often provide a great deal of the aesthetic pleasure if not the essence of the book, as in the Guilty Vicarage theory of Auden. The method used in the crime or crimes (usually murder) is bizarre or intriguing, and clues abound, both of the actual and red-herring variety, giving rise to many suspicions and cross-suspicions. (Which description fits Mrs James's, but owes even more to Symons' *Mortal Consequences*.)

P. D. James consciously moves in this tradition, with intriguing variations of course. Her series detective in six of the eight detective novels is Adam Dalgliesh, who is a professional policeman – the first big decision the detective novelist must make. But he is also very real in character and far from a plodding Inspector French type. Critics lead one to believe his major trait is that he is a poet, and a poet who has been published. Perhaps wisely, P. D. James seldom quotes anything of his lines. Indeed, in one or two of the novels, we scarcely realise he is a poet – in *Cover Her Face* (1962), I cannot recall any reference to his verse; though in *A Mind to Murder* (1963), the second novel, he is at a sherry party given by his publisher in his honour, when the murder is announced. (A ten-line metaphysical conceit is contained in *Unnatural Causes*.) Oddly, in *Shroud for a Nightingale* (1971), with which P. D. James first hit the world market, a fresh reader of her material would not really be aware that Adam is a series character at all.

Although the sleuth is characterised to some extent by the narrator, often entering his thoughts to give the reader background material, he is most strikingly analysed by possible suspects and subordinates. The Watsons in the latter group narrate next to none of the episodes, nor do they remain fixed through the novels. In *Cover Her Face* and *A Mind to Murder* Sergeant Martin far from idolises Adam (which is just as well, for through much of *A Mind to Murder* Adam is trying to 'pin it on' the wrong criminal). Sergeant Charles Masterson, who replaces Sergeant Martin in *A Shroud for a Nightingale* (1971), is younger, more ambitious, vain, and has a positive dislike for Adam. In *Death of an Expert Witness*, this figure becomes Inspector Massingham, perhaps the most satisfactory from the point of view of characterising his chief. They all lack the annoying qualities of Lugg and Fox, though they perhaps don't stand out as much in the reader's mind. Massingham is a biological quirk in a long family of Blimps – honest, down to earth, hardworking, perhaps ruthless and sensual; but a solid professional policeman.

Massingham wonders why witnesses and the bereaved 'seem to like him' (Adam):

God knows why. At times he's cold enough to be barely human. . . . What, if anything, he wondered, would move Dalgliesh to spontaneous pity? He remembered the other case they had worked on together a year previously, when he had been a detective-sergeant: the death of a child. Dalgliesh had regarded the parents with just such a look of calm appraisal. But he had worked eighteen hours a day for a month until the case was solved. And his next book of poems had contained that extraordinary one about a murdered child which no one at the Yard, even those who professed to understand it, had had the temerity even to mention to its author.

We know little, but enough, of Adam's background. He had a lonely boyhood – perhaps an only child – in a lonely vicarage in a lonely part of England. It is interesting to note the mixture of affection and superiority which he feels towards his father's former curate, in *The Black Tower* (1975) – which as an adult matches almost exactly his boyish feelings.

If Dalgliesh strikes his supporting policemen as cold and hard – driving for a narrower sense of justice – this analysis is tempered not only by his poetry and his inner fears and griefs which we occasionally get a glimpse of, but also by the love interests in the novels. The veil on these is perpetually trembling. For a time it appears that Deborah Riscoe, the widowed daughter of Eleanor Maxie in *Cover Her Face*, is to become the series love interest. This was held out as promise at the end of that novel, but still lies in the future at the end of *A Mind to Murder*. While their affair is never centre stage, it is over by the opening of *The Black Tower*. (Not appearing in *Unnatural Causes*, she breaks with him by letter at the end of the book, apparently because he cannot decide whether or not to marry.) In that novel, Adam has already risen professionally to the rank of commander, lives in a flat in Queenhythe of a very practical and artistic kind, and has already had several affairs, but all with sleek, sophisticated, unattached women – and women with whom no permanent attachment is perhaps possible. The affairs stay on a plane of museums, art, excellent cookery, and doubtless sex in an approved Masters-and-Johnson manner – but the inner character of neither partner is quickened. Yet the love interest is always there; there is even a slight romantic attachment set up between Adam and Mary Taylor, the matron of the hospital, though of course the reader learns later that any affair would be impossible. (Perhaps this can be related to P. D. James's theory that characters live their own lives, and that she isn't in full control of the threads of the plot – just as the novel itself has some kind of platonic pre-existence: in *Shroud* Adam's attraction to Mary Taylor is not intended to mislead the reader but comes early in the novel, perhaps at a stage of composition in which the author herself does not as yet know the ending.)

Adam's cold personality has perhaps been built deliberately through the years. P. D. James makes the point beautifully in the first novel. A woman disapproves of her son's engagement: '"Would you wish for such a marriage for your son?" For one unbelievable second Dalgleish [*sic* in *Crime Times Three*] thought that she knew. . . . He wondered what she would say if he replied, "I have no son. My only child and his mother died three hours after he was born."' We later learn this is an old grief, this death on an October day, fourteen years ago (*A Mind to Murder*). Out of the lonely boyhood, the grief in early adult life, Adam has built a cold professional exterior of detection and a warm inner life of poetry; and P. D. James has built an excellent, non-eccentric series sleuth.

Cordelia Gray, who is the dominant detective of *An Unsuitable Job for a Woman* (1972), where Dalgliesh enters only in the last chapter, has been found most fetching by all readers. Indeed, there has almost developed a kind of women's-magazine interest in Cordelia: will she succeed in marrying Adam or not? Readers and fans seem to hope so; the author professes to be unsure; no one seems to talk of the disparity in ages. At any rate, this gamin is delightful. She is far from upper-middle-class, and no blue stocking like Harriet Vane, although she has done a good job of self-teaching. (Does she pattern the author here?) Cordelia never had the stock children's classics, whether *Treasure Island* or *Winnie the Pooh*; she had the comics and TV. Later, perhaps a bit too self-consciously, she read right through the syllabus of Eng. Lit. She is a blessed relief from the 'Had I but known' heroine, though for a bit she does become the damsel in distress – and she's also an intriguing contrast to the undergraduates at Cambridge, only partly phony though they are. (We are told that in the detective novel which P. D. James has on the stocks, Cordelia is again the detective and main focus in *The Skull Beneath the Skin* (1982) where Dalgliesh is merely alluded to.)[2]

II

P(hyllis) D(orothy) James was born 3 August 1920 at Oxford and moved while young to Cambridge, the locale of the Cordelia Gray novel, and was educated there in the Girls' High School. She married Connor Bantry White in 1941, has two daughters and several grandchildren for whom she obviously has great affection. Dr White fought in the second world war, but was able to practise only briefly after the war, because of a prolonged mental illness which was never accepted as war-related. Mrs White held various positions in hospital administration from 1949 on to 1968, when she joined the Home Office – Criminal Policy Department, 1972–9. These experiences clearly provide an assured air of reality in her novels with their background in police procedure, juvenile problems, institutional administration. Few writers move with her surety in these areas which are the mainstay of much detective fiction – yet she avoids the boredom produced by many kinds of 'procedural' novels which can have a kind of inverted didacticism. She obviously has a great interest in art and literature, in the Anglican Church's traditions as well as its architecture.[2] In *Who's Who* she lists her recreations as exploring churches and walking by the sea – the last clearly providing inspiration for the opening of *Unnatural Causes* (1967). Her novels are published by Faber and Faber in England and by Charles Scribner's Sons in the United States, with a time lag for the first two novels, but with increasing success on both sides of the Atlantic beginning with *Shroud* (1971). With her first 'straight novel' *Innocent Blood* (1980) – which originally, it seems, was intended to have the much better title *Blood Tie*, her popularity as well as critical esteem was fully established, especially in America. Various of her works had won recognition in detective-writer circles before, both the short stories and the novels, but *Innocent Blood* was named a main selection of the Book of the Month Club. P. D. James retired, slightly early, at the end of 1979 and now has a new home in Campden Hill, London, even more suitable for visiting grandchildren.[3]

It is in P. D. James's adaptations of the formula of the classic detective story, in her insistent topics or themes, and above all in her interest in character that she has made a fresh mark. In all her novels she plays off her fiction against the classic formula. Perhaps the most dominant of these features is the closed setting in the novels, or the artificially limited 'circle of suspects all with motives, means, and opportunity', as Mrs James puts it. In three of the novels the closed setting is in a village with an additional closure, either in a district or Big House. In *Cover Her Face* it is the village of Chadfleet near London; in *Unnatural Causes* it is a village near Dunwich in Suffolk, and the house of Adam's Aunt Jane. In *An Unsuitable Job* there is the Callender Laboratory as closed house, and Summertrees and its shed, where both Mark (the victim) and Cordelia stay. (There is also in this novel, as in *Innocent Blood*, a nicely done tour of well- and little-known parts of London.) In the other five detective fictions, the closed society is even more limited to a single building or group of buildings: the Steen Psychological Clinic in *A Mind to Murder*, in London; Nightingale House and hospital in *A Shroud for a Nightingale*, in the country; Toynton (a kind of nursing home for victims of disseminated [multiple] sclerosis) in *The Black Tower*; and the Hoggatt Forensic Lab in *Death of an Expert Witness*. In *Skull* the isolation of the off-coast island is extremely significant.

These restricted settings and sets of characters allow James an intriguing puzzle element, but they also skilfully permit her a tone whereby Adam seems both amateur sleuth and professional policeman; and of course Cordelia engagingly acts as the amateur 'tec striving to become a professional on her first independent case. That is, with the exception of *A Mind to Murder*, Adam is physically removed from the scene of inner London and Scotland Yard. He is either on holiday (*Unnatural Causes*) by the sea – one of the few books, says James, which first came to her in a vision of a locality as she herself stood near the actual area, or is re-cuperating/convalescing, as in *The Black Tower*, where he must seek Scotland Yard help by mail, unofficially, through Bill Moriarity, CID.

Not only does Mrs James thus avoid too great an immersion in police methodology, but she gets far more than the miscellaneous house-party types of a Christie novel. After talking to a sister in *Shroud*, Adam reflects on her and the information she had given:

> He felt rather sorry for her. She had given him a depressing glimpse into the stultifying lack of privacy, and of the small pettinesses and subterfuges with which people living in unwelcome proximity try to preserve their privacy or invade that of others. The thought of a grown man peeping sur-reptitiously around the door before coming out, of two adult lovers creeping furtively down a back staircase to avoid detection, was grotesque and humiliating. He remembered the Matron's words. "We do get to know things here; there's no real privacy." . . . . Small wonder that Nightingale House bred its own brand of neurosis, that Sister Gearing felt it necessary to justify a walk with her lover in the grounds, their obvious and natural wish to prolong the final goodnight, with unconvincing twaddle about the need to discuss hospital business. He found it all profoundly depressing.

The closed setting then provides a closed world of pettiness, scheming, jealousy, crossed ambitions, in novel after novel. But the tone is not all that much different when Mrs James looks at the larger world in *Innocent Blood* and parts of *Death of an*

Expert Witness, for she by this stage of her career is much surer in the dramatisation of her worldview than in the earlier fiction, especially *Cover Her Face* and *A Mind to Murder* which, while good detective stories, are obviously apprentice pieces.

On the other hand, the accompanying literariness of the novels is both a strength and a source of one of the persistent criticisms of James's fiction. It is interesting to observe that while she shares the literary quality with many writers of the classic form – Dorothy L. Sayers, Michael Innes, Edmund Crispin, Emma Lathen, she does not really engage in that kind of didacticism which, fun though it often is, mars these novels in the eyes of many readers. It is a long and persistent strand in the classic form, from *The Nine Tailors* or *Murder Must Advertise* up to the exposés of the fast-food industries, Detroit, banking interests, and so on. P. D. James does not, though she makes good use of the settings, take us into the mysterious workings of mental clinics (*Mind to Murder*), hospitals (*Shroud for a Nightingale*), or Scotland Yard.

Her sleuth is interesting, furthermore, though not in his eccentricities. She has the best, as has been indicated, of both worlds. By separating Adam from his working locale, and concentrating on his 'poetic nature' now and then, she has developed a well-rounded character who pulls the series along. As she indicates in one of her prefaces, the writer must choose between amateur and professional. Yet in a sense she didn't. It is the amateur or the non-professional within the professional which enables Adam to do his best work. It is that poetic side which enables him to arrive at the understanding of character, which most often solves the crime.

We see this most keenly in his interest in the victim, paralleling the author's interest in character. 'Dead Men Tell Tales' is one of Dalgliesh's maxims. And in nearly every novel the victim is chosen by virtue of some character trait. We almost have a kind of persistent theme of the guilty victim, as it were: 'And at the heart of the mystery, the clue which could make all plain, lay in the complex personality of Sally Jupp,' the pretty, intelligent, ambitious, sly and insecure young mother who has just been killed in *Cover*.

The expert witness of the title of that novel, brings about his own death through jealousy, not the other way around as is usual. The murderer is not jealous of the victim, for the killer hadn't even been aware of the 'love triangle'. Yet the motives are embedded more deeply in character than greed or lust – as in the typical crime novel. The victim is insane through jealousy; the killer strikes, but not to keep his lover. 'I knew she didn't love me,' he says, 'but that wasn't important. She gave me what she could, and it was enough for me.' Even though he knows the affair will end, he kills not to make it last as long as possible, but to prevent exposure and scandal which might damage him in a custody suit over his children. The involution of motives based in characters' traits is most intriguing and uncommon.

More common is P. D. James's use of conventional signs for characterisation, at least the conventions of the classic detective story. She uses them extremely well, but there is a great reliance on reading character through the signs surrounding the individual. The shelf of books, the furnishings of a person's room, the pictures on the wall, the music listened to – all these are the rather too easy short cuts to character analysis. Yet within the genre of the detective story, if not the novel, they provide a good bit of the reader's pleasure.

If literature and the literary allusion are mainstays of James's fiction, there are certain other topics or standard themes which thread most of the volumes. While not necessarily used in the plot intrigue, they do provide a continuing kind of background material. A prolonged, sometimes incurable illness occurs in *The Black Tower* (multiple sclerosis); paraplegia and reaction thereto form a definite part of the background plot in *Unnatural Causes*; in *Cover Her Face* the father of the household is hopelessly invalided and in a virtual coma, offstage as it were for several years. We do not know whether this is disease or trauma, but his death is critical in the resolution of the interplay of motives and crime, though of course he had nothing to do with the crimes themselves. In *A Mind to Murder*, to give a final example, the mother of Nurse Marion Bolam is a long-time sufferer of multiple sclerosis, while the mother of Administrative Officer Enid Bolam (the women are cousins) had been mentally ill for years and had been treated by Dr Etherege, the Medical Director of the Steen Clinic. (This also illustrates the way in which P. D. James often has the past focusing down on the present crime.) It is not necessary, however, in this reader's view, to see any relation in this topic to the illness of Dr C. B. White and his wartime career; though of course his illness does relate to P. D. James's motive for writing at all – the need to supplement family income.

James is said never to have received a rejection slip, though the first three novels in comparison with her later work certainly strike one as apprentice stints, lacking the sure professional hand of *An Unsuitable Job for a Woman*, and in general the works starting with *Shroud*.

Other persistent topics are incest or its counterfeit (where the family structure, though not literal bloodline, is incestuous). The theme of incest is clearly evident in *Death of an Expert Witness*, *Innocent Blood, Cover Her Face* (where the mother for all her admirable traits has spoiled her son so completely as to make him almost a monster in his lack of feeling). Homosexuality is not often used as a specific murder motive, but cleverly thickens the texture of the background; it provides clues of the red-herring variety. Hilda Rolfe and Nurse Pardoe in *Shroud* are examples; another is Gabriel Lomas ('Ac/Dc') in *Innocent Blood*; and Julius Court and his friend in *The Black Tower* provide a more complicated instance.

But all in all, P. D. James has proven once again, especially through her interest in character, that the classic detective story gives us the best way of filling up that dead space between murder and solution. The abundance of clues, the abundance of suspects, the successive crimes to cover the original one: all these provide the intriguing puzzle. Other variants are to this reader not nearly so satisfactory as hers. The long romantic opening before the crime (Michael Innes) and the rather soppy kind of love affair (Agatha Christie of all people) are not nearly as satisfying.

Furthermore, P. D. James most often avoids what I take to be the general defect of the genre. The classic detective story or the puzzle novel has concentrated so much on the ingenuity of the crime that the resolution is often unsatisfying through one major defect – the lack of an acceptable motive within the murderer. All too often we think, 'Good Lord, is that why he did it!' It seems to this reader that Agatha Christie is one of the worst offenders in this regard. P. D. James, with perhaps the exception of the killer in *Cover Her Face*, avoids the problem.

This is not to say that the classic form doesn't give her other problems. And indeed, Mrs James falls into this difficulty at one remove, so to say. In *The Black Tower*, for example, the killer has plenty of motive for that crime, but the original crime or crimes which the murder is intended to cover up are simply incredible. The motive of the guilty victim, also, is insubstantial to a dangerous degree. Sally Jupp of *Cover Her Face* is the best example. Her teasing and making fools of others lead her not only to lie, but cause her death in a most unconvincing manner. It is hard to believe that any young mother would gloatingly tell the particular fibs which cause the killer to do her in – and indeed, the killer has been set up as so sound and sympathetic a character, that there is a good bit of reader disbelief on that score as well. Were it not for our acceptance of the conventions of the detective story, the novel would be no fun at all.

But most of the difficulties with P. D. James's novels are more precisely within the technique of fiction. The novels have a good many personages in them, and Mrs James simply lacks skill in introducing them. She seems to believe that she has a restricted cast, but the opposite is true. In *Death of an Expert Witness* there are about fifteen characters who are of a level of importance that they could be suspects; as in most of her novels, the reader has difficulty in sorting them out at first: there is no handy device such as a Conrad can use in setting up the watch in *The Nigger of the 'Narcissus'*. It almost makes one yearn for that old cast of characters and map provided in the detective stories of the twenties and thirties.

In the earlier novels, P. D. James was quite unsure in her use of technical point of view. More than once she uses a version of shifting, partially omniscient narrator. We are aware of the author's voice, which moves in and out of the consciousness of various characters. The result is very nearly an Ackroydal problem. In *A Mind to Murder*, for example, we often get the thoughts of a blackmailer and attempted murderer, without getting also those necessary thoughts which would give away the puzzle. 'He was almost untouched by Miss Bolam's death' is scarcely to be said of the thoughts of an accessory. Indeed, this person is the very one who bizarrely placed a patient's fetish on the victim's body.

Later use is much surer. As when Howarth, in thinking of his sister, is sick with jealousy of Lorrimer, ex-lover and later victim: 'It made no difference that the affair was over, that Lorrimer, too, was suffering. Reason couldn't cure it, nor, he suspected, could distance, nor time. It could be ended only be death; Lorrimer's or his own.' This misleading bit of information, clever and slick, is yet technically satisfactory.

However, even these later novels occasionally have problems with point of view. For example, it is either in Howarth's consciousness or the narrator's that we are told of Schofield, the husband whose death Domenica, Howarth's sister, had in a sense caused in a car accident. The dying Schofield lies to Howarth. The astounding thing is that 'he had hated his brother-in-law enough to die with that taunt on his lips. Or had he taken it for granted that a physicist, poor philistine, wouldn't know his Jacobean dramatists? Even his wife, that indefatigable sexual sophisticate, had known better.' The clause attributing sophistication to Domenica is simply psychologically impossible. Howarth could not think that thought. And yet, contained within that paragraph, there's virtually no other way to read it.

Other difficulties with James's practice are not so much technical, but arise from devices, good in themselves, which begin to wear with repetition. Too many of the novels are constructed on a pattern of interviews. Adam and his 'Watson' interview suspect after suspect and witness after witness in a separate room of the mansion or hospital offices, while the plot all too slowly builds up. (Oddly, this interview-pattern is just as strong in the books where Adam's Watson doesn't figure – *Unnatural Causes* and *The Black Tower*.)

James's use of the past also has become formulaic. It is not that she uses the present crime to resolve a past crime, or solves the present crime by solving an earlier crime, as in the manner of Ross Macdonald; but she does often use past events to thicken the quality of an interview. Thus, for example, the fairly recent death of a patient in *Shroud for a Nightingale* runs a thread through several interviews both with Adam and with his Watson, Sgt Masterson.

The war-crimes trial at the end of the second world war is part motive for the secondary murder. In every book we may count on the past impinging on the present but not always with clarification. Miss Eleanor Markland's illegitimate child was drowned in the well which nearly claims Cordelia as victim in *An Unsuitable Job for a Woman*, but that fact is scarcely more than coincidence, though it adds somewhat to the atmosphere of the novel. When past and present blend together in book after book, the device becomes mannerism.

What of the literary quality? Given the conventions of the classic form, it may seem unfair to argue that James is too literary. And, unlike the *TLS* reviewer, I am not offended by Philippa's remembering lines from Bunyan when she is told part of the grim truth of her real parentage. In his review of *Innocent Blood*, Mr Paul Bailey believes this overly literary quality 'trivialises them [rape and murder] with cleverness, and with an excess of epigraphs', in the 'straight novel'.[4]

The literariness does give rise to problems, but of another order. We enjoy her epigraphs but occasionally she overreaches. Schofield, in the paragraph quoted above, has attacked Howarth by saying, 'Remember me, Giovanni, in thy garden in Parma.' The line I take to be a reference to, but not quotation from, *'Tis Pity She's a Whore* — but without actual quotation, few readers, whether philistines or not, could identify this Giovanni from others in Jacobean drama. (Try it on your friends.) Nurse Fallon is another example in *Shroud for a Nightingale*, the novel in which P. D. James clearly hit her stride as well as her world market. Fallon is nicely characterised primarily by means of her bookshelf ('modern poetry . . . Austen . . . Greene . . .'), her few but perfect other belongings, her delicate and refined taste in tea ('the best China blend'), and so on. She is older than most of the student nurses and given considerable strength of character and good sense, as well as sophistication. One simply cannot accept that in the past she had a lengthy affair with a boorish and vain surgeon whose greed and desire for power complicate the ending of the novel. Or at least we could not accept this self-contradictory nurse unless we accepted the conventions of a classic detective story.

One other defect of P. D. James might be mentioned. Some of the books just aren't looked through or revised or proofread carefully enough. Did Adam's son and his mother die within three hours after he was born (*Cover Her Face*) or twenty-four hours (*Death of an Expert Witness*)? This is rather more than an example of our forgetful author, since so much is made of this with Adam, both in his poetry, his attitude towards lovers, and in his attitude towards children — the vision of William in his red wellingtons is an unforgettable image in *Death of an Expert Witness*.

So much for problems in P. D. James's use of the conventions, especially those related to character, in the classic detective fiction. Characterisation in these novels, regardless of her usage, is in and of itself a problem. It is at this point that the story element and the novel element come into conflict. Surely Symons is wrong in saying that 'the detective story par excellence could never really allow . . . characterisation . . . any approach to reality.'[5]

Not only did the classic story appeal through the eccentricities and full characterisation of the sleuth, as Symons would agree, but we value precisely those novels in which some attention was given to characterisation of the other individuals. We always preferred those classic detective stories with an intriguing cast of characters – Nicholas Blake, Ngaio Marsh, or more recently Emma Lathen. P. D. James has carried this much further than most of the other 'crown princesses' of Agatha Christie.[6] This is what we value, a greater depth of characterisation rather than a set of cardboard figures in a puzzle.

But this judgement does give rise to a paradox. We value the classic mystery in part to the degree in which it approaches the straight novel. Yet there is a real line, hard to define though it may be, beyond which the detective fiction must not cross. If the mystery in some chapters becomes a novel, the genres become confused and our critical strictures inevitably are misapplied. We then hold characterisation to the standards of the novel, not those of the detective fiction. We do this precisely because P. D. James's detective stories approach the quality of the straight novel throughout. In an odd sense, they are just too good. In *Innocent Blood*, the problem is the obverse.

For example, Philippa is much too self-composed at the time of the suicide. She is but eighteen years old and reacts to the death of a parent with the aplomb of a Sam Spade. This is unsatisfactory precisely because we are in the straight novel; Cordelia's reaction (*Unsuitable Job*) to the suicide of her partner, Bernie Pryde, is every bit as composed – the two girls are quite similar – but we accept it because we are within the tradition of mystery fiction.

It is true that P. D. James's detective fiction does rather struggle between that world and the world of the straight novel, to use Bailey's terms. Yet this concentration on character provides a realism, a toughness, a mature attitude toward life in the detective stories which are extraordinarily interesting. The evil is real in them and they come at that reality and that evil from what is fundamentally or finally a religious point of view, as is pointed out in the interview with Whale. Character makes for reality.

Perhaps mixed forms always give critical difficulties. *The Black*

Tower is unsatisfactory because it constantly threatens to move over into an area akin to religious fantasy. Though James regards this mystery novel highly, because Adam develops considerably in it, readers have not been greatly attracted to it. The flummery is not all caused by Wilfred running around in his monk's robe: it is inherent in the novel itself.

Indeed mystery novels apparently can have non-realistic elements in their essence that one would assume must be realistic – the details of the puzzle. Crispin, for example, can have all the characters mistake the firing of a blank for a real cartridge, which would seem impossible. Similarly, at least to a lay reader, James has some unrealistic touches. Even though she is the expert in real life as well as story-teller, it is hard for this lay reader to believe that a medical examiner/coroner would have slipped so badly on the causes of death in *The Black Tower*. On the other hand, the unrealistic medical touches in *Unsuitable Job* are nicely handled by having an aged and incompetent family doctor.

In P. D. James's 'straight book' (other than *Innocent Blood*) we have a different kind of reality. Oddly, this is far more a 'police procedural' book than the Dalgliesh novels. *The Maul and the Pear Tree*, written in conjunction with T. A. Critchley (apparently also of the Home Office), is an historical analysis of the procedures used just before the arrival of a true police force in metropolitan London. The occasion for this reconstruction is the Ratcliffe Highway Murders (1811) used most prominently by De Quincey in the well-known, but factually inaccurate, 'On Murder Considered as one of the Fine Arts' (1827), with its postscript (1854). *Maul* is an intriguing book, offering a convincing speculation for a better 'solution' than blaming John Williams. The description of the crowded districts in London (mainly Wapping) is even more convincing, and leads one to wonder whether we can someday expect an historical classic detective story from P. D. James – perhaps something more satisfying than Tey's *Daughter of Time*.

Her short stories are, as are most modern short stories in the genre, less satisfying. It is a paradox that the detective genre began as short stories and flowered with them (Holmes as well as his rivals), but that now most of the stories seemed decidedly O.Henry-ish in their quality. 'Moment of Power', 'A Very Desirable Residence', 'Murder 1986' (combining sci-fi), and 'Great-

Aunt Allie's Flypapers' (combining historical fiction; the early Edwardian scene, if not the Victorian, is interestingly portrayed in this bit of irony). Each of these (with the possible exception of 'A Very Desirable Residence') has an interesting aspect even within the O.Henry technique. In the science fiction, for example, the twists and turns in the surprise ending are carefully imbedded in, or are the output of, traits of character of the two policemen working at odds.

'Moment of Power' might offend readers through having an extra O.Henry twist: a minor character turns out to be the husband of the rape and murder victim. Yet the tone of the story has the impact of a Graham Greene novel, as we finally realise that the killer, whose mind alone the narrator looks into, had committed these deeds aged fifty. Now at sixty-six, though on the one hand he is haunted by symbolic dreams, on the other he is so worn down by life and years that he can scarcely remember the events, let alone feel remorse.

III

Clearly P. D. James is one of the most interesting of the new revivers of the classic detective novel. With whatever defects her books have, she is in the very forefront of the modern practitioners. Nor is she, like Conan Doyle, a writer who denigrates her detective yarns for her non-fiction and straight novel – she is, after all, returning to Cordelia with her last book. So much is clear. What is not clear, is why the classic detective story remains alive. It is clear why she is one of the best now writing, but what makes the form continue at all?

One aspect of the form and one of its enduring appeals is seldom mentioned: the pleasure the reader has in the mere tone of the book. The narrative stance, the commentary, the attitude toward life expressed in the style is even more important than the puzzle. This is seldom mentioned, and it is one of P. D. James's great achievements. That tone, so often conservative (Dorothy L. Sayers, Agatha Christie, and so on) in contrast to that of the crime novel, so often left-wing or radical, accounts for much of the appeal in the novels. In this P. D. James is quite splendid.

In so often taking Adam Dalgliesh away from Scotland Yard and its environs, she is able to expand on the cast of minor characters and consequently her narrative tone. The minor characters are often much like those to be found in a crime novel (as Symons would define it). So many of these minor characters have ancillary stories of their own, and their characterisations are full enough to give an additional fillip to the yarn: Dr Baguely and his awful wife in *A Mind to Murder*; Nurse Goodale and her fiancé the local vicar in *Shroud*; or Inspector Doyle and his unhappy wife in *Death of an Expert Witness* are examples.

But this is not quite accurate. The characters are not merely those who would not be out of place in a Dashiell Hammett or Raymond Chandler book; more to the point they would not be out of place in a Graham Greene novel, let alone his entertainments. Greene is clearly a favourite writer of P. D. James, as he was of Nurse Josephine Fallon in *Shroud*.

The minor characters, and the narrator's attitude and tone toward them, remind us inevitably of Greene. Mrs Meakin in *Expert Witness* is a good example. Mrs Meakin allows herself to be picked up by any man and 'bedded' in his automobile, even if it often means a long walk home after being abandoned. She's not interested in sex, but in that moment of quiet and warmth in the pub beforehand, when there is some companionability. Thinking she could be murdered, Sergeant Massingham, Adam's assistant, says, 'It's better to be alone than dead.' 'You think so, sir? But then you don't know anything about it, do you?' the middle-aged, broken, lonely woman replies. The narrator has all sympathy for her.

James's wording also often has that dying fall so characteristic of Greene: Hilda, the pathetic second wife of the trendy sociologist Maurice, in *Innocent Blood*; the Hilda who, sitting in her expensive house, is taken for the maid by Norman, who is himself a mottled figure of vengeance, straight out of Greeneland. We are told early of her that her 'only skills were cooking and deceit'. That trailing off, that easy paradox, is reminiscent of the greater writer. Or consider Jennifer Priddy of *Mind*: for the usual reasons 'she had to get married' as they say, only to miscarry; 'of course' as Greene would say. The whole Priddy family seems born to fail.

In *Shroud for a Nightingale* the drunken, voracious, almost nightmarish Mrs Dettinger, shrilly pursuing anything that wears trousers in a dance hall where she pays outrageously for lessons, is another such character. And Adam reprimands his sergeant harshly for feeling superior to this wreck. So whether it is detective fiction, non-fiction (Williams in *Maul*) or straight novel, the minor characters are of this order. *Innocent Blood* has perhaps the best and most typical example. Norman Scase, the bewildered revenger, finally finds peace with the blind girl who works the desk in his sleazy hotel, and both find companionability in her little dog. One character is positively Conradian. Dalgliesh and Taylor think of ordinariness:

> There had been a boy in his prep school like that, so ordinary, so safe, that he was a kind of talisman against death and disaster. ... Funny, he hadn't thought of him now for over thirty years. Sproat Minor with his round, pleasant, spectacled face, his ordinary conventional family, his unremarkable background, his blessed normality. Sproat Minor, protected by mediocrity and insensitivity from the terrors of the world. Life could not be wholly frightening while it held a Sproat Minor.

This acceptance of human frailty is dramatised in the tone of the books as much as in the minor characters. One example must suffice. In *Black Tower* Adam reflects on the loss of his wife: 'Grief for his dead wife, so genuine, so heartbreaking at the time – how conveniently personal tragedy had excused him from further emotional involvement.' Then his detachment from life is given the twist of a Greene: 'in the last fifteen years he hadn't deliberately hurt a single human being. It struck him now that nothing more damning could be said about anyone.'[7]

This pessimistic but accepting narrative tone becomes more and more prominent in Mrs James's later fiction; there is far more of it in *The Black Tower* than in the first novels. Finally, the narrative tone combined with the moral status of the minor characters in *Innocent Blood* makes it critically difficult to decide which the novel is closer to in its mixed character – the 'straight novel' containing elements of crime or the inverted fictions of Francis Iles. But even with this conservative, paradoxical, religious tone, P. D. James's other works are clearly detective fictions, not (still using her terms) straight novels.

Our enduring interest in the classic detective mode is not – as often enough it used to be claimed – just that we are law-abiding and law-loving members of the Anglo-American community. It is not our underlying sense of justice which constantly makes us interested in this kind of modern morality play, although P. D. James apparently subscribes to this view. Nor is it just that we are perpetually interested in the intellectual puzzle. Indeed, it can be very much doubted if any reader actually closes the book at some point, knowing he has all the clues, and genuinely works his way through to the detective's conclusion. Not even that old trick of the early Ellery Queen novels was followed by many readers, though that was often claimed in the higher criticism of detective fiction. What readers really want, one suspects, is to be pulled through the book by the puzzle element, get the solution, and then have a satisfying sense that the author had not only played fair but that 'I could have figured that out myself, in advance, if I had wanted to.'

Nor does the classic story retain its hold by a reversing of our law-and-order mentality: we are not cultural and moral snobs who enjoy seeing Superman Holmes rise above the law, claiming a higher moral justice, and deciding whether or not the criminal shall be caught and punished. (Freed because of a kind of admiration for the criminal, or freed technically because he has already suffered, and so on – the variations on this theme in the classic genre are legion.) The appeal of the classic form is that the story lies squarely in the area of tension between freedom and equality. These two contradictory principles of our society have always clashed; but we now see this tension as the essential and basic pattern of our post-second-world-war society.

James's novels exploit the tension. The murderer in a sense goes 'unpunished' in *An Unsuitable Job for a Woman*. The detective nearly misconstrues his case in *A Mind to Murder*. The killer is one of the most sympathetic characters in *Cover Her Face*; and it is the guilty bystander, Stephen Maxie, whom we dislike the most.

This tension between an individual's freedom to express himself or herself fully, between the detective's need to investigate freely but to treat everyone equally according to the rules; the tension, in a sense, between the welfare-state egalitarianism and a Friedmanesque liberty drives all the books. It comes from several dramatic devices, providing the power of her detective fiction. Is Domenica's freedom of sexuality good or bad (*Expert Witness*)? Should not only Adam but the assistant commissioner connive at letting Cordelia go unpunished for her crime, as they do, or should she receive the equal justice of punishment as an accessory?

The theme runs through all the books, but in certain ways is most explicit in a *Shroud for a Nightingale*, where Adam also comes cloest to the superhero sleuth. In one of the interviews Mr Courtney-Briggs challenges him – 'That question is hardly within your terms of reference.' Adam snaps back: 'That's for me to judge.' Or in an earlier interview he says, 'I'm in charge of this investigation. I do it my way,' to which his interlocutor responds, 'I see. You make up the rules as you go along. . . . Yours is a dangerous game.'

And indeed the rules are examined throughout the novel – Adam's rules, Judges' rules, society's rules, the author's rules. Adam at one time or another has everything both ways: makes up his rules as he goes along, as well as hides behind society's rules. The tension in the reader asks, what of the killer's rules? What of the Nazi's rules in the second world war? Adam can't ignore the Nazi past of the killer:

> 'I can't suppress evidence or omit relevant facts from my report because I don't choose to like them. If once I did that I should have to give up my job. Not just this particular case, my job'. . . .
>
> 'And you couldn't do that, of course. What would a man like you be without his job, this particular job? Vulnerable like the rest of us. You might even have to begin living and feeling like a human being'.
>
> 'You can't touch me like that. Why humiliate yourself trying? There are regulations, orders, and an oath. Without them no one could safely do police work'. . . .
>
> 'And you haven't any doubts?'
>
> 'Of course I have. I'm not as arrogant as that. There are always doubts'. And so there were. But they were intellectual and philosophical doubts, untormenting and uninsistent. . . .
>
> 'But there are the regulations, aren't there? And the orders. And an oath even. They are very convenient shields to shelter behind if the doubts become troublesome. I know. I sheltered behind them once myself. You and I are not so very different after all, Adam Dalgliesh'.

So finally Adam recognises that the rules have been violated by both himself and the killer. He also recognises that he wanted to enforce the rules but couldn't – there was no proof of the killer's guilt: 'He had found none, either at the time or later, although he had pursued the case as if it were a personal vendetta, hating himself and her.'

Though Adam admits that the rules are violated, he does not fully sense his own ambiguity. On the one hand he wishes them violated, on the other, enforced. Why vendetta? The author seems to say, 'Yes, the rules are violated, but I forgive both the detective and the killer.' She must mean this, otherwise the 'resolution' of suicide is not aesthetically satisfying. (We also remember the implication that if the rules had been violated and a husband arrested on suspicion, his suicide would have been prevented in *Expert Witness*.)

So Adam is in one sense the superman, in another sense frail: 'He, the most punctilious of detectives, had already spoken [to the killer] as if none of the rules had been formulated, as if he were facing a private adversary.' The result of all this is to make Adam all the more interesting. While he is strong, in his humanity he is weak and fallible. Even his strength of hardened consciousness, derived from the death of his wife and child, comes under authorial scrutiny.

He is such an intriguing character, then, that such details as the authorial error concerning the exact time at which his son and wife died is far more than an example of the forgetful author. It gives every sign of generating an abiding reader interest in the series figure. Might it not even give rise to a kind of Sherlock Holmesian biographical criticism of Adam Dalgliesh? If Holmes has his lost cases, if Watson has those intriguingly contradictory wounds from the Afghan war, where for example is that case or those cases in which Adam worked with poor old Bernie Pryde?

NOTES AND REFERENCES

1. Chandler's 1944 essay, 'The Simple Art of Murder', has been reprinted many times; the handiest, perhaps is in *The Art of the Mystery Story* Howard Haycraft (ed.) *(Simon & Schuster, 1946), pp. 222–37*. Symons's *Mortal Consequences*, 1973; [Bloody Murder], 1972) has the replacement of the Detective Story by the Crime Novel as its theme, virtually throughout. See also 'Is the Detective Story Dead?', a discussion between Symons and Edmund Crispin, *The Times Literary Supplement*, 23 June 1961, p. iv. Here Symons asserts that 'The detective story is more or less extinct; it exists still in the hands of a few very skilled practitioners, and as far as younger writers are concerned the detective story doesn't really exist any more. Nobody is writing detective stories who's under 40 years old.' Here Symons equates the detective story with the puzzle – 'a problem of detection' – and sees it as giving way before the crime novel, which in various different ways is concerned with the psychology of the characters. 'What the detective story

par excellence', he continues, 'could never really allow was characterisation, was any approach to reality.'

2. John Whale, 'Religion and the Art of the Thriller-Writer', *Sunday Times* 6 July 1980, pp. 14f.

3. Biographical information taken from reviews over the years, from *Who's Who* 1980 (which closed receipt of material in November 1979). The handiest compendium of details is in *Current Biography* for August 1980, pp. 19–22.

4. Paul Bailey, 'Between Two Worlds', *The Times Literary Supplement*, 21 Mar. 1980, p. 312.

5. *The Times Literary Supplement*, 23 June 1961, p. iv.

6. Perhaps it is as well to remark that James's style is simply much better than the Queen's. Christie simply wouldn't write the following passage of description from *Unsuitable Job*; it might seem to some readers to have a tinge of the purple, but, almost within the consciousness of the young Cordelia, it works extremely well:

> She was seeing Cambridge at its loveliest. The sky was an infinity of blue from whose pellucid depths the sun shone in unclouded but gentle radiance. The trees in the college gardens and the avenues leading to the Backs, as yet untouched by the heaviness of high summer lifted their green tracery against stone and river and sky. Punts shot and curtsied under the bridges, scattering the gaudy water fowl, and by the rise of the new Garret Hostel bridge the willows trailed their pale, laden boughs in the darker green of the Cam.

7. The parallels are so strong that, despite the biographical information available and P. D. James's explicit interest in Anglicanism and country churches, this reader would not be astounded to learn one day that she had converted to Roman Catholicism. While the narrator's tone is sympathetic to almost all religions, and Adam and Cordelia have both clearly lost their faith, yet there are a very great many intriguing 'clues'. *Black Tower* asks why Wilfred didn't do the logical thing and continue on to conversion to Roman Catholicism after his 'cure' at Lourdes? One remembers that Hilda goes to Westminster Cathedral for solace in *Innocent Blood*. Many of the details seem to outweigh the Anglicanism used with Mark Callender and his natural mother in *An Unsuitable Job*, where crucial evidence is contained in the *Book of Common Prayer*.

Against Mark, one must weigh Fredrica Saxon, who over a nine-month period of time is in effect driven to Roman Catholicism. The wording is reminiscent of that used of Sarah in *The End of the Affair*. Adam meets Fredrica in the Roman Catholic church to which he has gone to light his fourteenth candle on the anniversary of his wife's death. There Fredrica, in another of James's interviews, tells Adam of her affair and the way it had been broken off when her lover's wife would not give him a divorce. But it was already too late – she had started instruction. So, Fredrica concludes, her lover would have no reason to kill Administrative Officer Bolam: 'But you can see, can't you, that he had no reason to hate Bolam. I was the enemy.'

Adam does:

He felt profoundly sorry for Baguely, rejected by his mistress at the moment of a greatest trial in favour of private happiness which he could neither share nor understand. Probably no one could fully know the magnitude of that betrayal. Dalgliesh did not pretend to understand Miss Saxon. But it wasn't hard to imagine what some people at the clinic would make of it. The facile explanations came easily to mind. But he could not believe that Fredica Saxon had taken refuge in religion from her own sexuality or had ever refused to face reality.

CHRONOLOGY

Dates of first publication

NOVELS (published by Faber & Faber in UK and Charles Scribner's Sons in US)

1962 – *Cover Her Face* (US 1966).
1963 – *A Mind to Murder* (US 1967).
1967 – *Unnatural Causes*
1971 – *Shroud for a Nightingale*
1972 – *An Unsuitable Job for a Woman*
1975 – *The Black Tower*
1977 – *Death of an Expert Witness*
1980 – *Innocent Blood*
1982 – *The Skull Beneath the Skin*

NONFICTION

1971 – *The Maul and the Pear Tree* (Constable; not published in US)
1979 – 'Introduction' to *Crime Times Three* (*Cover Her Face, A Mind to Murder, Shroud for a Nightingale*)
1980 – 'Introduction' to *Murder in Triplicate* (*Unnatural Causes, An Unsuitable Job for a Woman, The Black Tower*)

SHORT STORIES (dates more difficult; first publications not seen)

1969 – 'Moment of Power'
1977 – 'A Very Desirable Residence'
1977 – 'Murder 1986' (1978?)
1980 – 'Great-Aunt Allie's Flypapers'

8 How Unlike the Home Life of Our Own Dear Queen: The Detective Fiction of Peter Lovesey

JAMES HURT

A love for the history of sport and for digging about in libraries for curiosities of the past would not seem to be obvious preparation for the writing of detective stories. But so it turned out for Peter Lovesey, former head of the General Education Department in London's Hammersmith College and the creator of Sergeant Cribb. 'It started', Lovesey has written, 'with Deerfoot,' an American Indian who in Victorian times held the world's record for the greatest distance covered in one hour.[1] Lovesey found his name and picture in a copy of the *Sporting Chronicle Annual* for 1898 which he picked up in a bookshop in Charing Cross Road, and they led him into the world of Victorian foot-racing as chronicled in the newspapers of the time. An article on Deerfoot led to other articles on track and field history and a job as a monthly columnist for a foot-racing magazine and eventually to a book, *The Kings of Distance* (1968), on five runners of the past, and to a book-length bibliography of the subject, *Guide to British Track and Field Literature, 1275 to 1968* (1969).

The transition from historian of sport to chronicler of fictional crime came in 1968, when Lovesey put together two newspaper items published ninety years apart. One was an account in *Bell's Life in London* for 1878 of an odd sort of endurance race called a 'Go As You Please' race, in which contestants covered as many miles as they could in six days and nights. The other was an announcement, in the personal column of *The Times*, of the Macmillan–Panther First Crime Novel Competition, with a first prize of £1000. Why not a detective novel set against a background of an 1879 'Go As You Please' race? The novel, *Wobble to Death* (1970), was written in three months and won the contest. 'And that,' Lovesey writes, 'as my Victorian newspapers might have put it, was the singular sequence of events which made me a crime writer.' Lovesey was launched as a detective writer; seven more detective novels, two thrillers and a number of short stories and television scripts had followed by 1980.

Wobble to Death introduced the main elements of Lovesey's detective fiction: Detective Sergeant Cribb and his assistant Constable Thackeray (the third recurring figure, Inspector Jowett, would not join them until the second novel, *The Detective Wore Silk Drawers*, 1971); a setting in the 1880s, built around some curiosity of Victorian social history; a violent, passionate crime which Cribb solves through his shrewd understanding of human nature; and a gallery of Dickensian comic secondary characters, as well as more sinister figures, including bewitching but perverse women and monomaniacal men.

Detective stories set in Victorian times, both by the Victorians themselves and by more recent writers, are commonplace enough: crime and its detection seem to flourish most luxuriantly in Holmes's London.[2] Lovesey's achievement is that the Victorian world he brings to life in his novels is not a vague, foggy world of generalised 'local colour', but a sharply realised world built up of hundreds of specific bits of Victorian lore. On the first page of *Wobble to Death* we are transported to the great Agricultural Hall in Islington, setting in the 1860s and 1870s of royal balls, animal shows, bullfights and evangelical meetings, and now, in November, 1879, of a 'Go As You Please' or 'Wobble' race, the creation, we learn, of a Sir John Astley the previous year. In the course of the novel, we receive a complete education in Victorian foot-racing: the competitors, the training practices, the advertising, the forms of competition. And all this inkhorn lore is introduced indirectly, in the course of building up a vivid and completely convincing fictional world. 'In writing period fiction,' Lovesey has said, 'one must avoid introducing gratuitous information. You know the sort of thing – a reference to horse-drawn cabs in an era when nobody would think of commenting on the horse because all cabs worked that way. ... I have come to the conclusion that it is best to assume an understanding with the reader that when he picks up the book, he steps into the period with you.'[3]

The endurance race itself becomes a lightly ironic metaphor for Victorian values. 'The public like these events,' proclaims the oleaginous promotor Sol Herriott. 'Endurance, persistence, the will to conquer – these are the qualities of our time, gentlemen.' And the racers themselves make up a little model of Victorian society, from the aristocratic Oxfordian and Guards captain, Erskine Chadwick, MA, through his working-class opponent Charles Darrell, and down to the desperate rabble doomed to failure on the outside track.

The crime is a double murder: Darrell, the second runner, dies of strychnine in his restorative tonic, and his trainer, Sam Monk, an initial suspect, is subsequently clubbed and then gassed. And so into the Hall and into detective fiction comes Sergeant Cribb: 'He died of poisoning, sir. Enough strychnine in the corpse to put down a drayhorse. Where shall we talk?'

The world of a detective novel is often created principally by its hero, and his approach to detection suggests the values and beliefs within which the novel operates. Cribb, in 1879, is 'in his forties' (perhaps forty-one, since in *Waxwork*, set in 1888, he is fifty). He is tall, thin and birdlike – 'he moves his head with a birdlike suddenness' – and he has an unusually long nose and a luxuriant set of side-whiskers, 'Piccadilly Weepers'. He has served in the army and became a detective sergeant in 1878; he seems permanently fixed in that rank, partly through the jealousy of Inspector Jowett, partly because of his own sharp tongue and unwillingness to cultivate friends in high places. In *Waxwork* he is described as 'sharp, too, in speech, quick to spot deceit. His sense of irony kept him tolerant of others in most situations. He often fumed, rarely erupted.'

Cribb's methods of detection are, for the most part, orthodox: 'suspects, means and opportunity, and possible motives'. Working in the 1880s, he experiences the advances of criminological science and technology, the 'Bunsen and beaker brigade', as he calls the crime laboratory technicians. But his chief asset is his understanding of human nature and his chief weapon the interview. 'There was more to detective work than clues and statements,' he reflects in *Waxwork*. 'It involved people, their ambitions and fears, innocence and guilt. You needed solid evidence to determine the truth, but you could divine a lot by meeting them face to face.' Cribb's characteristic posture, while investigating a crime, is sitting quietly (while he assigns the long-suffering Thackeray prodigious feats of leg-work). He is a masterful interrogator, and although he can spring into physical action when required, often he arrives at the truth of a crime by quietly talking with all concerned, probing quietly for the dynamics of human motivations behind the events.

Edward Thackeray, 'a burly, middle-aged man with a fine grey beard', is steady and reliable, 'a tower of strength at exhumations'. He has a healthy respect for Sergeant Cribb, but their relationship is strictly professional. (Both are married, but appear to be childless, and their wives and private lives never appear directly in the novels.) Cribb often uses him as a testing-ground: 'Cribb liked to affect ignorance with Thackeray. It brought out the constable's best qualities, and often encouraged a point worth taking up.' But Thackeray's deductions are invariably wrong, a lame parody of Cribb's own mental processes: 'The mind, Sarge. I fancy I know a bit about the workings of a woman's thoughts.' (He doesn't.)

Wobble to Death presents a broad gallery of richly developed secondary characters, not only the gentleman–racer Erskine Chadwick and the promoter Sol Herriott, but the brickmaker–racer Charles Darrell, the whisky-drinking Irishman Feargus O'Flaherty, and most notably the mysterious racer–doctor, F. H. Mostyn-Smith, a whimsical figure with his cases of herbal medicines and his mathematically precise schedules of running and resting.

But the most striking secondary figure introduces a type that is to figure very importantly in subsequent Lovesey novels: the passionate, imperious 'spider girl', who manipulates men through her sexuality and draws them to disaster.[4] Cora Darrell floats into the Agricultural Hall in the third chapter of the novel to inspect her husband's accommodations, and all activity immediately begins to revolve around her seductive figure. And the resolution of the novel turns around Cribb's realisation of the nature of the power she holds over at least three of the men associated with the race. Cora Darrell and her successors are among Lovesey's most compelling creations; he excels in tracing the mental makeup of such female vampires.

Lovesey has noted the problem, in writing a series of crime novels about the same detectives, of becoming stereotyped and repetitive; he has avoided this by varying the form of each of the Sergeant Cribb novels.[5] *Wobble to Death* takes place almost wholly within the claustrophobic confines of the sports hall and has a ready-made structure: that of the six-day race. *The Detective Wore Silk Drawers* takes Cribb and Thackeray out of the sports hall and out of London to the fields and villages of rural Essex for an investigation into the murders of a series of headless corpses fished out of the Thames, and ultimately into the world of illegal barefisted pugilism.

The first chapter of *The Detective Wore Silk Drawers* introduces the third recurring character in the Cribb novels, Cribb's *bête noire*, Inspector Jowett, a former fellow-sergeant who has been repeatedly promoted over Cribb's head, not through competence but through currying favour with his superiors:

> What was Jowett? A sandwich-man without boards, with a new message each time you met him. He was one of the few at the Yard who emerged unscathed from the Turf Fraud Scandal of 1877, when the Detective Department's three Chief-Inspectors stood in the dock at the Old Bailey accused of conspiracy, and two were convicted. Heads had rolled in plenty after that. Not Jowett's though. Who knew what he stood for?

What he currently stands for is the new Director's infatuation with the new 'French methods' of 'inspiration, intuition and flair'. Cribb is able to turn this infatuation to his advantage when he secures Jowett's permission to infiltrate the pugilists' circle with a young prizefighting constable named Jago.

The narrative structure of *The Detective Wore Silk Drawers* is considerably more complicated than that of *Wobble to Death*. The action moves back and forth between Cribb and Thackeray, in London and the countryside, and Jago, inside the sinister Radstock Hall, where he is investigating the criminal ring while being groomed to fight barefisted himself. There is a grisly second murder late in the book, and the plot climaxes in a sustained chase scene, with Cribb and Thackeray trying to get to the fight scene in Kent before Jago is maimed or killed by his opponent, Sylvanus Morgan, the giant black barefisted pugilist.

The details of Victorian boxing are recreated in great detail: training, gambling, ring procedure and the slang of the sport ('hat in the ring', 'throwing in the sponge', 'up to scratch', and so on). And at one point, a Victorian newspaper sports story is recreated: 'A spanking hit with the dexter mawley on Jago's left listener had him staggering. Then a stinger with the left on the knowledge-box completely knocked him off his pins to mother earth.' 'Capital writing!' exclaims Cribb.

Perhaps the most memorable feature of *The Detective Wore Silk Drawers*, however, is the creation of Isabel Vibart, a spider girl in the line of Cora Darrell, but vastly elaborated from her. Isabel Vibart operates Radstock Hall, ruling over the household: Robert D'Estin, her violent and half-crazed trainer and former lover; Edmund Vibart, her agent, brother of her dead husband, and a church organist; and Sylvanus Morgan, 'The Ebony', a powerful black fighter. Isabel wears black, less in mourning for her dead husband than for its sinister connotations. She wears a pendant of a cobra poised to strike around her neck, and revels in her collection of Indian art, dominated by a life-sized bronze statue of the Hindu goddess Kali, who 'is said to dance among the slain on the battlefield and eat their flesh'. She uses the fighters in her stable for perverse sexual gratification, delighting in imposing cruel and unnecessary torments on them while she watches them through a peephole. After a success, she gives the fighters highly sensual massages, culminating either in copulation or cruel scratches from her long fingernails. In a brutal and shocking scene, D'Estin rapes her, but even after the rape, she cows him into submission by her self-possession and scorn.

The foil to this demonic enchantress is Lydia Boltover, the proper young lady engaged to Constable Jago. Jago must struggle comically with the lure of Isabel Vibart by holding fast to the image of his Lydia in moments of weakness. Lydia is to have her successors in Lovesey's novels in a series of 'golden girl' ingenues, but few of them have the complexity or emotional power of their 'spider girl' antitheses.

The music hall was an inevitable setting for a Sergeant Cribb novel, and when Lovesey left the sporting world for other colourful aspects of Victorian life, it was to the music hall that he turned, in *Abracadaver* (1972). There is, after all, more than a little of the music-hall policeman comedy team about Cribb and Thackeray (as well as of the more general and archetypal relationship of straight man and buffoon that gave us also Holmes and Watson, Stephen and Bloom in *Ulysses*, and Didi and Gogo in *Waiting for Godot*), and they seem thoroughly at home in the world of the halls.

The formal innovation in *Abracadaver* is that it is told entirely from the point of view of Thackeray, from the moment he is rescued from his hated 'educational classes' at Paradise Street Police Station by a summons from Cribb to the climactic burning of the Paragon music hall. The precipitating crime here is not murder but a series of accidents, only apparently coincidental, to music-hall performers, none of which results in serious injury, but all of which expose the performers to ridicule and ruin their careers. This absence of a corpse becomes a running joke through the early part of the novel until a real murder is committed. 'We've taken on some odd cases, I know,' exclaims Thackeray at one point, 'but there's always been a corpse to make the whole thing worth while.' This line fairly represents the broad comedy of the entire novel. One of Lovesey's gifts is his command of various levels of comedy, from the dark, sardonic comedy of *Waxwork* to the genial whimsy of *Swing, Swing Together*. The comedy in *Abracadaver* is, appropriately, of a rough, knockabout, music-hall variety, and many of the characters, including Cribb and Thackeray themselves, seem at times like characters from music-hall sketches. Early in the novel, Cribb and Thackeray are outraged by a policeman sketch – Constables Salt and Battree – on a music-hall bill. 'Blasted scandal, it is,' growls Cribb; 'Home Secretary wants to look into it, in my opinion.' But the novel places them in a series of situations as ridiculous as anything on the stage of the Grampion: Thackeray as a sceneshifter during an obscene music-hall performance, dressed in bright yellow kneepants, and Cribb fighting off the advances of the eccentric Mrs Body in her private theatre box.

The novel contains two lengthy historical set-pieces: a detailed account in the third chapter of an 1881 music-hall performance, and another, in the tenth chapter, of another performance, as seen from backstage, with detailed recreations of Victorian stage machinery and organisation. An interview with a magician accused of injuring his assistant provides the occasion for another piece of detailed historical reconstruction, this time of the Old Bailey, its appearance inside and out, and the routine of guards and prisoners. All this material is handled with Lovesey's characteristic tact and unobtrusiveness, but provides much of the appeal of the novel.

The novel is rich in Loveseyan comic grotesques, especially the private detective Major Chick, who is pursuing his own line of investigation parallel to Cribb's, and who turns up, in good music-hall fashion, in a series of bizarre disguises at every turn of the plot. But the most grotesque figure is that of Mrs Body, mistress of Philbeach House for retired and distressed music-hall performers. Mrs Body is a tiny, doll-like figure with child-like blond curls, whose drawing-room features painted heads on the wall-paper, plaster heads on the sideboard, and egg-shell heads on the piano, all arranged to create the illusion of a music-hall audience, as seen from the stage. Mrs Body is another Lovesey spider girl, given a comic, music-hall treatment. She seduces men in her theatre-box/boudoir, but as Major Chick shrewdly realises, she is attracted only to men with obvious weaknesses. 'It's the runt of the litter that lady fancies, I can tell you,' observes Major Chick. The foil to Mrs Body is Ellen Blake, descended from Lydia Boltover as Mrs Body is sister to Isabel Vibart. She enters the novel singing 'Fresh as the New-Mown Hay', but by the novel's end turns out to be a complex version of the Victorian virgin. And once again, Sergeant Cribb's keen intuition of feminine psychology is the key to his solution of the case. 'What makes a young woman as vicious as that, do you think?' asks Jowett, with uncharacteristic respect for Cribb's opinions. 'A strong streak of Puritanism,' replies Cribb. 'And infatuation for a young man. A powerful combination, sir.'

Mad Hatter's Holiday (1973) explores the possibilities of the detective-story form in another direction, that of the modern art-novel. Lovesey has explained that in this book 'I experimented with pace, giving a slow, teasing build-up to the murder, and only introducing my detectives halfway through.'[6] Perhaps even more striking is the way Lovesey, without violating the conventions of popular fiction, gives the novel a Jamesian quality, through an adroit manipulation of point of view and the use of a number of well-worked-out symbols. *Mad Hatter's Holiday* is the first Cribb novel told primarily from the point of view of a character other than Cribb or Thackeray: Albert Moscrop, a notably subjective and obtuse observer. The theme of perception introduced by this use of limited point of view is further reinforced by a number of recurring symbols.

The date is September 1882, and Moscrop, manager of a London optical shop and a telescope hobbiest, is in Brighton for his solitary holidays. His delight is in peering at life through his binoculars, and within hours he has fixed upon a striking young woman as the object of his attentions, once removed. She turns out to be Zena Prothero, wife of the much older Dr Gregory Prothero, stepmother to the precocious fifteen-year-old Guy Prothero, mother of little Jason Prothero, and employer of the nursemaid Bridget. Moscrop, who feels most at home when he is 'invisible' in a large crowd, gradually insinuates himself into the Prothero party, alternately observing them safely through his binoculars and telescopes and arranging carefully staged meetings. Scotland Yard becomes involved when a young woman's dismembered body is found on the beach under the promenade; the subsequent death, apparently natural, of Guy Prothero of an acute asthma attack further complicates matters.

The book features a wealth of historical detail, including the vogue for telescopes and binoculars in the 1880s and the appearance of Brighton in 1882. But nowhere in the Cribb novels is historical material better integrated into the texture of the novel. The book is full of optical instruments – binoculars, telescopes, microscopes – which become a metaphor for perception itself. Cribb refuses to use them because they blind a person to what is near at hand; a man with a pair of binoculars is a perfect victim for a pickpocket, he points out. Moscrop is no Peeping Tom – he would not stoop to surveying the ladies' bathing-machines, for example – but he uses his instruments as a way of preserving his own detachment from life, which he rationalises as 'scientific objectivity'. But his view of life is intensely subjective and he misinterprets everything he sees, while it is Cribb who can, with his naked eyes, see beneath surface appearances to the truth.

The minute account of the pier at Brighton is similarly well integrated into the novel's symbolism. Thackeray finds murder unexpected in the gaiety of the seaside, but Cribb is not so deceived by appearances:

When you've had your eyeful of the scrubbed decks and the dapper little buildings, take a look underneath, right under the pier. I'll tell you what you'll see. Girders festering with barnacles. Slime and weed and water black as pitch lurching and heaving round the understructure fit to turn your stomach. That's part of your pier, too. Just as slums and alleys and back-streets lie behind the nobby hotels along the sea-front.

Crocodiles, too, are an image of the violence that lies beneath the tranquil surface of Brighton and of Victorian England. We first see Guy holding the infant Jason over the crocodile tank in the Aquarium with a teasing cruelty, the tank where a severed hand is later found. Moscrop later buys Jason a wooden crocodile, and a fireworks display celebrating the triumphant return of the British army from Egypt features a set-piece of a crocodile, representing Egypt. 'What cheers there were as the sparks spent themselves and the enemy was exposed as a charred and smoking ruin! Marvellous to be British, and in Brighton, and secure from such monsters!'

The two murders are well integrated into this scheme, both outbreaks of a monstrous reality that crack the façade of a carefully manipulated illusion. Zena, when the nature of the first murder is revealed, acknowledges her part in maintaining an illusion of a happy and tranquil household, shielding herself with sleeping draughts from acknowledgement of her husband's infidelities and her stepson's homicidal violence. But now there will be 'no escape from the truth. . . . I do not know whether the removal of our illusions is the best thing.' And the climax of the novel – the solution of the second murder – involves Cribb in a decision whether to reveal the truth or to collaborate in maintaining a comforting façade.

Lovesey's interest in feminine psychology is subordinated in this novel to the striking portrait of Albert Moscrop, but it persists in the vivid figure of Zena Prothero and the equally effective, though slighter, portrait of Samantha Floyd-Whittingham, Dr Prothero's copper-haired mistress, with an appetite for older men to which Thackeray almost falls victim.

If the Loveseyan spider girl is temporarily subordinated in *Mad Hatter's Holiday*, she returns, appetite unslaked, in *Invitation to a Dynamite Party* (1974), in the person of Rossanna McGee, the beautiful leader of a gang of Irish dynamitards. Lovesey has described *Invitation to a Dynamite Party* as 'my attempt to write a thriller – with the standard ingredients of kidnappings, secret organisations, beautiful women, dynamite and double-crossings – in the Victorian idiom'. The book is set against the background of the Irish bombing campaigns in London in 1884–5; Thackeray has unwittingly encountered the dynamite gang and been kidnapped by them, and Cribb infiltrates their group in the guise of a paid adventurer. The dynamitards plan to blow up a pier at Gravesend while the Prince of Wales is on it; the feat will be accomplished by a Holland submarine packed with dynamite. The book is structured around a series of cliffhanging crises and narrow escapes, and culminates in an escape by Cribb and Thackeray from the underwater craft and an aquatic chase scene after the escaping criminals.

The plot itself is an ingeniously constructed 'infernal machine', but it would seem a trifle too mechanical if it were not for a series of strongly drawn characterisations which humanise it. The thriller plot does not offer Cribb a puzzle to solve through his characteristic understanding of human nature – he saves his and Thackeray's necks and that of the Prince of Wales through an ingenious ruse – but the dynamite plot itself is given an interesting psychological basis through the character of Rossanna McGee. Rossanna is head of the gang through the circumstance of her father, Daniel McGee, having been horribly mutilated in an explosive accident. Most of his face has been blown away, and he wears a black silk mask to hide the horrid remains. Rossanna ostensibly acts as his interpreter to the gang. Rossanna swings between cold-blooded cruelty and a rather voracious sensuality. She shoots a weak comrade in cold blood and takes part in torturing Thackeray, but she also conceives a passion for Cribb and attempts to seduce him. She has not only Samantha Floyd-Whittingham's 'copper-coloured' hair, but her lust for older men as well. Cribb attacks her sternly when she shoots Malone, and is surprised to find that she responds amorously. He concludes that 'she was one of those unusual members of her sex uninterested in young men, preferring to submit to the authority of older, more masterful partners.' This touch and others like it subtly suggest an equation between passion and dynamite and provide a sexual undercurrent to the thriller plot.

A Case of Spirits (1975) presents Sergeant Cribb wrestling with a locked-room mystery, in which the problem is not only who the murderer is, but how the murder was done. The novel is set in 1885. (The Cribb novels are set in successive years of the decade of the eighties, skipping only 1883, 1886 and 1887.) Cribb and Thackeray are called in to investigate two burglaries that have occurred during seances. The case turns into a murder investigation when Peter Brand, a fraudulent medium, is electrocuted during a seance in which he sat in an electrified chair, maintaining a low-voltage electrical circuit with his hands in order to guarantee that he does not move during the seance. The problem is how the apparently safe mechanism suddenly transmitted a fatal shock and who manipulated it so it would do so. Cribb solves the problem with a classic 're-enactment of the crime' and a gathering of all concerned to hear his solution. As the *New York Times* reviewer commented, 'Traditionalism can go no further.'[7]

A Case of Spirits is an impeccably plotted novel with a number of curious and well-developed characters, especially prominent roles for Thackeray and Jowett (who becomes more and more a major comic creation), and a wealth of Victoriana, including not only the 'spiritualist' movement, but the novelty of electricity, the feminist movement and genteel pornography as well. But as in earlier Cribb novels, what unifies the novel is not the ingenious plotting or the historical lore, but the well-developed character relationships and motives. These turn, in *A Case of Spirits*, around Victorian sexuality and family life. The Probert family is a classic Victorian family. Sergeant Cribb fails to notice the self-effacing Mrs Probert when he first comes to the Probert establishment. 'There is no need to apologize,' she tells him, from her hiding place beneath a potted palm. 'My husband has failed to notice me for years now. I am quite resigned to it.' Dr Probert is a pompous, domineering Victorian father; Cribb thinks that 'the single thing in favour of the man was that his house had been burgled.' Probert opens his first conversation with Cribb bluntly: 'I don't propose to beat around the bush. My wife misunderstands me.' As for their daughter Alice, she seems to be in strenuous training to become an angel of the house, spending her time in good works. 'To see young Alice striding down the Hill with a marrow under her arm in search of a destitute family is a stirring sight, I promise you,' boasts her fond father.

Reality is somewhat at odds with this prim façade. The unobtrusive Mrs Probert, while she is supposed to be reading a collection of *Notable British Sermons* in her room, is really passing the time with a gentleman caller and a bottle of gin. Dr Probert comforts himself with his gallery of pornographic paintings, and young Alice, once down the hill with her marrow, hastens to an artist's studio to pose in the nude.

This sardonic portrait of the Victorian family is balanced by what amounts to a subplot, the story of Miss Crush, converted to feminism by a speech of John Stuart Mill in the campaign of 1865, and the mother of a child by a randomly selected sexual partner to whom she gave herself as her 'one foray into the enemy camp'.

Cribb has a keen sense of these various tensions and contradictions. He explains to Thackeray why Alice Probert consented to do nude modelling:

> It's well-known that girls often idolise their fathers – how else can they get to understand the opposite sex – and they only ask a modicum of affection in return. But how much notice did Alice get from Dr Probert? He was too devoted to the nymphs disporting themselves around the walls of his gallery to take any notice of his daughter or wife. So it's logical that she should behave as she did; he had shown her only one way to win a man's admiration.

Even Thackeray, who 'had never previously considered Cribb as an authority on the upbringing of girls', is forced to acknowledge, 'You make it sound quite sensible, Sarge.'

Victorian history provides not only the background but the form as well for *Swing, Swing Together* (1976). Harriet Shaw, a student at Elfrida College for the Training of Female Elementary Teachers near Henley, joins two fellow students for a surreptitious nude midnight swim in the Thames, and they see three men and a dog in a boat. An innocent schoolgirl lark turns into a murder case when a body is fished out of the river the next day, and Harriet is called to give evidence about the mysterious party in the boat. She joins Cribb, Thackeray and the attractive young Buckinghamshire constable Roger Hardy in a pursuit up the Thames of the mysterious suspects. (The names are important; when Cribb temporarily leaves the boat to continue the chase by train, the three left in the boat are Thackeray, Hardy and Shaw. Could Cribb's name be a joke as well? Is he a 'crib' for Victorian history?)

The Thames is swarming with vacationers recreating the boating excursion described by Jerome K. Jerome in *Three Men in a Boat (To Say Nothing of the Dog)*. Cribb and his party encounter one such group, with the fine names of Humberstone,

Gold and Lucifer, and they become major suspects. And of course Cribb's own group consists of three men in a boat (to say nothing of the girl). The form of the novel imitates that of *Three Men in a Boat*, as well, structured around a picaresque river journey from Henley to Oxford and divided into forty short chapters, all with Jerome-like chapter headings ('Original use of butter', 'River scene with figures', 'Something rather horrid', and so on).

Swing, Swing Together is the sunniest and most genial of the Cribb novels, a wonderful excursion into Victorian whimsical comedy. Much of its charm radiates from the character of Harriet Shaw, whose point of view shapes the novel. Harriet is a genteel young lady of eighteen, her head full of girlish fantasies: her first impression of Cribb is that 'he had reached what her mother called the dangerous time of life'. But she is also remarkably shrewd and resourceful; she takes an active part in solving the crime, and pursues Constable Hardy with as much determination as she does the criminals, though with different motives.

The sunny charm of *Swing, Swing Together* is all the more effective for the shadows in the book. The book's double vision of Victorian whimsy is suggested by the title, both a quotation from the 'Eton Boating Song' and a reference to hanging. In the background of the action is not only the 1889 vogue for *Three Men in a Boat*, but the terror in the same year of the Ripper murders and the pious cruelty of Victorian penology. The three men (not all in a boat) ultimately revealed as the murderers are driven by motives that suggest the inverted passions possible in a society that was expressed both by Gilbert and Sullivan and by Jack the Ripper.

Waxwork (1978), the last Cribb novel to date, is in many ways the most complex. Lovesey continues his practice of varying the form of each Cribb novel by taking on a retrospective plot in the manner of Agatha Christie. By the time Cribb enters the case, Miriam Cromer has made a full, detailed confession of the poisoning murder of the assistant of her photographer husband, has pleaded guilty at her trial, and has been sentenced to death by hanging. An anonymous communication to the Home Secretary has brought out one discrepancy in her confession, however, and Jowett assigns Cribb to conduct a detailed re-examination of the crime in the eleven days remaining before the execution.

It is hard to imagine two novels more different in tone than *Swing, Swing Together* and *Waxwork*. The whimsical gaiety of the previous novel is replaced in *Waxwork* by a dark, sinister quality. Even the comic office politics of Jowett become in *Waxwork* a cynical conspiracy to protect the reputation of those in high places even if it means hanging an innocent woman. The private crime of Miriam Cromer is tacitly contrasted with the public one of the commissioner of the Metropolitan Police, Sir Charles Warren, notorious for having put down a demonstration of the unemployed the previous year with a force of 4000 police and 600 guardsmen. The sardonic irony of the novel is heightened by the counterpointing of three plot threads. Against Cribb's slow progress toward the solution of the crime are set an account of the prison routine in Newgate, as Miriam Cromer is prepared for execution, and the preparation of James Berry, public hangman, to come up to London for the 'job'.

Cribb characteristically pursues his inquiry through a series of interviews. (He is alone: this is the only Cribb novel in which Thackeray does not appear.) Miriam Cromer's confession is a straightforward, fairly simple account of the crime, but once Cribb pulls one thread, the entire fabric begins to unravel, revealing a background of complex and perverse motives. If Harriet Shaw is Lovesey's finest 'golden girl', Miriam Cromer is his best realised 'spider girl', driven by compulsive desires and acting with icy cruelty. Her husband, Howard Cromer, is equally complex and equally perverse. He carries Albert Moscrop's tendency to keep life at a distance by viewing it through a lens to the point of madness; Cribb recognises that Miriam Cromer 'was more real to this man as a series of photographs than a wife'.

The climax of the novel comes when Cribb finally wins permission to interview Miriam Cromer herself in her prison cell. He has known all through the case that he will ultimately have to see her in person: 'Understand the woman, see her, hear her, and he would get to the truth.' When he does interview her, he is well armed with facts uncovered by patient investigation and with a theory of how the crime was committed. But finally, it is not facts but personalities that reveal the truth: 'people, their ambitions and fears, innocence and guilt'.

Waxwork recalls *Mad Hatter's Holiday* more vividly than any other earlier novel, not only in its concern with the dark underside of Victorian life – the underside of the pier – and with the Moscrop/Cromer habit of retreating from life into 'views' through a lens, but in its rich symbolism. The chief symbol is that suggested by the title. The 'waxwork' is immediately Madam Tussaud's museum, where the hangman Berry is having his statue made and to whom he intends to sell Miriam Cromer's clothing. But more generally the title refers to all the 'images' in the novel, not only the wax figures at Madam Tussaud's, objects of a prurient Victorian preoccupation with crime and punishment, but also the photographic images into which Howard Cromer has retreated, and even the mental images that Miriam Cromer has pursued in her misguided life. The climax of the novel comes when Cribb looks into Miriam Cromer's face and sees 'no longer the face in the photograph' but a real human being.

The Sergeant Cribb series of novels ends, for the moment, with *Waxwork*. Recently, Lovesey has occupied himself with two striking non-detective novels, *Goldengirl* (1977) and *Spider Girl* (1980), with a commissioned *Official Centenary History of the Amateur Athletic Association* (1979), and with a series of scripts, some original and some adapted from the novels, for British and American television. (The Cribb novels are eminently suited for film and television, with their vivid, colourful settings and their wealth of comic dialogue.)

The first eight Cribb novels have established Lovesey as one of the contemporary masters of the detective novel. Working with traditional materials, he has made them his own and has created a remarkably rich and varied range of novels that are at once witty and engrossing entertainments and convincing and thoughtful interpretations of Victorian life.

NOTES AND REFERENCES

1. Peter Lovesey, 'Becoming a Novelist', *Writer* 88 (Aug. 1975) p.21.
2. Lovesey has described the charms of Victorian England for the detective-story writer in 'Once Upon a Crime', in Dilys Winn (ed.), *Murder Ink: The Mystery Reader's Companion* (New York: Workman), 1977, pp.475-6.
3. 'Becoming a Novelist', p.22-3.
4. I have adopted the terms 'spider girl' and 'golden girl' from the titles of Lovesey's non-detective novels of 1977 and 1980, where they have a more literal meaning than I intend.
5. 'Becoming a Novelist', p.22.
6. Ibid., p.22.
7. 'Newgate Calendar', *New York Times Book Review*, 15 Feb. 1976, p.20.

CHRONOLOGY

Dates of first publication (published in UK by Macmillan):
1970 – *Wobble to Death*
1971 – *The Detective Wore Silk Drawers*
1972 – *Abracadaver*
1973 – *Mad Hatter's Holiday*
1973 – 'The Bathroom', in *Winters' Crimes* 5
1974 – *Invitation to a Dynamite Party* (American title: *The Tick of Death*)
1975 – *A Case of Spirits*
1976 – *Swing, Swing Together*
1978 – *Waxwork*
1978 – 'The Locked Room', in *Winters' Crimes* 10 (also in *Ellery Queen's Mystery Magazine*, Mar. 1979, as 'Behind the Locked Door')
1980 – 'How Mr Smith Traced His Ancestors', in *The Mystery Guild Anthology* (New York: Book Club Associates, 1980).

(The novels, except for *Waxwork*, were published in the United States by Dodd, Mead. Publisher for *Waxwork* was Pantheon. All of the novels have been published in paperback by Penguin.)

9 The Van der Valk Novels of Nicolas Freeling:
Going by the Book

CAROL SHLOSS

Without the police, one is in the indefinite world of a supervision that seeks ideally to reach the most elementary particle, the most passing phenomenon of the social body.
(Michel Foucault, *Discipline & Punish*)

They are part of the administrative machine, a tool of government control, and in our days the government, in order to make head against the pressures and distortions, the tides of economic change and the winds of upheaval, must possess a machine so complex and detailed that its tentacles can grip and manipulate every soul within its frontiers.
(Nicolas Freeling, *King of the Rainy Country*)

In *Because of the Cats*, Nicolas Freeling's second detective novel, commissaris Piet Van der Valk struggles to break the silence surrounding the death of a Dutch student. The dead boy's lover sits before him in the police bureau, prim, self-possessed and resisting: 'I don't see why I should be questioned about my private life as though I were a criminal or something.' This scene is worth isolating here because Van der Valk's answer to the girl allows us to locate the central conceptual categories that structure all of the Dutch mystery novels of this series: 'When someone dies by violence,' Van der Valk explains, 'he no longer has a private life. His actions . . . become legitimate subjects of inquiry'. As the two face each other in that stark room, they grimly re-enact the larger patterns of concealment and search that are most characteristic of Freeling's work as a whole: she, a young woman, tries to protect her private life by exempting emotion and subjectivity from surveillance. He, the representative of the public world, claims the right to observe, to probe, to bring into the open what had hitherto been beyond the legitimate offices of the state. Freeling describes their tryst as an act of love: 'He had just broken her; he felt as though he had raped her . . . he could not help it – at this moment he loved her.'[1]

This interrogation does effect a momentary union of opposites, but it is nonetheless a resolution of a very peculiar kind; for in a more general way, Freeling measures Van der Valk's talent as a detective by his ability to shed an official police identity and to enter into the subterranean world of the victim and his/her killer. Although the state empowers him and initiates each of his investigations, the procedures of state do not usually provide Van der Valk with any effective access to, or understanding of, criminal behaviour. We might say this another way by observing that the official world, as represented in these novels, is a singularly poor reader of criminal texts. In fact, the bureaucracy that Van der Valk is forced to inhabit so frequently occasions its own defeat that Freeling seems more interested in dramatising the tension between the methods of bureaucratic inquiry and the realities of Dutch bourgeois life than with criminal discovery *per se*. That is, he is concerned with the general relation of authority to the people it governs. Although his novels fall clearly into the pattern of police procedure, the genre that Jacques Barzun so disparagingly calls childish tinkering in sociology, they critique the very methods of inquiry that they purportedly espouse. We are told repeatedly that Van der Valk is a 'bad policeman', but we are to understand this personal deviance to be the source of his power. Where Marx or any of the critics of the Frankfurt School might look at the universe of these novels and see in it a world increasingly invaded or penetrated by capitalism's need to expropriate more and more areas of human existence, Freeling understands that world to be an example of civic privatism's successful resistance to state encroachment. His novels describe a world irretrievably polarised into public and private sectors, a world characterised by fundamental dissonance, a culture only superficially coherent. The official mechanisms of authority, as represented by the police, form a thin, ineffective superstructure which sits lamely over a block of civilian hostility and resentment. It is this gap between authority and the people it governs that

Van der Valk must bridge, and in the course of such stretching, Freeling reveals an interesting set of assumptions about the striated nature of contemporary European life.

Freeling's Holland is a land poised in precarious equilibrium between modernity and tradition, a land characterised by Calvinist rigidity, thrift and well-defined family roles. If these characteristics are attractive to Freeling, it is because they foster a moral clarity that contemporary life can often obscure. Its limitations derive from its virtues: the good burghers who perpetuate tradition are also complacent, self-satisfied and finally ossified in postures that have little in common either with Calvin's original teaching or with an adaptable social philosophy. Freeling understands this world to be law-abiding and, whether it is stolid and dull or savagely puritanical, it nonetheless produces a low rate of crime. In Holland, Freeling observes, 'our gangsters are simple-minded and pathetic oafs.'

Freeling's interest in traditional Dutch life can also be understood as a fascination with its mechanism for self-regulation. The villagers of these books ensure conformity through mutual observation. The streets become their look-out posts, their open windows invitations to judgement. In this world, visibility promotes virtue and secrecy itself becomes suspect: 'I felt the pressure of twenty pairs of unseen eyes going prickling over the skin of the back of my neck. . . . The muslin glass-curtains of the house across the street flickered as I turned to shut the door. These eyes were able to count the stitches that darned my left sock last week.'[2] Freeling emphasises the open-curtain habits in these small Dutch communities because seeing induces the effects of power even though power cannot be said to reside in the central government or in the formal mechanisms of a legal system. Rather the public polices itself; old notions of propriety are asserted by common housewives in defiance of the trends of modernity. They fear the shame of personal censor far more than any strictures of a formal legal code.

Freeling shows these people in the midst of an endless round of children and bicycles and neighbourhood shops; neighbours mind everyone else's business as they go about their own. 'Like Salem, the whole place sounded hysterical, neurotic. Neighbourhood squabbles tended to be started by virtuous housewives, shrilly accusing other virtuous housewives of immorality.'[3] The sinister cast this nosiness finally assumes can be taken as the measure of a threat perceived and obliquely dealt with through internal monitoring. It is, as Freeling shows, a momentary stay against change, an attempt to salvage familiar customs from the encroachments of technological advancement with its personal anonymity, the accountability of time, and mobility of population. 'The sleepy little place hardly knew itself now. ... The life of Zwinderen ... now was become the frontier of the big push at decentralisation, decongestion, full employment and Prosperity for all.'[4] In other towns, modernisation is less resisted but equally raw and self-conscious. Bloemendaal an Zee, for example, is full of

> brick-built houses; brick-paved streets. Plenty of glass and concrete; large, new, modern blocks ... it was built to house the young married couples, clamouring for living space sited conveniently near the industrial terrains that clutter round the North Sea Kanal. The townsmen are for the most part skilled technicians or rising executives.[5]

Freeling devotes a great deal of attention to these descriptions of place. They are integral to his purpose. In his eyes, crime belongs to its setting; it is always an inevitable, inextricable consequence of a way of life. Of Zwinderen he asks, 'What were the problems here, that had accompanied the laying of a thin veneer of glitter, a coating of wealthy materialism, on the old Calvinist roots of a stick in the mud country market town?'[6] Eventually Van der Valk discovers the unexplained suicides of this town to have been provoked by a religious woman whose resentment of industrialism was vented on the wives of successful businessmen. In another novel Freeling plays out the consequences of self-righteous materialism through the warped lives of well-to-do but neglected teenagers. The ennui and purposelessness of the very rich focuses a third investigation; the personal displacements of war – both the second world war and Vietnam – provide the context for still other inquiries. It would be fair to say that none of Freeling's criminals fits into the category of brilliant but warped minds. Neither do they belong to the group of petty violators of the criminal code. 'Not much interest or pride to be found in the identification and sequestration of criminals in ever-growing numbers, most of them either not really criminals at all or defined as such for the wrong reasons.[7] It would be better to observe that in Freeling's fictional world, the particular criminal is always emblematic of a large social problem and that his capture is the natural culmination of a private world entered into and understood by an empathetic mind:

> Society [Van der Valk] thought, was a fermenting mass, like a huge farmer's-pot of pig-swill, boiling on fires of hatred and envy, of bad education and war and outrage, of poverty and starvation, homelessness, joblessness. The scum rose to the top, where he was supposed to skim it off with a ridiculous tiny spoon. He could never reach the ferments and instabilities inside, let alone the fires below. He too was part of that sinister boiling in the pot. Tied, too, to these boys, with a strong band. What would he have felt, and done, had it been Arlette who had been raped? And what had he been like at eighteen years of age?[8]

From these examples and reflections, we can see that the nature of the crime – and the place of the crime – determine the mode of its discovery and that discovery entails Van der Valk's successful disclosure of an entire way of life. Where other writers might structure stories through the intellectual struggle between the criminal and the investigator or through the play of human intelligence as it decodes the material world, Freeling centres his novels around victims, their lifestyle, friends, home. The tangible world, the world of things that Jacques Barzun, for example, thinks so essential to detective fiction, is of little interest to Freeling. Where Barzun argues for detective literature as a 'romance of reason', where he considers the raw material of detection to consist of the physical objects that surround action, Freeling asserts the primacy of character and milieu and implicitly denigrates the materialism of his precursors. For him, the resolution of the tale is always achieved through knowledge of the victim; and the preceding struggle is itself emblematic of an equally pressing social problem since Van der Valk, as a police detective, is always locked into the difficulties of his own position: 'I am the government – the eternal enemy.' Though Holland's windowed homes and towns initially suggest social transparency, a congruence of inner and outer life, there is, in fact, a great deal that remains concealed from official scrutiny.

Van der Valk's failures in detection are, then, as important as his successes, for they signal a structural dissimilarity between the world of administrative action – the world to which he belongs professionally – and the cultural traditions of the country at large. Where a Dickens novel, to take *Bleak House* as one example, might show the police force to be continuous with crime, as corrupt as the world of crime that it seeks to monitor, a Freeling suspense story emphasises the distance between authority and its subjects. Van der Valk is not thrown into the slums nor is he tainted by the crime he must punish. Instead he must overcome the dynamics of exclusion: his initial bafflement at the crime is the measure of a social rift, the emblem of the official world's inability to penetrate the secret world which it has helped, by its own proceduralism, to engender: 'To call in an outsider, like me – mistake. They make resolute common front against me here. ... These people are scared sick of their government.'[9]

It is in recognition of this fear and resistance that Van der Valk assumes various disguises during investigations. These can be as simple as wearing ski sweaters in Austria or pretending to need a watch from a suspected jeweller or inventing a bogus complaint to be treated by a shady doctor. On occasion they become elaborate ruses or fully contrived secret identities. In *Double Barrel*, for example, Van der Valk parades around Drente as a government functionary making an ethnographic survey. These methods are condoned or even initiated by the police bureau; it is common knowledge that the police operate in the face of suspicion and hostility.

But if Van der Valk's tactics occasionally conform to what is officially required of him, they just as frequently do not. In fact, Freeling emphasises his protagonist's idiosyncracies, seeing in Van der Valk's humanity, his empathy, his commitment to private life the only secure foundations of social knowledge. Were he to adhere to condoned rules of evidence, the secrecy that surrounds these murders would never be pierced. It is for this reason that Freeling constantly reminds us that the physical objects of the world are, finally, inert, insufficient signs of past action, and that rules ensure their own defeat. In Bloemendaal an Zee, searching for a gang responsible for theft, rape and the death of one of their own weaker members, Van der Valk wanders, seeking passage through the inarticulate surface of middle-class professional life, wanting to understand the ways in which privilege and comfort can engender rage and the impulse to defile:

> This town was an oyster, at which he was picking with feeble fingers. To open it he needed a knife. Journalists in strange towns have this problem and know the solution. One's own impressions are meaningless and can be misleading; it is necessary to find a person who says words unthinkingly, even frivolously, that illuminate a tangled skein and drop, suddenly, the end of the thread in the reporter's hand.[10]

In this instance, Van der Valk's 'knife' is a Russian prostitute, a good woman whose impulses are neither legalistic nor greedy. She is someone who holds the confidence of otherwise conservative and upright businessmen; and while she never violates those confidences, she is nonetheless able to steer Van der Valk through the slippery surfaces of upper-middle-class convention. In retrospect, with both the gang and their middle-aged mentor arrested, Van der Valk can understand that this woman's speculations had obliquely provided him with the real beginnings of the case: 'He knew how often in police work one can have a sharp idea that someone is shady, and that in private one might hear illuminating things, even though on file there might be nothing "to his prejudice"'.[11]

This episode from *Because of the Cats* establishes a pattern; for Freeling's subsequent novels show us the consistency of these allegiances, the repetition of categories of opposition and reconciliation: Van der Valk calls attention to his own disposition to break rules and then shows that involvement to be more fruitful than all of the investigative machinery of state. Of an Austrian colleague he says, 'his theory was that you can find anything and anyone with a routine, if that routine is only well enough co-ordinated. Police departments are increasingly fragmented and where they fail is in the faulty liaison.'[12] Then, following hunches rather than computers, he manages to discover the criminal. This unorthodox conduct can be summarised by the phrase: '[h]e doesn't exactly go to work by the book.' To the extent that Van der Valk internalises the lives and habits of his victims, to the extent that their homes reveal – not bits of factual evidence, the knife, the poison – but their psychological proclivities, Van der Valk can solve the mystery of their demise. In fact, Holland's organisation and rigidity, the thick books of rules that Van der Valk tries so often to evade, can be seen in themselves as an *alazon*, for they perform the same function as the blocking character of classical comedy; they actually inhibit the recognition of the criminal's real identity.

Throughout all of these novels, we also find what might be called a helping figure – the person to whom Van der Valk confides or who can provide him with privileged knowledge of the victim; and in all cases, this helper is a woman. In *Because of the Cats*, it was Feodora, the prostitute; in *Love in Amsterdam*, the woman who had superseded the victim as wife of the accused looks back and recreates for Van der Valk the nature of the sexual struggle that had led her husband to abandon his previous mistress. It is also this woman who understands Elsa's murderer to have been someone familiar with the street she lived on, someone who would not have attracted notice in the neighbourhood. 'Woman's explanation, but anyway an explanation of something that bothers me, and has since I began this.' In *King of the Rainy Country*, Van der Valk is shot and wounded by his helper, a wealthy woman who is ashamed and angered that the police should discover the nature of her marriage and the humiliation of her husband's preference for the love of a sixteen-year-old girl. Here Van der Valk's successful understanding of private life actually elicits physical harm, a response more dramatic and telling than the nebulous, provincial resentment that usually surrounds his work. In *Double Barrel*, the novel in which Van der Valk assumes the disguise of a petty government functionary, Arlette, his French wife, becomes the helping figure: 'If you are to be the complete convincing, colourless if intelligent state functionary, you need a wife to do the housekeeping.'[13]

This book is pivotal for the group of novels under discussion, for in it Freeling extends and clarifies the implicit logic of his investigating methods. To this point, Van der Valk's wife had provided him comfortable relief from his work; she brought him out of the official work world into a place of warmth and repose. Her world was a round of housekeeping, neighbourhood gossip and shops – a world as unfamiliar to her husband as his endless paperwork was to her. But it is precisely at this juncture – the home – that Van der Valk gains his first natural access to the subterranean life of Zwinderen; it is through the casual talk of women at the shops and over the clothesline that he begins to understand the mass hysteria and Calvinistic zeal that has arisen out of overly ambitious plans for industrial development: 'I sat up. "What is it exactly that you get everyday in the shops?" "Well, one feels a strong hostility to the outsiders. . . . There's a hatred, almost, of all this progress."'[14]

It is not bureaucratic surveillance, nor even the disguised investigation of a sensitive man, that unknots the puzzle of multiple suicides in this provincial town, and Van der Valk's confusion gives the lie to his thought that an administrative machine might in theory supervise the entire social body. To the mayor, he says, 'patience and concentration. . . . If I could achieve a minutely accurate observation of everything I'd have this person for you tomorrow.' But the criminal knowledge he seeks is not a function of increased surveillance, for that which he needs to know will always evade formal inquiry. He does not need more 'minutely accurate observation' but knowledge of a substantially different kind. It is his wife who makes this clear to him.

Freeling's methodological shift, or rather his shift towards manifestation of a previously latent epistemological distinction, begins in *Tsing Boum*, where a foreign woman's death leads Van der Valk back into the political ramifications of the French involvement in Vietnam. Here Van der Valk and his wife adopt the daughter of the dead woman, a move which signifies the private union of the investigator and victim. It is in this work that Freeling first speaks of a 'penal marriage' – the psychological bond between the perpetrator and the victim – but that identification becomes increasingly less significant as the author explores the ramifications of Van der Valk's new symbolic family. The detective comes to see his wife – also a foreigner – as the key to Esther's fatally intrusive past; by observing her with the dead woman's child, he is able to unearth a probable network of private, lethal allegiances. What is most significant, however, is his wife's increasingly prominent role as an active investigator. Freeling tells us that

since the moment when she had 'known' instinctively that Esther had been at Dien Bien Phu, she had felt an uneasy identification, as though she was herself Esther [and] through

Ruth [the child] she was trying to penetrate the darkness much, had she known it, as her man was through the jungle of passions and loyalties of which Monsieur Marie and Colonel Voisin had been distant, uncomprehending spectators.[15]

Arlette van der Valk's growing involvement in her husband's life of detection prefigures the moment when she will assume his role in its entirety, for in the final novel of this series, Van der Valk is killed. There are several levels on which this rather disquieting strategy can be understood – from Freeling's dissatisfaction with his own creation, the colourless world of the Dutch bourgeoisie, to his desire to excel in a genre already excessively melodramatic. But the explanation that is most interesting shows the inevitability of this progression and understands the shift of the detective's gender to be implicit in all of Freeling's previous categories of explanation.

Van der Valk's death occurs at the moment when he himself is most aware of the limitations of police procedure, at a time when he has decided to begin an unofficial investigation of an urban boy's anxiety over his job. Freeling begins *A Long Silence* with an almost ritualistic denunciation of the ossified Dutch legal code: 'Everything in such jobs was cut and dried, dependent upon decisions taken thirty years before'; and he uses this as the rationale for Van der Valk's decision to move, for the sake of experiment, from policeman to private detective, to perform, at least temporarily, outside of the system whose inefficacy he has fought for so many years. It is in a private capacity that he probes the jewellery business that had disturbed the teenage boy; but it is in his public role that he is killed: knowing only that 'the police are onto them', the boy and store owner contrive Van der Valk's death. Having previously joined his murder victims in imagination, or through empathy, Van der Valk finally joins them in fact. The connection always previously implied between detective and victim is carried to its furthest extreme; the investigator becomes the victim; subject and object are joined. The private nature of Van der Valk's curiosity leaves the police bureau with no official record of his investigations and thus with no formal imperative to continue them. It is this lack of responsibility, coupled with ineptitude, that leaves Arlette the task of locating her husband's killers.

But the neatness of this official neglect can be deceptive; that is, it should not be considered a coincidence that official police investigations fail Arlette van der Valk at this moment. Freeling has consistently moved in the direction of 'investigative privatism'; he has led us to understand bureaucracy to be incapable of generating a mode of understanding continuous with, and thus adequate to, its object. Van der Valk, looking at his own notebooks before his death had 'wondered what some bright young PhD ... would make of all that if he were to drop dead suddenly'. But it is no accident that it is neither a PhD nor another policeman, but his own wife, his previous helper, who becomes the palaeontologist. It is a woman who reads the most significant of Freeling's criminal texts.

Arlette, without any of Van der Valk's wavering allegiances to official procedure, immediately understands the nature of her task: to interpret her husband's notebooks in the light of his character. 'It's like a crossword – if you understand his mentality you can read the clues.' Her subsequent inquiry never rises to the threshold of official notice. Armed with memories of intimate life with Piet, aided by people from her old neighbourhood and by her own imagination, she worries it out, 'stupidly, individually, honestly, personally.' But Arlette's methodological decision is far from being a reflection of inadequacy. Having helped foster Van der Valk's scepticism, she knows precisely why the official world will hinder her:

> They were all of them, vaguely, 'important people' with high intelligence, trained minds, logical reasoning powers and frequently with various useful official connections – well, that was just what was wrong with them. They would see her problem backwards – worse still they would take it away from her.[16]

The resolution of this investigation also marks a movement towards resolution of the thematic opposites that have structured the entire series of Van der Valk mysteries. The polarisations that Freeling has so often called into play are here made explicit and dissolved – at least to an extent – into a new order: Van der Valk, the police detective, immersed in the public world that is rational, detached, overspecialised and characterised by thought and balanced judgement, falls prey to the criminal forces that most fear discovery and betrayal by those characteristics. He pays the ultimate price of investigative failure. Instead the murderers are apprehended by a woman who never emerges from private life and who works entirely from intuition, involvement and feeling. This is especially interesting in light of Freeling's final summary of Van der Valk's personality: he is considered an irresponsible man 'with a tactless lack of respect for superior mediocrities and above all, a tendency to indiscretion'; and his career is described as one containing a few 'spectacular and brilliant successes.' But in point of fact, Van der Valk's 'brilliance' has never consisted of anything more than trust in the very qualities that his wife has never questioned.

We see, then, that the dissolution of opposites – to the extent that such harmony and balance are achieved in these stories – is not complete and it is certainly not achieved through the struggles of a brilliant man with criminal intelligence. In fact we might observe that Van der Valk's successes are achieved by an elaborate role reversal, that these novels begin to neutralise the antinomies of gender and of public and private by creating a husband who becomes increasingly like the wife who, in turn, eventually pieces together the story of his death. To the extent that Van der Valk had trusted his private instincts he had always achieved remarkable success; but it must be noticed that Arlette, who in becoming a detective crosses over to the social position of her dead husband, never assumes the characteristics lauded by the world. Though Van der Valk reverses gender roles, she does not. Instead, she retains firmly engrained habits of thought and being and remains immersed in a network of private communications which lead her directly to what she wants most to know. Because the shifting of roles remains asymmetrical, we can understand these books to be records of cultural crisis. Freeling's fiction represents a world whose antinomies or dissonances are incapable of full resolution. As such, his books serve as a critique of industrial Europe's social constructs rather than a legitimisation of them.

But we should also notice that the private world does not remain without critique. Arlette, who finds her husband's killers with remarkable ease, fails to 'bring [them] to book.' That is, she cannot shape her intuitive findings into proper cultural form; she is unable to transform moral certainly into legally admissible evidence. We see, then, in Freeling's work, a fictional world where 'going by the book' is fruitless: those who adhere to rules of evidence remain caught in a solipsistic world generated by that evidence, their very procedures guaranteeing eventual failure. 'One could not press people; one never got any information that way.' But on the other hand, those who can both find and interpret illicit evidence, the readers of subterranean private life, cannot bring the guilty to book. That is, they cannot re-enter the professional world of criminal investigation, at least as that world is currently constituted.

If Van der Valk had temporarily inhabited both worlds, he had done so as a maverick, a full citizen of neither place. Arlette, who later replaces her husband as Freeling's main protagonist, eventually gives up on the official world of bureaucratic regulation altogether. In *The Widow*, the initial book of a new series featuring a remarried Arlette, Freeling almost vehemently poses Arlette not only against the police, but against almost all the agencies of the government:

And all these people we have now? School doctor, nurse, social psychiatric counsellors – there seems no end to them. . . . And would the evidence be worth much? The children don't confide in these people, whom they view as the tame auxiliaries of authority, meaning repression.

Was she the cops or the social work or the Ministry of Education? No? Then something governmental, departmental, municipal? Neither? Then, if he might ask without seeming rude, what the hell was she?[17]

But Freeling has us understand the complete viability, indeed, the full necessity of Arelette van der Valk's work: 'the private advice bureau ... functions where no competent authority exists.'

When we pose Freeling's set of concerns about the discontinuities between public and private life against the formulations of the ideal police state quoted at the opening of this essay, we can judge how distant Freeling's representation of contemporary Europe is from the omniscient police machine brought under scrutiny by Michel Foucault. If absolute surveillance remains an implicit strategy of state control, then Freeling's novels can be read as records of that goal's failure. According to him, detailed knowledge of all citizens remains, and will remain, beyond the capability of any formal government structure: he envisions a state machine increasingly desiring control and yet increasingly inept and alienated from the very citizens it hopes to police. Van der Valk, the husband and the 'bad policeman,' and later Arlette, as representatives of that private world, illustrate a deepening schism between two modes of being and knowing in the world, two modes that have, traditionally and in recent times, been associated with gender distinctions. Adrienne Rich describes those two realms in this manner:

> For fundamental to woman's oppression is the assumption that we as a group belong to the 'private' sphere of the house, the hearth, the family, the sexual, the emotional, out of which men emerge as adults to act in the 'public' arena of power, the 'real' world, and to which they return for mothering, for access to female forms of intimacy, affection, and solace unavailable in the realm of male struggle and competition.[18]

And yet we can see that this dichotomy has a very different function in Freeling's work. Where Rich looks at a social world divided into public and private as an oblique mode of women's oppression, Freeling sees in unofficial life the grounds for reclaiming a public world increasingly alienated from itself, imprisoned by ossified procedures, unable to know itself fully and thus unable to generate a viable and holistic culture.

NOTES AND REFERENCES

1. *Because of the Cats* (Harmondsworth: Penguin, 1963), p. 131.
2. *Double Barrel* (Harmondsworth: Penguin, 1964), p. 51.
3. Ibid., p. 23.
4. Ibid., p. 78.
5. *Because of the Cats*, p. 5.
6. *Double Barrel*, p. 88.
7. *A Long Silence* (Harmondsworth: Penguin, 1972), p. 16.
8. *Because of the Cats*, p. 73.
9. *Double Barrel*, pp. 64, 74.
10. *Because of the Cats*, p. 15.
11. Ibid., p. 26.
12. *King of the Rainy Country* (Harmondsworth: Penguin, 1965), p. 44.
13. *Double Barrel*, p. 13.
14. Ibid., p. 120.

15. *Tsing Boum* (Harmondsworth: Penguin, 1969), p. 120.
16. *A Long Silence*, p. 133.
17. *The Widow* (New York: Vintage Books, Random House, 1979), pp. 181, 194.
18. Adrienne Rich, *On Lies, Secrets, and Silence* (New York: W.W. Norton, 1979), p. 215.

10 Simenon and 'Le Commissaire'

· PIERRE WEISZ

Sixty years of uninterrupted production, over five hundred titles under a dozen pen names as well as his own, translations in more than thirty languages including Chinese, Serbo-Croatian, Catalan and Yiddish, *aficionados* in all parts of the world and all classes of society, Simenon's achievement seems to defy the imagination. Although his place in world literature is now secure, he still appears to some as a phenomenon rather than a great writer, André Gide, Keyserling and François Mauriac, Céline, Jean Renoir, Henry Miller and Jean Cocteau (although *not* Agatha Christie) – the list of his admirers is long and distinguished, yet Georges Simenon seems to walk under a cloud: he is, after all, a writer of crime fiction. To our great delight.

What a blessing for us, that stain on the writer's reputation! More than a stain, rather a central flaw since his first work under his own name introduced a character that was to become a legend in crime fiction, Jules Maigret, *Commissaire de la Police Judiciaire*. In spite of later achievements, Maigret is still identified with Simenon, and much more closely than Sherlock Holmes with Conan Doyle or Lord Peter with Dorothy Sayers. Crime fiction naturally lends itself to the creation of serial heroes: when Poe created Dupin, he also created a tradition. Dupin *had* to appear in the three detective stories that he wrote. *Succès oblige*. This near necessity is at the heart of the genre. Crime fiction works within a triangle formed by the victim, the criminal and the detective. Everything proceeds naturally from the crime itself with the inevitable question: 'Whodunit?' A detective story cannot be a mere puzzle without becoming intensely boring, and Poe sensed the danger after *The Purloined Letter*, making sure that he would hold his readers' attention with murders most foul – and all the more enjoyable when savoured in the depth of a good armchair by the fireside. In true Oedipal tradition, the riddle has to be a matter of life and death. The reader tries and, in the best of cases, fails. Enter the hero who unmasks the criminal, solves the problem and so brings us peace of mind.

If the author is talented, a sort of psychoanalytic transfer has taken place, and the reader will from now on crave for his favourite analyst, be it Hercule Poirot, Ellery Queen or Charlie Chan. This explains why it is difficult to accept a Raymond Chandler without Marlowe or a Stanley Gardner without Perry Mason. Conan Doyle tried to kill Holmes and had to bring him back to life. If an author tires of the hero who made him famous, he almost has to write under a new name (although Agatha Christie did successfully impose Miss Marple). The limits of the genre are indeed narrow, but the variations are infinite: total liberty within a fixed form – such is crime fiction. Success is the only valid criterion. One can understand the faint disrespect that is attached to a genre that often comes so close to a parlour game, yet at the same time, all true lovers of the art know that it has produced masterpieces.

Maigret stumbled into this closed world almost by accident and established himself in the span of a few novels. From Dupin to Nero Wolfe, from Sherlock Holmes to Father Brown, the detective is expected to be, by tradition, a 'character' in the common, non-literary sense of the word. Dupin is an exotic Frenchman, Philo Vance an aristocratic aesthete, Holmes a freakish genius with a cocaine habit, Nero Wolfe an elephantine refugee from Montenegro. Most important of all, our fictional detective is usually an amateur. If murder is to be enjoyed, it should be a hobby, not a matter of routine. Maigret upsets the apple-cart. Although not the first policeman in crime fiction, he is the first true professional to meddle with the Art of Murder. Maigret smells cop. He fills his 'plebeian frame' with blood, flesh and bones. His physical presence is imposed upon the reader as it is upon witnesses, bereaved relatives, bartenders and prostitutes: 'He had a way quite his own to stand where he was.' Whether he stays still or walks – the two main 'activities' of police work – Maigret's great asset is *being there*: '[he was] cast in one piece against which everything seemed destined to break, whether he was moving forward or just standing, set on his two legs slightly apart.' This snapshot from *Pietr-le-Letton,* which marks Maigret's first appearance in 1931, was to be polished throughout some sixty novels. Maigret's clothes, tastes, habits are so ordinary that they would pass unnoticed if Simenon did not pointedly mention them again and again, thus making *le Commissaire* a striking antithesis to the great aesthetes of detective fiction. Maigret wears a bulky overcoat, a hat; he washes down his sandwiches with cheap beer; he drinks Calvados or *gros rouge* in little neighbourhood cafés; spurning Holmes' Latakia, he fills his pipe with *gris*, the coarsest grade of French tobacco. He is a common man. Larger than most.

Simenon is playing another game but he still makes use of the old material. Crime fiction never was entirely abstract or preposterous and it did keep tabs on the real world, evolving with the times, adapting its themes and techniques to a changing environment. Conan Doyle understood the importance of material clues and the place of science in police work. Professor Locard, the French criminologist, saluted Sherlock Homes as a forerunner of modern investigative techniques. A *Commissaire de la Police Judiciaire* could hardly ignore the realities of police work. What Simenon destroys, however, is the nineteenth-century sense of wonder which equates Holmes to a magician because he can trace a mudstain or identify a footprint. Maigret uses the resources of *l'Institut Médico-Légal* as a good cop should; he even has a special relationship with Moers, the lab technician at Quai des Orfèvres. In *Maigret and his Corpse*, he follows examplary police routine by determining the occupation of the victim from his hands, his feet, his clothes. He then proceeds to find out where he lived and where he was a short time before his death. A shirt, a pair of shoes, a stain of varnish on his trousers will play their parts. Such deductions will not, however, be presented as strokes of genius: Maigret simply has to justify his procedure before his superiors. In an almost perfect parallel to the Holmes–Watson situation, Maigret patiently explains facts and conclusions to a certain Juge Coméliau who does not view crime as a hobby. The reader finds his satisfaction; he does see bits of the puzzle falling into place, but he remains in a Paris that is not a tourist's playground or a high place of culture or a faraway dreamland. In Maigret's Paris most people are at work or eating, or sleeping; if they make love, body secretions and odours are present. Maigret's great idiosyncrasy is that he can feel other people live at their own rhythms, he can experience the exhaustion of their tired bodies, taste their food, hear their heart beats. The purely technical part of his work is no concession to the genre, it is part of the physical environment which conditions the problem.

The ideal triangle is still there: a victim, a murderer, a detective, but each element is treated in a new way. The victim usually comes first, which, after all, is only natural since its very existence is the source of the problem. Most authors treat it rather casually, reserving strange and striking characteristics for the criminal whose discovery has to be a dramatic climax. Simenon reverses the process. Maigret's first task or, rather, first labour is to *know* the victim. The corpse has to talk. Sometimes it talks before being killed, sometimes after, but the information released is always essential. *Mr Gallet, Deceased*, one of Simenon's first efforts, sets the pattern in exemplary fashion: the whole book is an investigation of the mysterious Mr Gallet, a very quiet, modest person who will prove to be an extraordinary combination of misery and guile, of guilt and innocence. Maigret will uncover dark secrets about most of the characters; he will upset their peaceful lives, ruin their little schemes and, in the end, wrap up the case by showing that murderer and victim are one and the same, that Mr Gallet died a double death as he lived a double life. Most writers would not get away with it: changing murder into suicide is one of the cardinal sins of crime fiction, and *aficionados* will not forgive where archbishops might. Strangely enough, the revelation does not frustrate the reader from his pleasure. The book does contain its share of problematic hardware in the form of a self-shooting device, but it is essentially devoted to searching the soul of a man, not his pockets. The answer is not so much the solution of a riddle as the resolution of a human paradox: the deep complexity of a nondescript individual. Maigret's approach does not entirely break with tradition; he still proceeds from the known to the unknown as does every other sleuth, but the object of his inquiry is highly original: he invades a domain that had always been the *chasse-gardée* of the novel, from Balzac to Dostoievski.

Establishing the facts is still a must. Maigret is the equal of his fictional peers but he treats very casually what used to be the bread and butter of crime fiction. Smaller versions of himself, Inspectors Lucas, Torrence or Janvier, deal with the material aspects of the investigation as they are supposed to in books as well as in life. Maigret's contribution is of a subtle order. If he decides to do leg-work, it is because he chooses to do so – one of the few liberties that Simenon takes with verisimilitude. Everybody can *understand*, but Maigret must *feel* in order to *know*. This is the poetic part of Simenon's creation. Maigret attunes his senses to the world. He takes in everything – the weather, the wet cobblestones, the smell of *fricandeau à l'oseille* and even the memory of the smell of *fricandeau à l'oseille*, and he gives the reader an uncanny sense of being there, whether the place is a train station in Belgium or a court-house in Arizona. 'It was full tide and a south-west storm made the little boats knock against one another in the harbour' – we are at a fisherman's village in Brittany. 'The houses glared white in the lowering light of late afternoon' – Loire Valley. 'The way the weather was going, it would rain all day, a cold and monotonous rain, with a low sky and the lights on in all the offices, with wet tracks on the floor' – Quai des Orfèvres in the Fall. Through a miracle of a sort, the perceptions of all kinds that Maigret soaks in seem to say something to readers in all parts of the world. The French text gives a sense of inevitability and still its many translations seem to be just as effective. 'Better put on your heavy coat,' says Mme Maigret, and a Japanese or Israeli reader prepares to face a Paris winter day.

Whether it is dialogue or description, a Simenon text seems deceptively simple. It says just what it means in the most economical way. There are very few adjectives and they all belong to everyday usage; verbs are all to be found in a pocket-dictionary; nouns stand for ordinary objects, well-known concepts or common feelings. Both Simenon and Maigret believe in essentials. 'Balzac is the novelist of the clothed man, I am the novelist of the naked man,' Simenon said in a radio interview. This does not keep him from being specific, taking us with each novel on a trip to a certain neighbourhood of Paris, a particular corner of provincial France, a city, a country, each with a flavour entirely its own. So much so that Simenon was long dubbed as a novelist of 'atmosphere', until the diversity of his characters and situations and the wealth of his invention made it obvious that he was not limited to local colour.

Although there undoubtedly is a Simenon manner that pervades all his novels, it can hardly be reduced to some ingredients of time, place and weather, or to the presence of the hulking commissaire solving crimes through the ingestion of vast quantities of food and beverages. It is rather characterised by the way Simenon uses his material, by the delicate balance he maintains between the various elements. He is very close to tradition and miles away at the same time. This is well illustrated by the difference between Maigret and Rex Stout's Nero Wolfe. A delightful heavyweight in his own right, Nero Wolfe also attaches deserved importance to what he eats and manages to eat very well indeed. But Wolfe is a gourmet. As we are treated to his table and share his sometimes simple but always delectable meals, we cannot help thinking that we are being 'entertained', that his faultless taste is part of a set of clever narrative devices. Maigret certainly knows his food but he picks it as best he can, like most of us. A Maigret novel often starts with the good news that Mme Maigret is preparing a great *cassoulet* for the commissaire's enjoyment, only to see him frustrated from his meal by some fulsome crime. For two hundred pages, Maigret carries in his head, nostrils and taste-buds the false memory of a summit of *cuisine bourgeoise* while gobbling stale sandwiches or greasy fries. Even the sacred monthly dinner at Dr Pardon's house will occasionally be interrupted by some unwitting criminal who, having disturbed one of the chief elements of order in this universe (Beef Bourguignon, that is), will thus have sealed his own fate. Every investigation is placed under the sign of a certain dish, a particular liquor or both. There are ham sandwich investigations, *rouelle-de-veau* investigations, sauerkraut investigations, some washed down with cheap beer, others laced with dry white wine, or digested with the help of a sturdy Burgundy. Every shot of Calvados, every gulp of brandy, every glass of vermouth adds to the commissaire's and our intimate, intuitive knowledge of some corner of Paris, some village in Normandy, some man with a knife in his chest or in his hand. Maigret eats it all, drinks it all and, in the end, knows it all. The body and the universe, we might say.

This appeal to our basic senses is no empty exercise; it brings us close to Maigret instead of setting him apart from the crowd as the 'great detective'. Maigret is not guided by a particular method or theory but rather by a deep-rooted feeling that all men are mirrored in each and every man. He will be able to solve his case only if he can apprehend the victim, the criminal, and their mutual relationship from the inside. This has little to do with the idea, sometimes expressed by other fictional sleuths like Hercule

Poirot, that the victim brought about his own fate. Simenon's murders are not the sanction of imprudent behaviour or light-headed rashness; they generally occur at the end of a causal chain, but that chain is so long that it is hardly possible to speak of cause and effect. A subtle interplay between chance and determinism, between freedom and fate results in a death, and there is no way to pin down any of these entities as the 'cause': two human beings crossed paths and a murder 'happened'; it cannot be ascribed to accidental circumstances, but individual responsibility seems inadequate to explain it. No spur of activity of the 'little grey cells' will deliver the guilty party.

This is why, aside from the investigation proper, Maigret usually goes into a sort of crisis of identification with both the victim and the killer. He immerses himself in the environment and opens up the gates of perception. The more important side of his work does not take place on the intellectual level. To questions about the case in hand, he usually answers with 'I never have ideas' or 'I do not believe anything'. Although he follows an intuitive path, he certainly does not solve his case through intuition: such a reversal of the rules of the genre would not be too effective and would leave the reader dissatisfied. In Simenon, the intuitive element does not replace logic, it is part of it; it puts Maigret on the right track without muddying up the issue. If the old comparison of the bloodhound applies to one sleuth, it is to Maigret. A complicated bloodhound, though, a human blood-hound whose perceptions go further than the sense of smell. Maigret knows that everything is both simpler and more complex than it looks. The simpler aspects are the causal chain that leads up to a murder, the more complex ones lie in the motivations. Maigret shifts the centre of gravity of crime fiction from the *who* and *how* to the *why*.

Local colour is thus not a device but an essential component of Simenon's novels. All authors of crime fiction situate every misdeed or murder in a world of its own; with Simenon, it is just as important to investigate that world as it is to solve the puzzle. This shift of focus changes all the rules. Simenon does not even have to start with a murder: the intimation of murder is enough. He does not have to wait till the last chapter to unmask the criminal: 'Whodunit?' is not the question. So we sometimes see Maigret looking for the victim even before the crime has been committed. We know that a crime is pending; we know that, contrary to thriller tradition, Maigret will be unable to prevent that crime, but we relish another kind of suspense based on character rather than events. In *Maigret et son mort*, for instance, if Maigret can learn enough about the future victim who calls him at intervals on the telephone, we know that he will be able to capture the killer. In *Maigret et le client du samedi*, we have the same pattern and quite another novel: the motivations, the setting, the characters are entirely different, but the main clue still is in the victim. At other times, the killer himself talks to Maigret for the better part of the book. Another kind of challenge: will Maigret find the words that will bring him to surrender? Usually, Maigret adopts a quietly amoral attitude: he is no judge; he is the perfect listener, gently encouraging the other fellow to go on talking and eventually to stumble on the only solution, which is to give himself up. Quite often, Maigret and the killer come face to face at Maigret's home. They talk and drink and a sort of complicity is established. Two members of the human race have to recognise their bonds in order for peace to be restored.

We could look at Maigret's cases from three main viewpoints: those where the investigation is confined to a well-defined environment; those where it has to go beyond those limits; those where it has to reach into the past in order to unearth a deeply buried secret. In the closed-field variety, the approach is, so to speak, horizontal. Maigret spreads his inspectors as well as his mental tentacles throughout a certain *milieu* and, having sifted clues and weighed characters, comes up with a solution that will satisfy both logic and psychology. The interest is focused on the individual in his 'natural' environment: the intimacy of the family in *Maigret se trompe*, the network of interferences between personal and professional relations in *Maigret et le marchand de vin*, the chance association of some soldiers on a binge in *Maigret chez le Coroner*. Maigret performs his task in a very static way: he mainly stands or sits around. The open-field variety, on the contrary, shows a sort of quest. The criminal is lost in the crowd and Maigret has to ferret him out. He walks. The investigation spreads to a broader group or area. This is the occasion for us to discover the hidden realities of a supposedly familiar world. Such is *Maigret et son mort*, where the commissaire takes us through the Marais quarter of Paris, with its refugees from central Europe. The third category shows Maigret travelling in time: a 'vertical' approach. The present does not seem to hold the answers to his questions; he has to go into the past, just as he would go to another part of town or take a trip to another country in order to get the evidence. Material clues play an essential part here. Some discrepancy will put Maigret on the trail, he will start digging into the past of the victim, he will discover past associations, the memory of friends that would be better forgotten, of a sin that never led to atonement; a motive will finally emerge, a mask will crack. We could see *Maigret in New York* and many others in this light.

Needless to say, Simenon did not write novels in order for us to classify them. Most of the time, there is no definite border between novels of various moods. The restricted group, the small town, the emergence of the past; if one element is dominant, all are generally present at the same time. It is difficult to treat Simenon in a systematic way. Just as Maigret will not confine himself to a 'method', Simenon will not let himself be pinned down under a critic's magnifying glass. We have to open up, to take in what we are given. Perhaps one fruitful approach would be to extend Maigret's special relationship with his murderers and victims to include the author and the reader. Is there, in this respect, something peculiar to the work of Simenon that makes it different from the rest of crime fiction? The detective novel has always given a special place to the reader by inviting him to match wits with the sleuth. Most stories reach a point where it is theoretically possible to solve the case and, although authors play with a stacked deck, the reader usually lets himself be drawn into the game. This trait is unique in the field of art in so far as it challenges the public to participate in the creation itself. Perhaps this is the reason why so many addicts of fiction feel the itch to write a detective novel. Simenon does not elicit exactly the same responses. There is a body, a crime, a puzzle, and we do want an answer, but we rarely try to second-guess Maigret. The game he plays is so close to life that it has no fixed rules; the puzzle he is putting together is so complicated that it can be arranged into different pictures. We are quite content to put our trust into the good commissaire and let him assume the burden. Burden of proof it is not, but burden of guilt. Every Simenon novel shows that the line is thin between criminal and victim, so much so that Maigret sometimes does not bother to deliver a killer to justice. Crime and punishment are identified to each other, a lesson that we also received from other quarters. It is not too much to say that there is an affinity between Simenon and Dostoievski. A Simenon novel differs from 'serious literature' in only one way: it accepts the conventions of a genre by replacing analysis with formal investigation. We might say that Simenon has created a new genre which combines two apparently irreconcilable approaches to literature.

The Maigret–Simenon relationship falls in with the tradition of the mainstream novel rather than that of crime fiction, which is not surprising since Simenon concentrates on character rather than oddities. Maigret's personal habits, his love for little cafés, his closeness to people of all callings and descriptions, his taste for the simpler pleasures of life are direct transpositions of Simenon's own tastes and idiosyncrasies. Maigret's investigations, his travels, his encounters always run parallel to Simenon's own experiences. Although sequences might be different, Maigret's biography would very much read like the author's. Maigret, however, is no duplicate of Simenon. His 'job', in the first place, is different. A writer (or a man in the street) can take his time analysing characters; a detective has to conclude his inquiry. The natural limits of the genre impose a certain one-sidedness on Maigret, a quantitative rather than a qualitative difference. There are, however, differences of another order.

There is an aloofness about Maigret which is certainly not shared by Simenon. He keeps the world at a distance. He understands all passions and vices but seems immune to them. If not entirely innocent, his pleasures are none the less severely limited to those that will not shock bourgeois morality. Mme Maigret is a provider of good food and tender care, but a mistress she is not. Maigret, 'who always regretted not having a child', goes to the conjugal bed only to get a restful sleep. He, who penetrates the most carefully hidden secrets in the sexual life of others, will not ever yield to the temptation of the flesh. The closest hint that he is not totally indifferent to sex is a touch of jealousy he feels when a prostitute falls in love with a criminal from whom Maigret expected her to worm out information. Apparently a curious return to the old values of crime fiction, which forbade the hero to engage in such lowly matters as sex and love. The reasons, however, are quite different. Crime fiction used to sacrifice the human element to the intellectual pleasure of solving riddles. A Simenon novel, based on opposite principles, generally has its share of sex and love, often described in starkly naturalistic style, but they exist for the reader's sake, not the

Commissaire's, whose function it is to bring order to the world. The priest is not supposed to dally with the parishioner he is confessing; the analyst is not supposed to join the patient on the couch.

Simenon has been reproached by some bilious critics with rehashing his material and churning out his novels like so many hot cakes. To the sympathetic reader the astounding abundance of his production does not seem repetitive. It is true that the general trend of his novels is predictable, but it reminds one of five-finger exercises composed by a master. Is it coincidence if Simenon is a great admirer of Bach? Old Johann-Sebastian did not lose his genius while composing for Anna-Magdalena. In the post-war period of the Maigret saga, Simenon collects vignettes. The virtuoso is using his well-honed technique for his own pleasure and ours. There is no artificiality in these *pièces de circonstance*. Simenon always keeps to what he knows, emotions, anecdotes, countries, people. In mature life, he discovers humour, which certainly does not diminish him.

It would be unfair to leave Simenon without saying a word on his non-Maigret novels. A Simenon novel without Maigret does not essentially differ from his detective stories. It also is an attempt to capture the 'naked' man, but this time without a go-between. It is, most of the time, a confession in the first person. Freed from the conventions of crime fiction, Simenon goes deeper in his analysis and covers a broader spectre of themes. Revolt, hatred or ancient sin does not always lead to murder, since the accent is more on analysis than on detection. It still is a sort of investigative literature, involving the reader and inviting him to discover a certain logic of feeling and passion.

Throughout his long career, Georges Simenon has shown rare unity of inspiration. He has succeeded in the paradoxical endeavour to bring together two genres that were apparently impossible to reconcile. We can understand Agatha Christie, who once refused to comment on his talent: their approaches to literature are so different that they hardly belong to the same trade. Crime fiction changed a lot since Commissaire Maigret made his first appearance in the 1930s. Writers like Raymond Chandler and Dashiell Hammett have also brought a valuable contribution, bringing it closer to the great current of realism which started in the nineteenth century. In Simenon's own words, it has introduced 'a new way to look at man'.

BIBLIOGRAPHY

Adam, vol. 34, nos 328–30, 1969 (special issue on Georges Simenon).

Lacassin, Francis and Sigaux Gilbert, *Simenon* (Paris: Plon, 1973).

Narcejac, Thomas, *Esthétique du roman policier* (Paris: Le Portulan, 1947).

Ritzen, Quentin, *Simenon, Avocat des hommes* (Paris: Le Livre Contemporain, 1961).

Stéphane, Roger, *Le Dossier Simenon* (Paris: 1961).

CHRONOLOGY

Dates of first publication (the Maigret texts and translations):

	ORIGINAL TITLE
1931	*M. Gallet decédé* (Fayard)
1931	*Le Pendu de Saint-Pholien* (Fayard)
1931	*Le Charretier de la Providence* (Fayard)
1931	*Le Chien jaune* (Fayard)
1931	*Pietr-le-Letton* (Fayard)
1931	*La Nuit de carrefour* (Fayard)
1931	*Un Crime en Hollande* (Fayard)
1931	*Au Rendez-vous des terre-neuvas* (Fayard)
1931	*La Tête d'un homme* (Fayard)
1931	*La Danseuse du Gai-Moulin* (Fayard)
1931	*La Guinguette à deux sous* (Fayard)
1932	*L'Ombre Chinoise* (Fayard)
1933	*L'Affaire Saint-Fiacre* (Fayard)
1932	*Chez les Flamands* (Fayard)
1932	*Le Fou de Bergerac* (Fayard)
1932	*Le Port des brumes* (Fayard)
1932	*Liberty Bar* (Fayard)
1933	*L'Écluse no. 1* (Fayard)
1934	*Maigret* (Fayard)
1943	*Maigret revient* (Cécile est morte; Les Caves du Majestic; La Maison du juge) (N.R.F.)
1944	*Signé Picpus* (L'Inspecteur cadavre; Félicité est là) (N.R.F.)
1944	*Les Nouvelle enquêtes de Maigret* (N.R.F.)
1946	*La Pipe de Maigret, et 'Maigret se fâche'*, (Presses de la Cité)
1946	*Maigret a New-York*, (Presses de la Cité)
1947	*Maigret et l'Inspecteur malchanceux*, (Presses de la Cité)
1948	*Maigret et son mort*, (Presses de la Cité)
1948	*Les Vacances de Maigret*, (Presses de la Cité)
1949	*La Première enquête de Maigret*, (Presses de la Cité)
1949	*Mon Ami Maigret*, (Presses de la Cité)
1949	*Maigret chez le coroner*
1958	*Maigret et la vieille dame*
950	*L'Amie de Madame Maigret*

1950	*Maigret et les petits cochons sans queue*
1950	*Les Mémoires de Maigret*
1951	*Un Noël de Maigret*
1951	*Maigret au Picratt's*
1951	*Maigret en meublé*
1951	*Maigret et la grande perche*
1952	*Maigret, Lognon et les gangsters*
1952	*Le Revolver de Maigret*
1953	*Maigret et l'homme du banc*
1953	*Maigret a peur*
1953	*Maigret se trompe*
1954	*Maigret à l'école*
1954	*Maigret et la jeune morte*
1954	*Maigret chez le ministre*
1955	*Maigret et le corps sans tête*
1955	*Maigret tend un piège*
1956	*Un Échec de Maigret*
1957	*Maigret s'amuse*
1958	*Maigret voyage*
1958	*Les Scrupules de Maigret*
1959	*Maigret et les témoins récalcitrants*
1959	*Une Confidence de Maigret*
1960	*Maigret aux Assises*
1960	*Maigret et les vieillards*
1961	*Maigret et le voleur paresseux*
1962	*Maigret et les braves gens*
1962	*Maigret et le client de samedi*
1963	*Maigret et le clochard*
1963	*La Colère de Maigret*
1964	*Maigret et le fantôme*
1964	*Maigret se défend*
1965	*La Patience de Maigret*
1967	*Maigret et l'affaire Nahour*
1967	*Le Voleur de Maigret*
1968	*Maigret à Vichy*
1968	*Maigret hésite*
1968	*L'Ami d'enfance de Maigret*
1969	*Maigret et le tueur*
1970	*Maigret et le marchand de vin*
1970	*La Folle de Maigret*
1971	*Maigret et l'homme tout seul*
1971	*Maigret et l'indicateur*
1972	*Maigret et Monsieur Charles*

TRANSLATION

1932	*The Death of Monsieur Gallet*
1932	*The Crime of Inspector Maigret*
1934	*The Crime at Lock 14*
1939	*A Face for a Clue*

1969	*Maigret and the Minister*
1970	*(Maigret and the Calame Report)*
1967	*Maigret and the Headless Corpse*
1965	*Maigret Sets a Trap*
1962	*Maigret's Failure*
1957	*Maigret's Little Joke*
1958	*(None of Maigret's Business)*
1974	*Maigret and the Millionaires*
1958	*Maigret Has Scruples*
1959	*Maigret and the Reluctant Witnesses*
1968	*Maigret Has Doubts*
1959	*The Short Cases of Inspector Maigret*
1961	*Maigret in Court*
1962	*Maigret in Society*
1963	*Maigret and the Lazy Burglar*
1964	*Maigret and the Saturday Caller*
1973	*Maigret and the Dosser*
1973	*(Maigret and the Bum)*
1965	*Maigret Loses His Temper*
1966	*Maigret on the Defensive*
1966	*The Patience of Maigret*
1967	*Maigret and the Nahour Case*
1968	*Maigret's Pickpocket*
1969	*Maigret in Vichy*
1969	*(Maigret Takes the Waters)*
1968	*Maigret Hesitates*
1970	*Maigret's Boyhood Friend*
1971	*Maigret and the Killer*
1971	*Maigret and the Wine Merchant*
1972	*Maigret and the Madwoman*
1975	*Maigret and the Loner*
1972	*Maigret and the Flea*
1973	*(Maigret and the Informer)*
1973	*Maigret and Monsieur Charles*

Various novels also published in English under variant titles. All titles from 1946 onwards are published by Presses de la Cité.

11 The Education of Martin Beck

BERNARD BENSTOCK

Rarely has the detective fiction subgenre, despite its solid base within popular culture, been employed as a medium of social comment, although like genre painting and other second-level art forms it often mirrors with precise accuracy facets of the known world. Inadvertent sociological observations and the political predilections of individual authors have frequently surfaced in crime literature, particularly because it does pretend to deal with an aberrant stain in existing society, and certain political events have on occasion had their impact on crime novels. The Swedish wife–husband writing team of Maj Sjöwall and Per Wahlöö, however, set out in their Martin Beck series purposely to examine the condition of Sweden's society through the detective story medium, and their ten novels, published between 1965 and 1975 (ending with Wahlöö's death), are a progress through the changes in the effects of the famous 'Middle Way' policies that have governed the nation for four decades. Much that occurred in Sweden during that decade brought those policies into question, and in 1976 the Socialists were voted out of office, a year after the last Beck book culminated in the assassination of the prime minister by a 'welfare child'.

Nothing in the Beck novels would ever give the impression of a sociological tract: political elements emerge subtly and discreetly and develop intrinsically from the plot materials and the conditions of the ageing members of Beck's police. The often restrictive conventions of the crime genre are adhered to by the Wahlöös with apparently effortlessness, and if any single factor impresses the casual reader of their novels, it is the enormity of the violent act that triggers the activity of the Martin Beck squad. The naked body of a raped woman is dredged up inadvertently from a canal (*Roseanna*); pre-pubescent girls are found raped

189

and strangled with their own jump-ropes in park playgrounds, where aged mugging victims have been severely bludgeoned as well (*The Man on the Balcony*); all nine passengers in a city bus are machine-gunned to death in a late-night rainstorm (*The Laughing Policeman*); a house explodes into flames while under police surveillance, several survivors jumping naked out of windows into a cold winter night (*The Fire Engine that Disappeared*); a business tycoon is shot at a dinner party in an elegant hotel, falling face down into the mashed potatoes (*Murder at the Savoy*); a police official, terminally ill in a hospital room, is viciously slashed to death with a bayonet in the dead of night (*The Abominable Man*); the putrid corpse of a recluse is discovered in an overheated room several months after death (*The Locked Room*); a compliant woman, expecting sexual advances, is strangled instead and gratuitously punched in the groin after her death (*Cop Killer*); a dictator's car is blown up along with various onlookers and police horses during a state visit, his head landing in the lap of a police official (*The Terrorists*). Such highly sensational touches, even to the extent of the ludicrous and the grotesque, are characteristic features in a Beck novel, with only *The Man Who Went Up in Smoke* offering an unsensational initial circumstance, the disappearance of a Swedish traveller in Hungary, whose murder is eventually disclosed as barely more than accidental.

The sensation of horror is invariably balanced by a comic flair that often proves hilariously absurd. In *Roseanna* a murder suspect, easily exonerated under questioning, none the less talks himself into a burglary confession; in *The Man on the Balcony* professional psychologists attest that the murderer is either (a) oversexed or (b) undersexed; in *Murder at the Savoy* Beck immediately spots the secret police agent assigned to his case – he wears the most ostentatiously garish clothes; in *Cop Killer* the only fatality in a bloody shoot-out is that of a policeman stung by wasps when he hides in a ditch, giving the title of the book an ironic twist. The wildest humour is occasioned by the various 'Keystone Kops' on the force, particularly the radio car team of Kvant and Kristiansson, who invariably run afoul of the explosive Inspector Larsson and become his personal *bêtes noires*. When they accidentally apprehend the Balcony Man about to commit his fourth sex-murder, it is only because they have stopped in a wooded area to relieve themselves against a tree; when they discover the bus massacre it is only because they have purposely strayed out of their assigned area in order to avoid anything that might interfere with their going off duty in a few minutes (and they obliterate all footprints with an enormous number of their own). In *The Fire Engine* they fail to report a false alarm, obfuscating the crime; in *Murder at the Savoy* they fail to apprehend a murder suspect when they misinterpret as a personal insult a comment that has nothing to do with them. Yet a Larsson dressing-down is not the ultimate punishment: Kvant is killed in *The Abominable Man*, Kristiansson wounded, and when the latter recovers he is teamed with an overenthusiastic Kenneth Kvasto, a bane to his determination to avoid any confrontation with trouble.

Incompetent cops of various types augment the duo of K and K, especially the cloddish Bo Zachrisson, who at one instance is discovered by a furious Larsson to be moonlighting as a janitor. Zachrisson has a penchant for firing off his gun, once emptying it at an embezzler but succeeding only in hitting Larsson's shoeheel; in *The Locked Room* he wounds a police dog and hits a steam pipe, inundating and scalding the entire stake-out squad. Larsson's expensive clothes are ruined in this escapade, as they so often are throughout his expoloits, especially since he insists on crashing through locked doors. In the final novel, when all of the Stockholm police and recruits from all the outlying areas are massed against the potential assassination of an American senator (heavily based on Barry Goldwater), Larsson takes the precaution of assembling all the dangerously incompetent and assigning them where they can do no damage. But the chief superintendent, a political appointee, mistakes the list marked 'CS' by Larsson (for Clod Squad) as the 'commando section', and delegates them to guard the senator and the prime minister of Sweden, resulting in the death of the latter. Rarely are horror and humour separated from each other in the Beck novels.

As intricately convoluted as are the plotlines in the Wahlöö books, the major emphasis, as in the best detective fiction, is on the detective – and in this case the detectives. Beck's team as such has certain constants and many variables, and as a unit undergoes significant transformations. It begins with Kollberg and Melander, with whom Beck works particularly well, and Kollberg remains Beck's closest friend throughout, despite changes in their professional relationship. Melander is an odd character, and although valued for his prodigious memory, he never is drawn into the personal relationships that are so important in the sociographic structure of the Beck team. The second novel, where Beck travels to Hungary, leaves the Stockholm component with only ancillary functions in the case, but with the third the team seems fully established. To Kollberg and Melander are added Gunvald Larsson (a decidedly hostile element), the insignificant Rönn, and the vacationing Stenström, with Hammar named as chief superintendent. But Beck has been promoted to superintendent, separating him from Kollberg and Melander (with whom he is none the less reunited for this case). Stenström, however, is one of the victims of the machine-gunning in *The Laughing Policeman*, and the unit coheres to solve the case, producing the most concentrated activities in which every member plays an important role, even 'visiting' police contribute a particular 'find', and Stenström himself has left behind a final discovery that is put into place. Only the bigoted Ullholm, not part of the team and destined for the Clod Squad, fails to do his bit.

In *The Fire Engine* the group is directly labelled 'Hammar's team', consisting of Beck, Kollberg, Melander, Rönn (Hammar, however, is slated soon for retirement, an omen of eventual disintegration of the cohesive unit). Despite that integral group the real operatives who solve the crime are Larsson, the forensic expert Hjelm, Benny Skacke (Stenström's replacement), and Per Månsson, the inspector in Malmö, who had previously assisted Beck. The venue moves to Malmö in the sixth book, Beck sent down to supervise the investigation (Månsson assisting, along with Skacke, who had been transferred). In Stockholm meanwhile, Kollberg is enlisted much against his will to carry on the local part of the search, along with an equally reluctant Larsson, and Stenström's fiancée, now with the Vice Squad. Divisions within the team are apparent by their geographical separations, but also by the mutual antipathy of Kollberg and Larsson, the latter an increasingly important operative.

Serious elements of disintegration are discerned in *The Abominable Man*, where a disaffected former policeman sets out to assassinate various police officials, some 'abominable' and some (like Beck) commendable. It is certainly the bleakest, most despondent of the Wahlöö novels, and Beck is left for dead – the assassin's bullet in his chest – at the conclusion. Kollberg, who had been seriously stabbed at the end of *The Fire Engine* and has totally lost his already jaded taste for police work, once again finds himself having to work closely with Larsson, and it is Larsson who emerges as the undisputed hero of the book. (Beck, on the other hand, is teamed with Rönn, whose abilities he never rated highly.) Although *The Locked Room* is something of a comic romp after the sombre predecessor, convalescent Beck is almost completely abstracted out of it, devoting his time to a minor case that proves to be connected with the major one undertaken by Larsson, Kollberg and Rönn. As a comic opening for *Cop Killer*, a relatively relaxed detective story, Beck and Kollberg are reunited, but in ill-fitting uniforms as a radio car team on a stake-out, humiliatingly recognised and scoffed at by the burglar—murderer they cannot manage to catch red-handed. Beck is soon displaced from Stockholm again, finding himself on a murder case down in the country, while Skacke finds himself uncomfortably having to work with Kollberg, whose stabbing he feels clumsily responsible for, precipitating his transfer. Gunvald Larsson, meanwhile, self-willed and obstinate as ever, but a highly effective police officer, is now a chief inspector, a promotion the unpopular and abrasive Larsson had given up on.

That Kollberg finally resigns from the force at the end of *Cop Killer* (replaced by Benny Skacke), pausing just long enough in the handing in of his letter of resignation to put the final piece of the puzzle in place, leaves Beck a tired and lonely police official in the final novel, and once again the target of an assassin frustrated by Beck's brilliant manoeuvre in preventing the killing of the American senator. Kollberg, who had many years ago accidentally killed a man in the line of duty, and has since never carried a gun despite the dangers and the regulations, is now at work as a part-time sorter of guns in the Army Museum and proves useful in that capacity to Martin Beck. But more important is the permanent friendship that remains for the two of them as the last book closes. In the long interim between *Roseanna* and *The Terrorists* many changes had taken place in Beck's life outside his job in the the police, and the rapport with Lennart Kollberg has been the one constant factor.

The Martin Beck that we first met was a vaguely unhappy man, disappointed with his wife and distanced from his young children, easily prone to catching cold and discomforted by the coffee he drank, with aversions to riding the subway and to driving a car. That he is wrenched away from the beginning of a tranquil family vacation to fly to Hungary in *The Man Who Went Up in Smoke* is highly annoying, yet his stay in Budapest proves idyllic, and he returns after solving the case with no great enthusiasm for the restored vacation. In the third book he invents a reason to go to Motala, just to get away from his nagging wife, and even contemplates sleeping on the living-room divan when back at home. The latter becomes a reality in the fourth book, and while he confesses to himself a dislike for his son as well, he has established a better relationship with his daughter Ingrid. When she considers herself to be old enough, Ingrid moves out, suggesting that her father do the same. Over the length of several books, then, Beck evolves into a bachelor, living alone, with his digestion improved, and even spends a night at the Savoy in bed with the former fiancée of the dead Stenström – two lonely people finding momentary gratification together.

The grim *Abominable Man* contains fewer personal elements than any of the other novels, although it opens with Beck and his daughter having a restaurant meal together in a prelapsarian tranquillity before the horrors begin. In *The Locked Room* the unhappy and dream-troubled Beck is at loose ends, feeling trapped and forced to give up smoking, almost regretting having left his wife. Even his one non-vocational interest, sailing ships and naval battles, has become jejune, and his mother, whom he had previously visited on occasion, is now in a nursing home, and obviously near death. While involved with his insignificant murder case Beck meets Rhea Nielsson, a strong-minded, independent and socially committed woman, with whom he glides into a relaxed and rewarding love affair. Separated from her during his case in southern Sweden (*Cop Killer*), he keeps in telephone contact, realising that he is in love with Rhea. In the ultimate volume she plays a part in relation to the terrorist plot Beck is in charge of preventing, identifying the assassin after a casual crossing of paths, but more importantly saving Beck's life (although neither of them ever will ever know it): Beck's queasiness at the prospect of a long car trip results in his staying in Stockholm the night that the frustrated hit man stakes out his flat, but it is the naked Rhea whom he sites with rifle through the window, eventually deciding against squeezing the trigger. Had she not been with Beck, Heydt would have gunned him down in revenge. *The Terrorists* ends with a joyous New Year celebration consisting of Kollberg, his wife, Martin Beck and Rhea, after Beck has tracked Heydt down at the border.

A decade or so of Beck's life, roughly between the ages of forty and fifty, unfolds during the ten volumes, and although just a thin cord of personal continuity, these events bind all aspects of the professional circumstances into a tight fabric. At no time in the Wahlöö books is criminal investigation conducted by characterless bloodhounds, but as Beck's life is interwoven with his police work, so is even the least of his associates a human entity in operation. Kollberg marries and settles into a life of sexual pleasure, good eating and child-rearing, getting fat in the process and disenchanted with his work. Melander has developed a reputation for being more often in the washroom than in his office; Skacke devotes himself diligently to a career leading to commissioner of police, marrying Monica along the way without letting his private life interfere with his ambitions; Månsson has become a weekend husband with a bachelor flat during the week, and when his love affair in Copenhagen becomes too much of a good thing, he ends it to return to his 'balanced' life. Larsson has broken with his upper-crust background, left-leaning in his politics and sexually puritanical, yet meticulous in his fashionable clothes and East German sports car. With Rönn, also something of an outcast in the department, he has formed a close friendship outside their professional orbit, going off on quiet fishing vacations in the north, and when he and Beck discover that neither one of them has ever killed in their entire police careers, a bond begins to form between the two enemies: what began as a team of Beck–Melander–Kollberg has evolved into a team of Beck–Larsson–Rönn based on new awarenesses of mutual respect.

Looking back from the perspective of the completed series, the first two books are almost peaceful and idyllic. They are both summer books, and although Roseanna's body is dredged up from the river, precipitating the criminal investigation for her sexually repressed murderer, it was from a leisurely floating pleasure cruise that she had disappeared. Beck and Ahlberg, his regional counterpart, dedicate themselves to solving the crime and become confirmed friends in the process. The pursuit drags on from the summer murder through the autumn investigation and the winter capture: time is not a factor and normal life remains constant despite the murder case. Identifying the body is accomplished by Interpol, and Beck establishes telephone contact with an American police captain, Elmer Kafka of Lincoln, Nebraska, who assists in dredging up background information on the sexually assertive and independent victim. The seemingly hopeless narrowing down of suspects (passenger lists are inadequate for a boat that takes on casual deck passengers without reservations) becomes possible through a fine bit of reasoning which brings in all the casual photos taken by the various passengers, and an unknown man is discovered in the background with Roseanna. Even when Bengtsson is isolated, and a convincing profile of him established, there is no way of proving his guilt except through entrapment: the precision-timed trap with an enticing policewoman as bait captures him, although the vagaries of ordinary events interfere to foil her rescue almost completely. None the less, despite the heinous crime and the diligent police work, life seems to go on regularly and decently. The crime seems only an individual aberration, rather than diagnostic of social malaise, the unfortunate bringing together of the sexually aggressive woman and sexually disturbed man, a confrontation that was sheer accident in an otherwise logical world.

In *The Man Who Went Up in Smoke* a mildly disgruntled Beck is deprived of his summer vacation (on an island with his family) and sent to a Budapest that proves to be near-paradise: Old World charm, tranquillity in a crime-free Communist country, good food and warm weather, pleasant people throughout, and beautiful, old-fashioned boats – a Beck passion. The irritant, however, is that a Swedish journalist has disappeared in Budapest without a trace, and his editor threatens to publicise the case and cause diplomatic embarrassments. Beck unofficially is sent to investigate quietly, but under a rigid time-restriction, and he manages to unearth an ugly situation: three Germans (a nymphomaniac, a latent homosexual and a manic–depressive) have been involved with the Swede in a complex drug-dealing network, using Hungary (where such dealings would never be suspected) as a conduit, and Beck is almost killed by them in their attempt to cover up their criminal business. This is the first indication of a condition that will be found throughout the Beck novels, prising up the rock that reveals the horrors crawling under it. But as in *Roseanna* the latent horror is in sharp contrast with an otherwise halcyon world, where Beck meets his Budapest counterpart, the highly efficient and low-keyed Vilmos Szluka (a nice balance for the American Kafka) who saves his life. The murder of the journalist, however, has strictly Swedish origins, and police teamwork succeeds in apprehending his killer. But Beck derives no satisfaction from arresting Åke Gunnarsson and preventing his suicide, since the murderer is demonstratively a better person than the despicably abusive drunkard of a drug-dealer, and the homicide basically accidental (the cover-up even brilliant). Whereas unfortunate coincidence sparked the horror in *Roseanna*, an unavoidable and unfair set of circumstances here serve to mar an otherwise decent world – circumstances that flare forth overwhelmingly in the successive books.

The Man on the Balcony immediately posits two crimes occurring simultaneously and threatening to continue at an accelerated pace. They are crimes in the parks and playground of Stockholm, paradise not only lost but violated. Beck's surreptitious vacation to visit Ahlberg (a last respite in the pastoral environs of the Roseanna case) returns him to confront the spectres of the sadistic mugger and the sex-murderer of children. Every adult male is now a potential child-rapist and killer, and even when the criminal is known and pursued, an innocent look-alike is mistakenly snared in the police dragnet while the real murderer is about his business stalking a fourth victim. Police work here depends upon the fingering by a jealous mistress of the mugger (in bed with a compliant, Roseanna-like alternate); the mugger giving evidence inadvertently against the more heinous criminal; the almost inarticulate child who had held on to a train ticket; a forgotten crank call that complained of a man on a balcony behaving mysteriously; a policeman accident-ally spotting the crank in a pastry shop; and the two absurd policemen urinating in the woods and having their attention drawn to the real villain and his prospective victim. Vicious crime, however, is not the only symptom of the post-Edenic world: Beck is depressed by the new location of his office; anti-American demonstrations over the Vietnam war are breaking out; technical advances in police tactics fail to offset the waves of crime; there are signs that the welfare state is failing in its care of the needy; vigilantes among the middle classes are taking the law into their own hands, and Kollberg is attacked by them in a park, mistaken for the dangerous offender, and for the first time he is threatening to leave the police department.

Intimations of something rotten in the Swedish state explode into grotesque horrors and chaos in *The Laughing Policeman* with the most startling opening in any crime story. That the mass machine-gunning occurs on the last run of the bus during a torrential downpour co-ordinates time and the elements in a near apocalypse. All occasions inform against Beck and his squad: he himself has moved out of his wife's bed; Kollberg is fat and flabby; Rönn a decided mediocrity constantly rubbing his red nose; Melander a bore and a skinflint; Larsson misanthropic and bullying; and the dead Stenström's fiancée distraught. (The one fortunate circumstance is that the squad functions extraordinarily well, with nine distinct achievements by nine of the operatives in resolving the case.) The complexities of the case, however, are manifold: identifying all nine victims, tracing their lives back to possible causes for this particular crime (and in doing so, the rock has been prised up again and various crimes, misdemeanours and unpleasantnesses uncovered). The *clou* is an unsolved murder sixteen years old, so that the two cases intertwine, and the obvious assumption is that the old one was committed by a sex-maniac and the new one by a maniac. Both hypotheses prove wrong when Beck confronts the solid businessman who had killed a nymphomaniac, an embarrassing hindrance to his impending marriage, and sixteen years later eliminates both the blackmailing accomplice and the tenacious policeman that had got on his trail, obfuscating the double murder by accounting for seven other casual victims to cover his tracks. That he had done the mass killing with a machine-gun used in the Finnish War, in which he boasts that he wiped out three Bolsheviks, adds a political note that will become increasingly important as the series develops.

Unrelenting winter has set in with *The Fire Engine that Disappeared*, where the opening scene is almost as magnificent as in the preceding novel: Larsson on surveillance on a freezing night sees the house he is watching explode into flames, and he manages to catch several people jumping or thrown out of the windows, some children, some horribly in flames, some stark naked. A public hero now, Larsson refuses to allow the case of accidental fire to remain closed, devoting himself to a thorough investigation that unearths cases of prostitution and drug dealings. Whereas he and Skacke are energetic in their detective work, Beck is generally abstracted from the case and Kollberg downright uninterested in it. Yet with Melander meticulously surveying the site of the crime, Beck's intuitive processes mastermind a hypothetical reconstruction with the aide of Kollberg and Melander, much to the discomfort of the unimaginative Rönn. Suicide, a (presumably accidental) fire, a second suicide, which is also a murder by a timed device that causes the fire – all eventually lead to a manhunt for a suspect who himself proves a murder victim, disintegrating in a submerged automobile. A network of relatively petty Swedish criminals had run afoul of a larger international syndicate for their attempts to usurp power, and a hired assassin has been skilfully at work in eliminating them. Skacke's diligence has identified the hit man, but when he and Kollberg attempt to apprehend him, Skacke misreads the signals, allowing the assassin to knife Kollberg before Skacke shoots him dead. This gratuitous horror, following upon the senseless killing of Stenström in the preceding book, contributes to the sense of impending doom that reaches even into the inner circle of the Beck team.

Murder at the Savoy is something of a respite after *The Laughing Policeman* and *The Fire Engine*: the scene shifts to the southern port city of Malmö (where the Wahlöös had themselves moved), away from what has already been designated as the most polluted city in Europe. This is the domain of Inspector Per Månsson, who has found flavoured toothpicks to compensate for having given up cigarettes, and despite the murder at the elegant hotel, the atmosphere remains warm and relaxed throughout. Beck is called in to supervise, and has Månsson as his confrère, with the transferred Skacke to assist, while Månsson's Danish counterpart Mogensen assists in Copenhagen. Essentially, this is a straightforward murder (an almost casual homicide): a wealthy businessman shot in the dining-room, while addressing associates and wives, by a gunman quietly passing through – and out. Delving into the lives and affairs of the dead man and his cohorts again prises up the rock, especially in Stockholm where Kollberg and Larsson are enlisted against their volition. The victim is discovered to have been unscrupulous, a purveyor of arms to colonial powers, while his wife is having an affair with his second-in-command and his Stockholm manager involved in grand embezzlement (his 'secretary' at the dinner was actually a prostitute hired for the trip). A singular lack of suspects – all possible suspects are witnesses instead – and evidence makes the murder investigation seemingly impossible, and the government is panicked over political and diplomatic implications, all of which leave the non-political Beck totally indifferent. When a child on a Danish beach finds a saturated gun box, the single clue appears to lead to a former employee, long-sacked as redundant, deprived of his flat and divorced by his wife. He had only coincidentally spotted the industrialist in the hotel while passing by, on his way from his recreational target practice, and availed himself of an opportunity for revenge without any hope of actual escape. His arrest offers no pleasure to Beck: the justified murderer is certainly a better human being than his pernicious victim.

If the unconscionable capitalist is a likely murder victim, so is the martinet Chief Inspector of Police Nyman (ironically a loving family man at home), and the brutal murder of this presumably terminal hospital patient is enacted before the eyes of the readers of *The Abominable Man*. (That we later learn that his illness had just been diagnosed as curable serves as an added irony.) It becomes apparent that a major vendetta has been planned for policemen in general and certain high officials in particular, including the Chief of National Homicide, Martin Beck, but despite the race against time, there is no list of logical suspects. When a former policeman, who had campaigned against police brutality and blamed the death of his wife on Nyman's conscious negligence, is identified, the case appears too old to be having such late repercussions. But Åke Ericksson has been driven to desperation by being deprived of his child by the welfare service, and by the loss of his flat, and barricades himself on a rooftop heavily armed, intent on killing as many policemen as he can. The official solution is Chief Superintendent Malm's use of helicopters and commandos, but Ericksson is as intelligent as he is determined, and the overkill method fails. Beck, with a sense of guilt despite his relative innocence, attempts to scale the roof and is shot in the chest, finally rescued by Kollberg. Larsson takes two volunteers to the roof, refusing to shoot or allow Ericksson to be bludgeoned by Nyman's vindictive subordinate, bringing him down alive. The grim events had been immediately preceded for Beck by a pleasurable dinner with his daughter at the Golden Peace Restaurant and ends with his near fatality; throughout he had an intuituion of danger, of retribution or nemesis, and risked his life as a form of penance for sins committed by others, although he never openly admits it. Instead, he has become withdrawn, not even confiding in Kollberg, accepting Rönn as a partner without being able to establish rapport with him. The Martin Beck of *The Abominable Man* is on the verge of being suicidal.

The Martin Beck of *The Locked Room* has returned from the dead, a burnt-out ghost assigned to a hopeless case of a decomposing recluse in a room long since locked, while the rest of his 'team' is attached to a robbery squad headed by an overeager district attorney. Robbing from banks has been designated a crime that cannot be tolerated, and Bulldozer Olsson had declared war on an ingenious team of thugs that he blames for every robbed bank. But it is a desperate young mother who has cleverly robbed a bank and in the process accidentally killed a customer, and her link is coincidentally with a drug dealer who has been supplying necessities to the ingenious thugs for their final grand operation, a caper on which they intend retiring. The skein of threads are multiply interwound, and Beck's murder case actually brings him to Mauritzon, the dealer–supplier, while Olsson masterminds a stake-out based on evidence volunteered by Mauritzon, accidentally apprehended carrying his drugs for consignment. Beck solves his locked-room case, even hearing Mauritzon admit his guilt (the tape-recorder, however, is not functioning properly), but Malm refuses to believe the solution, and Mauritzon is convicted instead of the robbery-shooting, a situation that drives him to the edges of insanity. The stake-out is a glorious fiasco, elaborately staged in Stockholm while the successful haul actually takes place in Malmö. Beck was to have been rewarded with promotion to commissioner, essentially withdrawing him from active service, but his 'failure' over the locked room loses him the unwanted promotion. The bank thieves have luxuriously retired to the continent, as has the young mother and her child with the bank proceeds. Crime pays handsomely in this case, and it is apparent that our sympathies are directed toward the outcasts, rather than the defenders of society.

Not quite as comic, but equally relaxed is *Cop Killer*, despite its disturbing title. The longest of the Beck novels it begins a process of summing up, even recapitulating events from the earliest two books: the murderer of Roseanna has served his term in jail, and having taken up residence in a small town, finds himself the prime suspect in the murder of another woman; the killer of the Swedish journalist has also served his sentence, and is a local reporter covering the case, befriended particularly by Kollberg and, because of his unique condition, is made privy to the story of Kollberg's having once killed a man. The Wahlöös, who have often shown their skill in juggling two interlocked plotlines at once, here take on a third as well far into the novel, and all three come superbly together at the closure. The unsuccessful Beck–Kollberg surveillance of a bank-robber and killer called The Breadman is soon forgotten as Beck is assigned to the murder of a woman in a remote village, where he and Kollberg set to work with the local officer, Harrgott Allwright (renamed Herrgott Content in the next book by a different translator). During the course of their frustrating investigation, a pair of petty thieves are involved in the same area in a shootout that leaves one of them dead, two policemen wounded and a third dead from (what the police refuse to divulge) wasp stings. The escaped youth, who never fired a shot, steals a car that belongs to the murderer of the woman, and through a mutual acquaintance finds himself hidden away in a cabin with The Breadman. Beck locates the murderer, the woman's married lover; Kollberg pauses long enough in writing his letter of resignation to spot and identify the car, admitting to a 'hunting instinct'; Larsson and Rönn frustrate Malm's blitzkrieg-ambuscade in capturing the pathetic 'cop killer' and the Breadman unharmed. *Cop Killer* evolves as the most benign book of the series, an idyllic pastoral in which Beck and Allwright enjoy the beauty and the tranquillity of country life (pheasant-hunting and mushroom-picking), and the charms of the villages and picturesque churches. Allwright's constable admits to Beck that he rebelled against the inevitability of being brutalised by police life, and had opted for the country assignment where he could be a policeman without being a sadist.

Tripartite plotting again becomes the forte in *The Terrorists*, as the authors continue to demonstrate a talent for making the impossible look remarkably easy. International terrorist atrocities, performed by skilled paramilitary professionals without a designated political cause, are certainly the subject matter of the novel, but all the thematic warps in the first nine books are interwoven with that woof. The projected visit of the American senator causes the Swedish government to send Larsson to a Central American country in order to learn how those experienced in preventative methods have perfected their expertise: instead he witnesses the explosion that decimates the visiting despot. Bulldozer Olsson, meanwhile, is prosecuting a young mother for bank robbery, but her defence attorney, a Swedish Clarence Darrow known as Crasher Braxén, has her acquitted, rendering the charges against her ludicrous; and Beck is at work on finding the murderer of a pornographic film maker, collaring the unfortunate father of a girl he had driven to drug addiction and prostitution. As the senator's visit takes stage-centre, all efforts are geared toward preventing his assassination, Beck's methods proving even more ingenious than those of Heydt and his three cohorts, but Heydt and two Japanese terrorists find themselves having to remain in hiding, trapped in Stockholm. And because the Clod Squad bungles the final stages of the state visit, the young woman that Braxén had defended succeeds in shooting the prime minister of Sweden as he is playing host to the American. While Braxén dedicates himself to defending her once again, the hunt for the terrorists continues, Larsson engineering the disarming and capture of the two booby-trapped Japanese. As Christmas approaches, the team splits up to watch the three escape routes deemed most logical for Heydt to take, Larsson particularly eager to snare Heydt (which probably would have meant his having to kill for the first time in the line of duty). Beck and Skacke, however, are at the correct exit in Malmö, and it is the wounded Skacke who makes the necessary kill.

Martin Beck is understandably disconcerted to have become known as the 'Swedish Maigret', but none the less gratified that he is recognised as a public figure. Without the paternalism displayed by his prototype toward his associates (gathering Janvier, Torrence and the young LaPointe around him), Beck does operate as the leader of a functional band of detectives, with mixed and changing attitudes toward them; he is disdainful of higher authority, and highly subject to the common cold. Whereas in the scores of Simenon *romans policiers* there is rarely a note of disenchantment with the efficiency of police operations, in the Wahlöö books there is constant questioning of the place of the police in society. Kollberg, the implied pacifist who carries a major portion of reader empathy, is stunned by a description of the police as a 'necessary evil' ('"Well, that's the last straw if we have to regard ourselves as a necessary evil", Kollberg muttered despondently'), yet that seems the best that can be said for them as the Beck novels progress. Kollberg has previously been rather modest in what he could claim for police necessity, realising that the inevitable capture of a murderer depended on 'giving luck a helping hand, of making the net of circumstance that was eventually to catch the criminal as fine-meshed as possible'. Policemen like Kollberg and Beck are a product of a 'substantial shake-up' dating from the 1950s, with 'an infusion of fresh leadership and fresh air', when 'military thinking ceased to be so popular, and reactionary ideas were no longer necessarily an asset.'

If the abominable Nyman was now a fossil, the fresh leadership of Martin Beck was soon threatened by a reactionary resurgence. The first two books reflect those honeymoon years, but by the third Beck admits to himself, 'All that the police really succeeded in doing was to stir up the dregs – the homeless, the alcoholics, the drug addicts, those who have lost all hope, those who could not even crawl away when the welfare state turned the stone over.' That they concerned themselves diligently with routing demonstrators at the American Embassy is emphasised continuously in all the later volumes, descriptively on the first pages of *The Laughing Policeman*, and caustically as well: 'the police commissioner had said in a public statement that many of the regular duties of the police would have to be neglected because they were obliged to protect the American ambassador against letters and other things from people who disliked Lyndon Johnson and the war in Vietnam.' Such misdirection is venial compared to the zest with which the police attack the demonstrators, as Allwright's assistant complains:

> I used to be on the force in Malmö and I thought it was sheer hell. People looked at me like I wasn't human, and I noticed myself that I was starting to get funny. I was at a demonstration there in 1969, and we were beating people with our billy clubs. I hit a girl myself. She couldn't have been more than seventeen, and what's more, she had a little kid with her.

Police brutality becomes a comonplace that even Larsson finds that he must ignore as he wonders, 'how many policemen had worked over presumably innocent people in patrol cars and local stations. Probably too many to count. He minded his own business.' Kollberg, on the other hand, views the situation as diagnostic: 'No, it was no fun . . . being a policeman. What could a man do as he witnessed the gradual decay of his own organisation? As he heard the rats of fascism pattering about behind the wainscoting? All his adult life he had loyally served this organisation.'

More police, more technology, more firepower are the solutions of the political appointees like Malm, and the commissioner of police who lurks behind him and remains unavailable to anyone, in combating the 'swift gangsterisation of society' viewed by Kollberg. The progression of the Beck series depicts an escalation of hostilities between a disaffected society and its nominal defenders, and the Wahlöös document the fictional events with statistics on police budgets, comparative crime figures, and political and sociological news items for the decade under surveillance. In contrast to the faceless, nameless Police Head we find a Per Månsson who gives interviews and talks to people, even refusing to disperse crowds that gather at the site, allowing them the right to congregate, observe and even speculate. Along with Allwright, Kollberg and Beck he represents the cop committed to a responsible role in law enforcement, the infusion of 'fresh leadership and fresh air'. At another level are the Melanders and Rönns and Skackes who undertake their jobs as responsibilities, doing the necessary police work without any apparent policies or politics, professional experts who conscientiously perfect their abilities. The wild card in the bunch is Gunvald Larsson, perhaps the most interesting cop created by the Wahlöös, who does not officially enter the scene until the third book, but plays increasingly important roles thereafter. His characteristics are complex: a fiery temper, a tenacious commitment, a direct approach, a refusal to toady to higher authority, even an antisocial personality. He has severed his roots with the haute bourgeoisie, as contemptuous of his family as they are ashamed of him, and exists mostly as a loner, practically a teetotaller and certainly a sexual prude, and he sports a wardrobe that consumes most of his salary. Yet he emerges as the viable successor to Kollberg and potential inheritor of Beck's mantle. Larsson continually expresses his disdain for capitalism, and his suspicions of the political right, even to the extent of berating a secretary who had taken her holiday in Greece, lecturing her on social consciousness (while snubbing her sexual advances): 'Don't you know that the military junta there allows tens of thousands of people to rot away in political prisons and the people are tortured to death every day?'

As outspokenly political as Larsson appears throughout, Martin Beck remains doggedly nonpolitical until the very end, when it must be assumed he has become aware of a change within himself to mirror the changes he experienced. The basic statement of his contempt for politics is heard in *Murder at the Savoy*, 'that Martin Beck detested everything even remotely related to politics and that he promptly retreated into a shell every time there was any mention of demonstrations, assassinations or political involvement'. Which makes for a comic juxtaposition thereafter is an *unpolitisch* protagonist at the centre of an increasingly political drama. It is in *Murder at the Savoy* that a reprehensible capitalist is the unmourned murder victim, his empire rotten with slum landlords, jerrybuilt housing, extortionate rents, political chicanery, and ecological destruction, and Beck finds that he 'didn't feel good at all' that 'a shipyard janitor ... would be tried for ... murder, and then have to rot away the best years of his life in a prison cell'. It is in this novel that Månsson remembers his depression childhood, conscious of the vast gulf separating the rich from the economically deprived; that the parvenu capitalists are described as gaining a foothold in the ruling centres of Swedish government; that Larsson gets an opportunity to harass and humiliate his snobbish sister − in the line of duty; that the police are credited with gratuitous brutality in 'patrol cars and local stations'; and the so-called welfare state is dissected:

Behind its spectacular topographical façade and under its polished, semi-fashionable surface, Stockholm had become an asphalt jungle, where drug addiction and sexual perversion ran more rampant than ever. Unscrupulous profiteers could make enormous profits quite legally on pornography of the smuttiest kind. Professional criminals became not only more numerous but also better organised. An impoverished proletariat was also being created, especially among the elderly. Inflation had given rise to one of the highest costs of living in the world, and the latest surveys showed that many pensioners had to live on dog and cat food in order to make ends meet.

Beck could hardly persist in his innocence of such politically potent events, and by *The Abominable Man* he proves to be aware of his daughter's political militancy, if not his own, when Rönn slanders women as carelesss drivers; 'If my daughter could hear your now you'd get a real lecture,' he comments, obviously with malicious delight. His antipolitical stance is still intact in *Cop Killer*, although Rhea has added her influence to that of daughter Ingrid, but 'whenever people started talking politics he went as silent as a clam.' Yet in *The Terrorists*, before the assembled police higher-ups (including the head of the Security Police), Beck denounces the American senator: 'He has always been the most active of what they call hawks in Vietnam, and there's no doubt that he worked for the fascist junta in Chile, which was responsible for the murder of President Allende and thousands of other people.' When the commissioner protests, 'I thought you were nonpolitical,' Beck insists, 'I am. I'm just recounting certain facts.' (Larsson of course is even more vocal about those facts: '"If I were free this particular day, I might go out and demonstrate against this bastard myself", said Gunvald Larsson. "He's a lot worse than Reagan."'

Beck's startling shift may have been engendered by his not only sleeping with Rhea, but sleeping with a poster of Mao Tse-tung over the bed: 'Martin Beck never expressed opinions on political matters and said nothing this time either.' Rhea jovially offers to take it down rather than 'compromise' him, 'but the thought of the tremendous dismay the poster would cause in certain circles decided him at once to leave it there.' He himself had come to understand something fundamental in his own world when he sat and talked with an old seaman in order to dredge up background material on the corpse in the locked room:

It was often interesting, listening to old workers, and Martin Beck couldn't understand why almost no one took time to do so. This man had seen a lot of things, both ashore and at sea. Why didn't such people ever get a word in on the mass media? Didn't politicians and technocrats ever listen to what they had to say? Certainly not; for if they did, many fateful errors in matters to do with employment and the environment could have been avoided.

The final phase of Beck's tenuous politicisation certainly begins in the courtroom at his first appearance in *The Terrorists*. As a witness in the trial of Rebecka Lind, the putative bank robber, he contributes easily toward her exoneration, and in the presence of Rhea he hears Crasher Braxén's defence of the girl and condemnation of a heartless society masquerading as a benevolent democracy. In his later defence of Rebecka, now the assassin of the prime minister of Sweden, Braxén makes his most potent political accusations:

> We have lived through Hitler and Mussolini, Stroessner, Franco, Salazar, Chiang Kai-shek, Ian Smith, Vorster and Verwoerd, and the generals in Chile, men, who, when they have not led their people to the edge of disaster, have in their own self-interest treated their own citizens in the manner of a military power oppressing an occupied country.

Crasher's condemnation of right-wing dictatorships is apparently hyperbolic for 'middle way' Sweden, but the evidence has been accumulating of a phony socialism dusted off for the annual May Day celebration, of the destruction of 'a natural wilderness that should of been protected by law', of 'gross ecological malfeasance, typical of the anti-humanitarian cynicism ... characteristic of what the government called A More Compassionate Society', of a 'so-called Welfare State' that 'abounds with sick, poor, and lonely people, living at best on dog food'. Martin Beck has had a unique moment of glory, heading the campaign against the terrorists with even the security chief having to take orders from him and listen to his denunciation of fascism, and he succeeds in putting Heydt and the terrorists out of commission. As he relaxes from his successful exploit, a saviour of Swedish society, Beck refrains from any Braxén-like pronouncements. Instead he celebrates the New Year with those he loves, playing a word game in which Kollberg chooses the hardest letter in the alphabet to deal with, allowing the last book in the Beck decalogy to close with the most difficult name for 'middle way' Sweden to deal with:

'My turn to start? Then I say X — X as in Marx.'

CHRONOLOGY

Dates of first publication. The Martin Beck series by Maj Sjöwall and Per Wahlöö is published in Stockholm by P. A. Norstedt and Söner (about whom the Wahlöös include an in-house joke in one of their novels), and is available in English in Vintage Paperbacks (Random House) (the second and third volumes transposed in the series): (English title in brackets)

1965 – *Roseanna (Roseanna)*
1966 – *Mannen som gick upp i rök (The Man Who Went Up in Smoke)*
1967 – *Mannen pa balkongen (The Man on the Balcony)*
1968 – *Den skrattande polisen (The Laughing Policeman)*
1969 – *Brandbilen som försvann (The Fire Engine that Disappeared)*
1970 – *Polis, polis, potatismos! (Murder at the Savoy)*
1971 – *Den vedervärdige mannen från Säffle (The Abominable Man)*
1972 – *Det slutna rummet (The Locked Room)*
1974 – *Polismördaren (Cop Killer)*
1975 – *Terroristerna (The Terrorists)*

Index

(Includes authors and titles mentioned in the texts, but not in notes, bibliographies or chronologies. In most cases names of fictional characters are not included, unless they are serial characters or of more than passing interest. Titles beginning with the indefinite article are alphabetised under A; titles with the definite article under the second word of the title.)